Education for Awakening

An Eastern Approach to Holistic Education

Yoshiharu Nakagawa

To my parents,
Sueko and Morio Nakagawa

Acknowledgements

This book is based on my doctoral dissertation at Ontario Institute for Studies in Education of the University of Toronto. During my stay in Toronto from 1996 to 2000, many people supported me to continue and complete this study.

Among them, there are several individuals whom I would like to thank for their encouragement and support. Special thanks to Professor Jack Miller, who kindly wrote a preface for this book, for encouraging and supervising this work. Also, special thanks to Professor Clive Beck and Professor Vivian Darroch-Lozowski at the University of Toronto, and Professor Aostre N. Johnson at Saint Michael's College for valuable advice and comments, which greatly improved my ideas.

I wish to express my gratitude to Professor Atsuhiko Yoshida, who stayed in Toronto on his sabbatical, for reading the manuscript and making a number of suggestions, most of which I have been able to include in this work.

I gratefully acknowledge helpful discussions with my friends, Susan Allen and Isabella Colalillo-Kates. Susan, Ms. Martine Johnson and Ms. Amy Kirtley were very helpful in editing this work that was written in my second language.

Special thanks are due to Mr. Tomikichiro Tokuriki and Matsuku for permission to use the woodcut prints of the Ten Oxherding Pictures.

Also, special thanks to Dr. Ron Miller for his decision to publish this work through The Foundation for Educational Renewal. His decision made it possible for my first book to appear.

Table of Contents

Preface

John P. Miller

In 1994 I had the opportunity to go to Japan to work with educators there interested in holistic education. I was impressed by the dedication and enthusiasm of the people that I met then and on my subsequent visits to Japan. I met Yoshi Nakagawa in 1994 and along with several other individuals he has provided leadership in the area of holistic education in Japan. Japan is reexamining its educational system and looking for ways that can stimulate individual student creativity.

This book, I believe, is one of the most important books in the growing field of holistic education. It is a powerful synthesis of Eastern and Western thought that provides a significant theoretical contribution to the field. The amount of literature that he has integrated into his presentation alone makes this an important work. But Professor Nakagawa has not just reviewed this literature; he has integrated it into a conceptual framework that provides a new perspective on holistic education. The five dimensions (objective, social, cosmic, infinite, and universal) that he describes should stimulate thinking about the way that we view holistic education. Through this framework Professor Nakagawa argues that we need to integrate Eastern and particularly Buddhist perspectives into how we approach holistic education.

The beauty of this book is that the ideas are presented clearly and concisely but in a manner that does not compromise their depth and complexity. One's admiration of this book increases because Professor

Nakagawa has written this book not in his native tongue, Japanese, but in a second language to him, English.

I believe that holistic education is a global phenomenon. This book supports that claim as it provides a voice from Asia to the ongoing conversation and dialogue about the future of holistic education in the twenty-first century. I am also confident that we will hear from others around the world as the conversation continues and widens. In the meantime we can be grateful for this book and its contribution to that dialogue now.

Introduction

TOWARDS AN EASTERN PHILOSOPHY
OF HOLISTIC EDUCATION

The purpose of this study is to explore a theoretical foundation for holistic education from diverse perspectives of Eastern philosophy.[1]

"Holistic education"[2] appeared as a concept in North America in the late 1970s. This contemporary trend of holistic education has so far considerably enlarged and altered our basic understandings of education. Many theoretical attempts at contemporary holistic education have enlarged worldviews of education to embrace the realms of nature and the universe. They have attempted to establish all-inclusive comprehensive worldviews in which the entire enterprise of education can be located.

However, Eastern philosophy is able to provide further conceptions of holistic education. Eastern ideas of holistic education remain not only on the ecological and cosmological levels of nature and the universe but also go beyond them to embrace the ontological ground of nature and the universe. In this regard, the ideas of contemporary holistic education are still not comprehensive enough.

From the viewpoints of Eastern philosophy, even the universe is not seen as the all-embracing ultimate reality. In other words, whereas contemporary holistic education is concerned with the aspects of *Being* and *Becoming* (evolution) of the universe, Eastern philosophy is concerned with the deeper aspects of *Non-Being*.

Therefore, Eastern views of holistic education significantly differ from the ecological and cosmological views of contemporary holistic education. Contemporary holistic education tends to highlight "interconnection" of all beings as the foundation of education, which in most cases refers to the ecological and systemic connections in nature and the universe. By contrast, Eastern philosophy celebrates "interpenetration" that does not have ecological and systemic connotations but means absolute freedom (liberation) in all relationships.

Eastern views of holistic education have not been well explored even among thinkers of contemporary holistic education who have been interested in Eastern thought. The task of this study is to realize what Eastern philosophy can bring to the discussions of holistic education.

A primary difference between contemporary holistic education and Eastern views of holistic education consists in their basic worldviews or ontologies. While contemporary holistic education tends to celebrate a web-like horizontal interconnection of the universe, Eastern philosophy involves ideas of *multidimensional reality* or *vertical depth.* In addition, the multidimensional ideas of Eastern philosophy have always acknowledged the deepest dimension of reality as well as other surface and intermediate dimensions. Traditionally, this deepest dimension has been diversely called *Brahman, nirvana, sunyata, Tao, wu, li, mu,* and so forth. It is this inclusion of the profound dimension that is responsible for the special characteristics of the Eastern philosophy of holistic education in both theory and practice.

However, it is also important to stress that this book is not intended to oppose an Eastern view of holistic education to Western ideas. It ultimately seeks to enlarge the framework of holistic education by integrating both Western and Eastern perspectives. In fact, the rise of contemporary holistic education has made it possible for the first time[3] to realize such an integration, for it makes space for Eastern thought to take part. Holistic education becomes an arena where fruitful encounters between Eastern and Western philosophies can take place.

TOWARDS A RECONSTRUCTION OF EASTERN PHILOSOPHY

Eastern philosophy can transform existing ideas of holistic education. On the other hand, it goes through transformations on its own side. It is no longer an archaic legacy but a vital storehouse from which we can draw treasures for the future of the world. In this regard, this book is an effort to explore certain possibilities of Eastern philosophy in the present world situation and to apply them to a particular field of education. This attempt may belong to what David Ray Griffin (1989) calls "constructive" or "revisionary" postmodernism that "seeks to overcome the modern worldview ... by constructing a postmodern worldview through a revision of modern premises and traditional concepts" (p. x). Drawing upon "premodern" Eastern philosophy, this study tries to illuminate "postmodern" elements hidden in it.

Eastern philosophy is not the mere negative, nihilistic, and pessimistic philosophy it has been considered. It is not an otherworld-oriented transcendentalism detached from the mundane world but a radical immanentalism through transcendence; that is, it reveals an infinite depth of reality in finite actual beings of this world. Eastern philosophy is not a pessimistic attempt to escape from this world but a passionate seeking for the fulfillment of being in this world. It is never a mere life-negating philosophy but an absolutely life-affirming philosophy, a philosophy of absolute affirmation through absolute negation. Neither is it a mere romantic or idealistic speculation but a very practical, operational philosophy with certain methodologies. All of these aspects can contribute to "constructive postmodernism" (as distinct from "deconstructive postmodernism").

The basic position of Eastern philosophy is a *radical reconstructivism through a radical deconstructivism*. It is this position that makes Eastern philosophy an important strand of postmodern thought. As you read this book, you will find this critical element in many forms of Eastern philosophy. However, the foremost expression of this understanding has been put forward by the Mahayana Buddhist philosophy of Emptiness (*sunyata*) and Suchness (*tathata*).

Eastern philosophy is now being applied to a range of particular fields. Though this book will focus on the field of education, we are also witnessing growing interest in the Eastern ways of thinking and practice in such fields as comparative philosophy, transpersonal psychology, holistic health and medicine, physics, ecology, and cognitive science.

Eastern philosophy is able to provide effective solutions to difficulties in modern education. Modern education in our industrialized society has lost its ability to cope efficiently with serious problems such as the relationships between humans and nature, and between individuals and society. It also lacks the ability to awaken us to the true meanings of personal and collective life, for it has ultimately served to reproduce the system of modern society. Eastern philosophy, on the contrary, has been concerned with issues neglected in modern education, including humans' belonging to the cosmos, liberation in society, various forms of spirituality, and the meaningfulness of life. In particular, it has been the study of the true Self, which reveals undivided relations of the Self with the other realms (nature, the universe, and the infinite reality). In this way, Eastern philosophy can provide valuable alternatives to modern education.

However, problems exist within Eastern traditions themselves. To become a significant current in postmodernism, they have to undergo critical examinations of their own traditional ways. Most traditions of Eastern philosophy seem to retain crucial drawbacks in their archaic outlooks with much technical jargon difficult to comprehend and extremely complicated systems developed over a long period. These elements make it virtually impossible for most of us, including Easterners, to access them.

In addition, academic orientations to the studies in Eastern thought have been strictly pedantic and have not allowed creative interpretations to develop. What have been accumulated in academic institutions are numerous amounts of philological studies. This conservative climate of study has in fact been an obstacle to the creative development of Eastern philosophy. If Eastern philosophy is to influence the future of philosophy, it must break its fixation with the past.

THE PROGRAM OF THE FOLLOWING CHAPTERS

To grasp the essential structure of Eastern philosophy, Chapter 1 will examine the remarkable ideas of four Eastern (Japanese) philosophers, namely, D. T. Suzuki, Kitaro Nishida, Shin'ichi Hisamatsu, and Toshihiko Izutsu. This study particularly owes the idea of multidimensionality to the groundbreaking studies by Izutsu.

The essential structure of Eastern philosophy is based on multidimensional ideas of reality. On this basis Chapter 2 will introduce a framework of holistic education called *the five dimensions of reality*. This scheme intends to incorporate Eastern as well as Western perspectives. Briefly, *Dimension I* means the objective reality of individual beings. *Dimension II* is the social reality underlying the phenomenal objective distinctions. *Dimension III* is the cosmic reality of nature, life, and the universe, with which many contemporary holistic theories are concerned. *Dimension IV* refers to the infinite reality as the deepest dimension of reality, with which Eastern philosophy has been mainly concerned. *Dimension V* is the universal reality in which the infinite reality manifests itself in all beings. Throughout this study, this multidimensional theory of holistic education will serve as the guiding principle.

Chapter 3 will examine theories of contemporary holistic education from the vantage point of the multidimensional theory. I will classify six major orientations of contemporary holistic education—perennial philosophy, indigenous worldviews, Life philosophy, ecological worldview, systems theory, and feminist thought. Then I will discuss some of the fundamental problems inherent in these orientations.

Chapter 4 will explore Buddhist ideas of relationships developed in early Buddhism and Mahayana Buddhism (the Madhyamika and Hua-yen schools) to highlight multidimensional ideas of relationships. This chapter will clarify an ontological difference between interconnection and interpenetration.

Chapter 5 will explore Eastern views of relevant pedagogical concepts to show constructive contributions of Eastern ideas to our understandings of education. It will focus on Hinduism and the aim of education, and Taoism and the concept of nature. Then issues such as language and silence (Buddhism, Taoism), learning and unlearning (Taoism), and human development (Taoism, Zen Buddhism) will be discussed.

Chapters 6 and 7 will focus on the practical aspect of Eastern holistic education. Chapter 6 will explore the Eastern ways of contemplation and art. To present an integral view of the educational way of contemplation, this study will integrate somatic education developed in the West with Eastern meditations. The Eastern way of art will be explored as a form of contemplation and spiritual practice.

Lastly, in order to focus on discussions about personal and social transformations, Chapter 7 will examine social implications of Eastern philosophy, that is, multidimensional implications of the Eastern way of action. Then, it will examine the concept of caring with reference to the Eastern concept of compassion (Pure Land and Shin Buddhism). Finally, it will call for a society of Enlightenment.

This study is entirely based on literature research and hermeneutic interpretation of materials; in most cases I will try to draw on the basic literature of Eastern philosophy that includes original classical scriptures and sutras, their interpretations and commentaries by scholars and thinkers, teachings of Eastern thinkers, and other writings on Eastern philosophy by both Eastern and Western authors. Among others in Eastern philosophy, this book will particularly refer to Buddhist literature.

I am also strongly inspired by the work of Japanese scholars such as D. T. Suzuki, Toshihiko Izutsu, Keiji Nishitani, Shin'ichi Hisamatsu, Shizuteru Ueda, Masao Abe, and Muneyoshi Yanagi as well as that of Jidu Krishnamurti, Aldous Huxley, Ken Wilber, and John Miller.

NOTES

1. In this study "Eastern philosophy" denotes various traditions of Eastern thought. Geographically, they cover vast areas of Asia from the Near East through the Middle East and the South East to the Far East. Therefore, representative traditions of Eastern philosophy include Hinduism, Buddhism, Taoism, Confucianism, Sufism, and others.

2. In this study, the ideas of holistic education that first appeared in the late 1970s are referred to as "contemporary holistic education." However, the "holistic" ideas of education are not new but have existed across the ages and cultures, if we regard holistic education as a form of education that is oriented towards wholeness. This study will include both old and new forms under the umbrella of "holistic education." The general sense of holistic education involves *ideas, theories, methods, and practices that are oriented towards the wholeness of Existence, the human being, and education.* In this context, "Existence" includes culture, society, nature, the universe, and the Infinite. The wholeness of "the human being" includes aspects such as the body, emotions, the mind, the heart, the soul, and the spirit. The wholeness of "education" means any forms of implementing holistic ideas that include methods such as imagery and visualization, art, body-mind approaches, and contemplation.

3. Prior to holistic education, in the West there have been pioneering efforts to bring Eastern ideas into education in such fields as humanistic psychology/education and transpersonal psychology/education. However, the efforts found in humanistic psychology/education have been limited. Transpersonal psychology, though it has successfully incorporated a large part of Eastern thought, has not developed a branch of transpersonal education very well (see Nakagawa 1996b).

The Structure of Eastern Philosophy

What is Eastern philosophy? To grasp the essential structure of Eastern philosophy, we will look at the remarkable ideas of four Japanese thinkers: D. T. Suzuki, Kitaro Nishida, Shin'ichi Hisamatsu, and Toshihiko Izutsu. They have provided the essential characteristics of Eastern philosophy and, at the same time, exemplified how meaningful encounters between Eastern and Western thought can take place.

D. T. Suzuki's View of "Eastern Perspective"

Daisetz Teitaro Suzuki (1870-1966) has been called the first "Zen thinker." While most of his work dealt with Zen Buddhist philosophy, his personal life was largely occupied with the Western way of life; he was a rare Easterner who could deeply incorporate it in his own existence. In other words, he lived at the same time in two fundamentally different worlds; that is, the irrational world of Zen Buddhism and the rational world of Western thinking. However, as Shizuteru Ueda[1] (1997) suggests, it is through an existential tension created by such an opposition of the two worlds that Suzuki realized "Zen philosophy," which was none other than an integration of the Eastern and Western ways of thinking.

Interestingly enough, in his last years Suzuki came to stress the meaning of "the Eastern" more than ever. In one of his last essays (originally published in 1963), he celebrated "Eastern Perspective" (*toyo-teki na mikata*):

> I would like to strongly emphasize "Eastern Perspective." I would like
> to posit this in opposition to what is Western, scientific, logical, con-
> ceptual and so forth in our time, and to let it to be widely known not
> only to Eastern people but also to Western people in general in order to
> celebrate the significance of Eastern culture. My point is that this East-
> ern Perspective has a role to play in cultivating the world-culture to
> come. (Suzuki 1997, 15, trans. Nakagawa)

Eastern Perspective is different from the Western perspective that is
based on "dualistic divisions" of things. It refers to the state of "unitary
One"—*Tao, li, t'ai-chi,* absolute Nothingness, absolute One, or Emptiness—before a dualistic division takes place (p. 20). The "unitary One"
does not mean the union of the two separate realms such as subject and
object, or God and human, but the undifferentiated primordial state
prior to division of any kind.

At this point, Eastern Perspective differs from Western mysticism that
seeks for *unio mystica* between God and human. Suzuki (1982, 100-101)
said: "As long as mysticism is understood as the union of 'subject' and
'object,' I cannot approve of the use of the term for the Buddhist experience." Eastern Perspective denotes the non-dualistic ground ontologically prior to dualism.

Suzuki (1972/1994) also often used the terms "the metaphysical Unconscious" and "the cosmic Unconscious" to describe the non-dualistic
ground beneath the layers of "the psychological Unconscious." In terms
of *satori*, he defined them as follows:

> Psychologically speaking, satori is super-consciousness, or conscious-
> ness of the Unconscious. The Unconscious is, however, not to be iden-
> tified with the one psychologically postulated. The Unconscious of
> satori is with God even prior to his creation. It is what lies at the basis of
> reality; it is the cosmic Unconscious. This Unconscious is a metaphysi-
> cal concept, and it is through satori that we become conscious of the
> Unconscious. (p. 88)

As stated here, the non-dual primordial ground, or the cosmic, metaphysical Unconscious, can be attained not by the intellect but by "spiritual intuition" called *satori.* Therefore, Suzuki (1964/1991, 95) regards
satori as "the *raison d'être* of Zen without which Zen is no Zen." *Satori* is

not an objective perception of things but "the perception of Reality itself" (p. 93), through which we become conscious of the cosmic Unconscious.

The Western way of thinking, based on a dualistic division of subject and object, has developed an intellectual and logical analysis of the objective world that has resulted in remarkable developments in science and technology. In contrast, from a Buddhist point of view, logical analysis means "ignorance" (*avidya*): "'Ignorance' is another name for logical dualism" (1964/1991, 52). And logical and analytic thinking has to be transcended in an intuitive perception of *satori.*

However, Suzuki's celebration of Eastern Perspective does not necessarily imply that he fell into a narrow view that only affirms the Eastern view. Perspectives of both East and West are equally important. In fact, he was fully aware of the danger that some can erroneously use the idea of Eastern Perspective as a totalitarian ideology to arouse emotional bonding among people. In this respect, he was very critical of "Japanese sentimentalism" and emphasized the importance of rational and critical thinking to overcome an Eastern collective mentality.

Suzuki's "Eastern Perspective" was really meant to integrate the positive aspects of East and West to provide an enlarged vision for a forthcoming "world-culture." According to Ueda (1997), his attempt was "to explore the possibility of a new 'one world' that would connect the East and the West in a positive way, and to expand and deepen the new possibility of the human being in the world" (p. 321, trans. Nakagawa). Therefore, Eastern Perspective is *not* bound to its geographical, historical, and cultural backgrounds but refers to the existential and ontological dimension of the human being. Ueda remarks: "'Eastern Perspective' is not 'the view of the East' confined only to the East. It was indeed historically realized in the traditions of the East, but in its quality it is a possibility or a possible way of perception for all human beings" (pp. 335-36, trans. Nakagawa). The East and the West denote "the different possibilities of the way of being-in-the-world" (p. 336, trans. Nakagawa) that can be unified in a multidimensional way. In other words, the non-dualistic dimension is the ground on which the dualistic dimensions unfold.

Nishida's Philosophy and Zen Buddhism

Kitaro Nishida (1870-1945) has been considered to be the first authentic philosopher in modern Japan. Even more than his life-long friend D. T. Suzuki, Nishida was heavily involved in Western philosophy. Even so, he was deeply rooted in the Eastern tradition of contemplation. Throughout his life as a philosopher, his whole effort was devoted to attaining a meaningful synthesis of the two different traditions. Though he was keenly aware of their fundamental differences, he grasped them as a positive whole out of which a unified "world-culture" could emerge. In a lecture delivered in 1928, he remarked: "I think ... that in the East there is something fundamentally different [from the West]. They compensate for each other to form a human culture and to reveal a complete humanness" (Nishida 1966, 405, trans. Nakagawa). Masao Abe[2] (1990, xxv) points out the basic character of Nishida's philosophy as follows:

> He recognized a kind of universality in Western philosophy and logic but did not accept it as the only universality. Realizing the uniqueness of the Eastern way of thinking, Nishida took absolute nothingness as ultimate reality and tried to give it a logical foundation through his confrontation with Western philosophy.

Throughout Nishida's endeavor, "he neither established a new Eastern philosophy nor reconstructed Western philosophy but created a new world philosophy" (Abe 1990, xxv).

Nishida was not only a penetrating thinker but also a spiritual seeker. The formation of his philosophy was inseparable from the fact that he had seriously practiced Zen for ten years in his 30s. Once he wrote in his journal: "the purpose of *sanzen* is liberation from the world of birth and death. There is no other aim" (cited in Ueda 1991b, 180, trans. Nakagawa). These words tell us how serious his intention toward spiritual awakening (*satori*) was. His practice in Zen colored his concerns in philosophical thinking that were the radical inquiry into the self, the world, and life.

Nishida embodied both the Western way of intellectual reflection and the Eastern way of contemplation. This created a tense situation for him because of the discrepancy between the two ways; that is, Zen tends to reject any intellectualization in favor of immediate experience. On the other hand, for philosophy the experience of Zen seems to be too alien to be grasped in philosophical speculations. Nishida's unique creativity found its expression in this difficult situation. As Ueda (1994a) points out, "in the person of Nishida Kitaro, for the first time in world history, Zen and European philosophy truly encountered one another" (p. 42; 1998, 24).

The first achievement was *An Inquiry into the Good* (originally published in 1911), which soon became an epoch-making publication in the history of Japanese philosophy. It was also epoch-making in the entire history of philosophy for it was the first original attempt to integrate Western philosophy with Zen Buddhism. However, it appeared as a genuinely "philosophical" work. In other words, the integration it achieved was not a superficial linking of the two realms but penetrated into the "structure" of his philosophy. Ueda (1982b; e.g., 1991b, 1994a, 1998) describes the structural aspect of his philosophy as follows:

> In general, philosophy and Zen—crudely put, thinking and non-thinking—stand opposed to one another. This tension, however, became something creative in Nishida through Zen and philosophy bringing one another into question. In the light of Zen, philosophy was made into a question about the origination of principles. In the light of philosophy, Zen was made into a question about the possibility of the project of building a world and the possibility of cultivating a logic. (p. 167)

Philosophy seeks fundamental principles that are capable of grasping all phenomena in a systematic manner. Zen raises the question in philosophy about how fundamental the principle of a philosophy is, for Zen attempts to provide the most *radical* experience from which a fundamental principle for philosophy can arise. Nishida proposed his fundamental principle in the formula that "pure experience is the sole reality." The "pure experience" is the radical dimension Zen realizes, and the formula signifies the fundamental principle on which one can build a system of philosophy. As philosophical investigation does not include a practical avenue to "pure experience," Zen can provide philosophy with a path to "pure experience." On the other hand, philosophy can provide Zen with conceptual tools and methods of theoretical speculation for Zen to construct its own worldview. Their mutual interaction can transform both philosophy and Zen. As Abe (1990, xii) states, "Nishida transformed Zen into philosophy for the first time in the history of this religious tradition and, also for the first time, transformed Western philosophy into a Zen-oriented philosophy."

The "Eastern" component in Nishida's thought is "pure experience" (*junsui-keiken*), the fundamental ground for all beings. In Nishida's (1990, xxx) words:

> Over time I came to realize that it is not that experience exists because there is an individual, but that an individual exists because there is experience. I thus arrived at the idea that experience is more fundamental than individual differences, and in this way I was able to avoid solipsism.

The "experience" in this context is totally different from the ordinary sense of experience that takes place in the way that the pre-existent self experiences something as its object. Here the experiencing self and the thing to be experienced are already separated. On the other hand, Nishida regards "pure experience" as "more fundamental" because on this level there arises no separation between subject and object. As Abe (1990, xvi) comments on this: "In actual experience it is not that *the self experiences* something but that *the self as well is experienced*." This means that the self and other beings articulate themselves from the fundamental, non-dual, pure experience.

The pure experience cannot be recognized by the mind but must be directly intuited. Nishida (1990, 3) says:

> To experience means to know facts just as they are, to know in accordance with facts by completely relinquishing one's own fabrications. What we usually refer to as experience is adulterated with some sort of thought, so by *pure* I am referring to the state of experience just as it is without the least addition of deliberative discrimination.

"To experience" is to be immediately aware of what *is*. Any kind of intervention of the mind such as "fabrications" and "deliberate discrimination" disturbs the purity and directness of experiencing. Nishida goes on to say: "When one directly experiences one's own state of consciousness, there is not yet a subject or an object, and knowing and its object are completely unified. This is the most refined type of experience" (pp. 3-4). Pure experience is the primordial experience that happens when the function of the mind is transcended. And this is what a Zen state of *satori* means.

After *An Inquiry into the Good*, Nishida continued to deepen his philosophy and articulated the philosophy of the "place" (*basho*). This is also important in our discussion of Eastern ontology, for he put forth the idea of "Absolute Nothingness" (*zettai-mu*). Nishida discerned the two different ontological modes of place: "the place of being" and "the place of Absolute Nothingness." These two places are always connected in such a way that "the place of being" of any kind is *in* "the place of Absolute Nothingness." Though the place of being can be *a* place only if it is defined by its "outside," the place of Absolute Nothingness has no "outside." As Robert Schinzinger (1958, 38) comments on this, "Being is always a 'being in ...', a 'having its place.' But that which is only place and does not have its place in something else, cannot be called 'being.' Therefore it is called 'nothingness.'" Absolute Nothingness is an ontological place in which a being is able to be.

Ueda has refined Nishida's Absolute Nothingness in his concept of "Infinite Openness," (*die unendliche Offenheit*) which reveals the positive aspect of Absolute Nothingness:

> If there is a definite place, in the last analysis, it is in Infinite Openness (*die unendliche Offenheit*) that transcends and encompasses the place. Being-in-a-place means eventually that a being is always simultaneously in Infinite Openness. By being in a place, at the same time, a being is in Infinite Openness. (1991b, 314, trans. Nakagawa)

The ultimate ontological ground is infinitely open. Both Nishida's Absolute Nothingness and Ueda's Infinite Openness are uniquely Eastern views of ultimate reality. These concepts emerged, as Abe (1990, xxiii) suggests, from the Buddhist idea of *sunyata*: "It [the logic of absolute nothingness] is a logic of Oriental *nothingness (sunyata)*."

Nishida's philosophy[3] has had a certain effect on studies in education among his followers. Yet it is more important for our present concern to recognize how Nishida approached both Eastern and Western traditions and how it became possible to develop a philosophy based on Eastern conceptions, which would encourage the philosophy of education to realize an internal integration of the Eastern and Western perspectives.

HISAMATSU'S IDEA OF "EASTERN NOTHINGNESS"

Shin'ichi Hisamatsu (1889-1980) was one of the representative religious thinkers of the Kyoto school of philosophy that was founded by
Nishida at the Kyoto University (the former Kyoto Imperial University).[4] Hisamatsu was at the same time a Zen Buddhist, committed to a
Rinzai school. In his practice of Zen, it is said that he had an experience of
kensho, an in-depth insight into the true nature of the Self, which formed
a critical moment in his practice and life. Hisamatsu's clear understanding of religious matters seems to come from his own experience of *kensho*.
Generally speaking, in the Eastern traditions of thought, one principal
criterion used to evaluate the quality of thought is whether or not a
thinker has had such a profound experience. As Hisamatsu (1939/1987)
himself said, "in Zen, if it were not for *kensho*, all perceptions would be
delusion" (p. 132, trans. Nakagawa).

Hisamatsu coined a concept called "Eastern Nothingness"
(*toyoteki-mu*) to clarify the heart of Eastern philosophy. In his anthology
Eastern Nothingness (originally published in 1939), he celebrated Eastern
Nothingness as "the essential moment of what is particularly called 'the
Eastern'" (1939/1987, 7, trans. Nakagawa).

> Here, what I call "Eastern Nothingness" is the fundamental moment
> which particularly characterizes Eastern culture as distinct from West-
> ern culture. If sages in the East had not found this "Nothingness" and
> not transmitted it in an extensive way in the East, a cultural form that is
> called "Eastern" would not have appeared. Therefore, this Nothing-
> ness is the foundation and at the same time the expression of Eastern
> culture. Accordingly, without this moment, what is the Eastern cannot
> be fully understood in its inner significance. (p. 37, trans. Nakagawa)

Hisamatsu saw Eastern Nothingness as the ontological foundation of
Eastern culture, including philosophy, religion, and art. Whereas Western philosophy is a philosophy of "Being," Eastern philosophy is a philosophy of "Nothingness." "Everything in the West is based on actual
beings and their cognition.... It is in this sense that the West is the world
of 'Being' and Western culture is the culture of 'Being'" (p. 24, trans.
Nakagawa). Western philosophy is based on the worldview of Being in
which fundamental existence is embodied in actual beings. Obviously,

due to this worldview, Western objective science and technology have successfully explored the world of actual beings. On the other hand, to comprehend what is the Eastern, the position of Being must be subverted into the position of Nothingness. In other words, Eastern philosophy sees Nothingness as a deeper dimension than that of Being. Accordingly, Nothingness can be realized only when Being is negated through and through. "The basic way of the East lies in that 'Being' becomes 'Non-Being,' or 'Nothingness,' through self-destruction of 'Being'" (p. 34, trans. Nakagawa).

Let us take the concept of "transcendence," for instance. From the viewpoint of the "logic of Being," a transcendental reality means a supreme Being like God. By contrast, according to the "logic of Nothingness," what *is* is none other than a transcendental reality, for the logic of Nothingness negates any substantial concept of Being including a transcendent being and ultimately does away with the division between the sacred and the profane. Nothingness is not apart from Being but is "present" in Being itself. This view that "transcendence is presence" is the hallmark of Eastern spirituality. In this regard, Hisamatsu (1982) saw Zen as the negation of holiness:

> Zen ... negates this transcendent and objective holiness which is so radically separated from us just as it denies a Buddha existing apart from human beings. As such it is radically nonholy. Retrieving the holy Buddha, ... it realizes the Buddha within these human beings, a "nonholy," a human Buddha. (p. 173)

This is "a sort of Copernican effort to bring the transcendent objective holiness down to the ground of the human self and to grasp it as the subject of the self" (1982, 174). The self is identical with Buddha; however, "[t]his does not mean, of course, that man in his 'usual state' is a Buddha.... It is precisely the position of Zen to negate absolutely that 'usual state' of man" (p. 176). Only absolute negation leads to absolute affirmation of what is. Right beneath an ordinary being is an infinite depth of Nothingness.

To realize Eastern Nothingness in our existence requires us to cease to be a "usual" being. Particularly, this means moving away from the ordinary function of thinking. In the East, thinking has never enjoyed a supreme position among other human faculties. Hisamatsu (1939/1987) says: "The reason why thinking is disregarded, or regarded even as a disturbance to the realization of truth, is that in the East the metaphysical does not belong to the thinkable" (p. 31, trans. Nakagawa). Therefore, Eastern seekers have explored numerous ways of contemplation to transcend thinking.

Hisamatsu celebrated Eastern Nothingness as the heart of Eastern philosophy; however, at the same time he emphasized that what is the Eastern is not necessarily confined to the geographical realm of Asia, just as natural science has been called "Western" science because it has developed in the West. He did not intend to oppose the Asian to the European but rather, like Suzuki and Nishida, tried to reveal Eastern Nothingness as an ontological and existential dimension of the human being and thereby to bring about an enlarged vision of reality: "If we say the 'Eastern Metaphysical' [Nothingness], it sounds as if it is something regional, but the Eastern has never such a connotation. The 'Eastern Metaphysical' as such does not belong to the East nor to the West but it is universal" (1939/1987, 17, trans. Nakagawa).

Based on the preceding discussion, three characteristics of Eastern philosophy become evident:

First, Eastern philosophy has a certain ontology that sees reality as a multidimensional, stratified structure and assumes the deepest dimension. Suzuki's "Eastern Perspective" and "the cosmic Unconscious," Nishida's "pure experience" and "Absolute Nothingness," and Hisamatsu's "Eastern Nothingness" denote this deepest reality.[5] They do not signify a mere negative state in the sense that nothing exists; rather they imply the deepest open ground of reality from which all beings arise as they are.

Second, the idea of *multidimensional ontology* opens a new ground for integrating the Eastern and Western views to provide an enlarged vision of reality. The three thinkers tried in one way or another to articulate frameworks of "world-philosophy." In their views, both dualistic and non-dualistic perspectives, Being and Nothingness, have their own places in a comprehensive worldview. In this regard, what is the Eastern is an existential and ontological category.[6]

Third, schools of Eastern philosophy have always emphasized the importance of contemplative practice for the in-depth realization of what they say. The intellectual approaches are limited in this regard. In other words, personal transformation or self-cultivation through contemplative practice forms an integral part of Eastern philosophy.

An Eastern philosophy of holistic education is to include these aspects as its essential components. Thus, I turn to the thought of Toshihiko Izutsu, who has remarkably succeeded in delineating the fundamental structure of Eastern philosophy. His thought provides the best introduction to the Eastern philosophy of holistic education.

IZUTSU'S RECONSTRUCTION OF EASTERN PHILOSOPHY

Toshihiko Izutsu[7] (1914-1993) was one of the most remarkable Eastern philosophers in the twentieth century. His main concern was to reconstruct Eastern philosophy as a form of postmodern philosophy. After his enforced return to Japan in 1979 following the Khomeini revolution in Iran (where he had devoted himself to the studies of Islamic philosophy), he became more concerned with reconstructing Eastern philosophy as a whole. In 1982, Izutsu (1983) described his state of mind in his groundbreaking study *Ishiki to Honshitsu* [Consciousness and Essence] as follows:

> For these ten years, matters about Eastern thought or Eastern philosophy have come to urgently capture my mind.... In my youth, I was greatly affected by European literature and philosophy and was passionately absorbed in them. However, I could not forget the fascination of what is "the Eastern," and eventually I moved between East and West. But now, when I am almost seventy, I have come to truly feel that the "roots" of my existence have been in the East. I happened to find myself in such a situation. For me it meant a finding of *my East* within myself, though it is still vague and rambling. (p. 427, trans. Nakagawa)

The results of his studies appeared in a series of extraordinary articles (1983, 1985, 1989, 1991), which have encouraged us Easterners (Japanese) to review our own traditions of Eastern philosophy in the global context of the present time.

Izutsu regards "Eastern philosophy" as including various traditions of philosophical thought developed in the vast area of Asia, ranging from the Far East to the Middle East to the Near East. "Eastern philosophy" in this sense is so broad and diverse that it is not possible to identify its consistent development and coherent system, compared to the case of Western philosophy. In his words, "there is no general unification nor organic structure in Eastern philosophy as it is given to us.... The philosophy we find primarily in the East is, concretely put, multiple traditions of philosophy that co-exist but are entangled with each other in complicated ways" (1983, 428, trans. Nakagawa). The multiple bodies of Eastern philosophy are mainly due to the history of Eastern philosophy that goes back to ancient times with their regional diversity and different ethnic cultures.

Generally speaking, most studies in Eastern thought have been philological studies on classical texts within each tradition. In Izutsu's notion, they have been "past-oriented," objective, and accordingly not creative. Also, these scholastic studies have never tried to synthesize different traditions to yield a comprehensive system of Eastern philosophy. Faced with this prevalent situation, Izutsu took an alternative approach; he required that studies in Eastern philosophy be "future-oriented" and become a "creative source" for our future life. He was strongly convinced that Eastern philosophy must and can respond to the challenges of the present situation of the world and bring about a new perspective for a forthcoming global society.

> For years, I have conceived an opinion that it is not enough to store the traditions of Eastern thought ... as precious cultural heritage.... If we really respect the various traditions of thought that we inherited from the past, we should not commit follies to leave them as *the legacy of the past* and to let them remain dried up. But rather we have to make every effort to positively review them in response to the challenges of contemporary philosophy, and if necessary, we have to dare to deconstruct them and to reorganize them into a new form of Eastern philosophy that can be committed to the future. (1991, 467, trans. Nakagawa)

To develop a new "future-oriented" Eastern philosophy, the traditions of Eastern philosophy have to undergo a radical transformation. In this context, Izutsu introduced a "methodological operation," which was entirely new to conventional studies. The operation has two phases; the first phase is to apply a method called "meta-historical structuring" to the bodies of Eastern thought. He explained it as follows:

> Briefly speaking, this operation begins by disentangling main philosophical traditions in the East [from their historical backgrounds] and then, in the present context, places them on a theoretical plane on which they are going to be rearranged. In other words, it attempts to liberate the traditions of Eastern philosophy from their temporal dimension and to recombine them in a paradigmatic way in order to artificially create a new space for thought-connections that are capable of including them all in its structural framework. (1983, 429, trans. Nakagawa)

The method of meta-historical structuring has a twofold aspect in itself: (a) it hermeneutically sorts out the fundamental patterns of Eastern thought, and (b) it develops a more coherent structural system by rearranging the patterns. This method is concerned with "a new structuring, or hermeneutic reconstruction, of Eastern philosophy as a whole" (1991, 105, trans. Nakagawa). In this process, it is crucial not only to read texts in a "precise" or "objective" way but also "to read old texts in an entirely new way from the viewpoint of the present context" (1991, 468, trans. Nakagawa). Izutsu called it a "creative reading," which, "in addition to the philologically precise reading of a given text, and based on this reading, attempts to creatively explore a possible path of thought it suggests" (1991, 468, trans. Nakagawa).

The second phase of the methodological operation has to do with the "subjectification" or internalization of Eastern philosophy in our own existence. It is "to take the system of fundamental patterns of Eastern philosophy thus realized on ourselves and to subjectify it. Then, on this [subjective] foundation, we are going to establish our own viewpoints of Eastern philosophy" (1983, 429, trans. Nakagawa). This second phase has a complementary function to the first. Although the first phase still remains on an objective plane, the second phase requires us to understand the fundamental structure of Eastern philosophy from within. Here, Eastern philosophy comes to terms with the transformation of our own consciousness. It is through this transformation that we can create a new form of Eastern philosophy.

THE FUNDAMENTAL STRUCTURE OF EASTERN PHILOSOPHY

One of the remarkable patterns found in Eastern philosophy is, according to Izutsu, the idea of multiple dimensionality. "The thought-space thus created [by the methodological operation] will certainly have a multidimensional and multistratified structure" (1983, 429, trans. Nakagawa). In *Sufism and Taoism* (1983/1984), he says, "Existence or Reality as 'experienced' on supra-sensible levels reveals itself as of a multistratified structure. The Reality which one observes in this kind of metaphysical intuition is not of a unistratum structure" (p. 479). For example, he delineates "multistratified structure" in the philosophies of Ibn Arabi and Lao Tzu (1983/1984, 481). Ibn Arabi's strata contain:

- The sensible world
- The stage of Images and Similitudes
- The stage of the Divine Actions (the stage of Lordship)
- The stage of the Divine Attributes and Names (the stage of Divinity)
- The stage of the Essence (the absolute Mystery, abysmal Darkness).

Likewise, Lao Tzu's strata consist of:

- The ten thousand things
- Being (Heaven and Earth)
- One
- Non-Being
- Mystery of Mysteries.

What follows will delineate a multistratified structure of reality, which Izutsu (1981a, 1983, 1985) recognized as a representative pattern in Eastern philosophy.

First, the most superficial level of the multidimensional structure is the empirical world of myriad beings (or things). This is the level of so-called naive realism that perceives things as objective, separate, discrete, tangible, and solid entities. However, in the Eastern view, this worldview of separation and diversity (multiplicity) in naive realism is just a surface view of reality that is nothing but a production of the mind, or what Izutsu calls "subjective fabrication" and "semantic articulation." In this regard, he refers to contemporary semantics to describe how this empirical world arises for us. We are strongly inclined to believe that we are living in an objective world of concrete things independent of us:

> In truth, however, this seemingly intrinsic order of the world is but a subjective fabrication. The immediate reality, what is initially given, is a welter of sense impressions, a tremendous tangle of incoherent and elusive sense-data. (1981a, 435)

It is the "semantic articulation" of the mind that molds the immediate inarticulate state of sensory experience into an ordered world of things. "The essential mechanism of the mind ... is such that it immediately transforms this bewildering chaos of sense-data into an ordered world by producing within itself sensory images having their structural basis in the semantic evocations of words" (1981a, 436). The mind articulates the immediate reality into a "meaningful" world by forming "sense-images" in accordance with the "semantic configuration" of language. This is the basic mechanism that gives rise to the empirical world we experience in our ordinary state of consciousness.

Second, as the deeper levels of consciousness are cultivated, the world becomes more subtle and fluid. Each being begins to lose its solid appearance as a separate object. On this second level the vast realm of "imagination" exists. Izutsu (1985) observes: "Things liberate themselves from their individual material forms firmly held in the dimension of ordinary sense and transform themselves into fluid and creative images" (p. 33, trans. Nakagawa). The "fluid and creative images" are distinct from the surface "sensory images," for the former involve "mythic, mythopoeic, archetypal, or symbolic images" (1981a, 441) that abide in the deeper unconsciousness with no factual references in the empirical world. In short, Izutsu calls them the "symbolic images."

This second realm of the symbolic images produces a "symbolic picture of reality," or the "symbolic articulation of reality," which is entirely different from the common-sense articulation of reality in the surface level. Due to the "mythopoeic" nature of the symbolic images, they have found their expressions in myths, legends, fairy tales, fantasies, dreams, symbolic arts (mandala, icon), sacred words and sounds (mantra), and others. The symbolic images can be activated in altered states of consciousness such as shamanic experiences, visualization, magico-religious rituals, and psychotherapeutic experiences like pychosynthesis (Assagioli 1965/1971) and holotropic breathing (Grof 1985). The world of the symbolic images has been explored under the concepts of the "collective unconscious of archetypes" (Jung), the "mythic images" (Campbell), and the "symbols and metaphors of transformation" (Metzner 1986).

In this regard, Izutsu refers to the concept of *mundus imaginalis* coined by Henry Corbin. According to Corbin's (1995) own exposition on "theosophy" in Islamic philosophy (especially Sohravardi's theosophy), there are three universes corresponding to three modes of perception; that is, the "physical sensory world," the "suprasensory world of the Soul," and the "universe of pure archangelic Intelligences" (p. 8). The corresponding three organs of perception are the senses, the imagination, and the intellect. The *mundus imaginalis* designates the intermediate world, "a world as ontologically real as the world of the senses and the world of the intellect, a world that requires a faculty of perception belonging to it" (p. 9). The imaginative consciousness is a psycho-spiritual organ that can perceive the imaginative world. Corbin uses the term "imaginative" instead of "imaginary" because the latter implies something unreal or utopian. The "imaginative" world is real in its own right and has an "immaterial materiality."

For example, Jalal al-Din Rumi (1994, 145-46) remarks in his discourse as follows:

> The human imagination and inner workings are like an entryway through which one comes first before entering a house. This whole world is like a house, and everything that comes inside the entryway must of necessity appear in the house.... Imagination, thought, and ideas are the entryway to the house.... And everything ... that appears in this world appears first in the entryway; only then does it appear here.

Rumi correctly knows that the images constitute the intermediate stratum of reality: "In comparison with the world of concepts and sensibles, the world of mental images is broader because all concepts are born of mental images; but the world of mental images is narrow in relation to the world where mental images are given being" (p. 203).

Eastern philosophy has a variety of descriptions of the *mundus imaginalis* (e.g., Izutsu 1983, chaps. VIII-XI). The *I Ching* appeared in ancient China, for example, and depicts a symbolic system of the universe with the eight basic trigrams and the sixty-four hexagrams. These trigrams and hexagrams are archetypal images (archetypal diagrams) articulating different aspects of the universe (e.g., Wilhelm 1950/1977; Izutsu 1980). The schools of Esoteric and Tantric Buddhism have been mostly concerned with the symbolic world of images. They have described this realm in the forms of *mandala* symbolism and have invented methods of contemplation using visualization to activate the imaginative states so that they could symbolically realize the Buddhist universe.

The symbolic images are valuable, even though they appear to be absurd or insignificant to our common-sense mind, because they represent deeper worldviews unattainable in our ordinary state of consciousness. According to Izutsu (1981a, 443),

> the symbolic images ... are extremely valuable in that the figures of the things looming up through the mist of these images do represent the primeval configurations of a reality which are psychically far more real and more relevant to the fate and existence of man than the sensory reality established at the surface level of consciousness. The world-vision presented by the images ... is, in other words, a direct reflection of reality as it is viewed at a deeper level of consciousness, and as such it reveals the primeval structure of Being which remains hidden from the view of the empirical eyes....

Izutsu regards "the house of the symbolic images" as *mundus imaginalis* and also posits the fundamental place that generates the images at the bottom of *mundus imaginalis*. He calls the place the "linguistic *alaya-vijnana*," or the "linguistic Storehouse Consciousness," relying on the idea of *alaya-vijnana* developed in the Yogacara School of Mahayana Buddhism. The "linguistic Storehouse Consciousness" in question is the underlying matrix where all images (including the sensory images as well as the symbolic images) are conceived and, to use Yogacara terminology, stored as *bija*, or "psychic seeds," which tend to transform themselves into actual images.

The third dimension is called "ontological Chaos" after Chuang Tzu's conception of "Chaos." One of the famous parables by Chuang Tzu refers to "Chaos" as follows:

> The emperor of the South Sea was called Shu [Brief], the emperor of
> the North Sea was called Hu [Sudden], and the emperor of the central
> region was called Hun-tun [Chaos]. Shu and Hu from time to time
> came together for a meeting in the territory of Hun-tun, and Hun-tun
> treated them very generously. Shu and Hu discussed how they could
> repay his kindness. "All men," they said, "have seven openings so
> they can see, hear, eat, and breathe. But Hun-tun alone doesn't have
> any. Let's trying boring him some!"
> Every day they bored another hole, and on the seventh day Hun-tun
> died. (Watson 1968, 97)

This parable describes Hun-tun (Chaos) as a deeper dimension of organic continuum, which must be killed by the discriminative analysis by Shu and Hu. On this level of the chaotic reality, every being becomes a "fluid state" in which the distinctive boundary completely dissolves away and each interconnects with each. This is the dimension of interconnectedness of all beings. This "ontological fluidity" also means an "ontological transparency": "On the world of the surface consciousness, A is A, and B is B through and through. And they mutually obstruct; that is, there exists an ontological resistance between them" (Izutsu 1985, 34, trans. Nakagawa). By contrast, in the state of fluidity the ontological resistance disappears, and all beings become non-resistant and mutually transparent to each other. Boundaries become so fluid and transparent that every being mutually immerses. The "ontological Chaos" is "a reality of fusion of beings in which every being ... kaleidoscopically mingles with each other and penetrates into each other" (1985, 35, trans. Nakagawa). However, the third dimension of the ontological Chaos is not the final dimension in the structure of multidimensional reality.

The fourth, deepest dimension is "Non-Being" (Nothingness). In this stage, "Chuang Tzu's 'Chaos' turns into Lao Tzu's 'Non-Being'" (1985, 36, trans. Nakagawa).[8] Izutsu explains this as follows:

Here consciousness is no longer "consciousness of something" but absolutely pure "Consciousness" itself.... It is not even a consciousness *of* "Non-Being" but rather "Consciousness" *is* completely identical with "Non-Being." In other words, this is a situation in which the metaphysical reality in its state of non-articulation manifests itself as "Consciousness" in absolute subjectivity. This mutual identity of both sides means the Absolute Unarticulated. (1985, 36, trans. Nakagawa)

He calls this deepest level "the ultimate Zero Point of Consciousness and Existence." In the traditions of Eastern philosophy, the ultimate Zero Point has been named in various ways: *nirgna Brahman* (formless Absolute) in Vedanta philosophy, *wu* (Non-Being) in Taoism, *sunyata* (Emptiness) in Mahayana Buddhism, *wu-chi* (the ultimate Principle of Non-Being) in Neo-Confucianism, and *mushin* (No-Mind) in Zen. (This ultimate point corresponds to Suzuki's "Eastern Perspective" and "Cosmic Unconscious," Nishida's "pure experience" and "Absolute Nothingness," and Hisamatsu's "Eastern Nothingness.")

The Eastern way of contemplation helps us to realize the ultimate Zero Point; however, this is not the final phase of contemplation but covers only the first half of the Eastern way of contemplation. Eastern spirituality does not abide in a transcendental realm, but, on the contrary, once it attains that point, it returns to all the other levels. In other words, the Zero Point marks the turning point of contemplation from the "seeking mode" to the "returning mode."[9] "The long way of contemplative practice comes to 'Non-Being' and thus attains its goal, but one starts with the point, turns back the same route, and again returns to the world of ordinary consciousness" (1985, 37, trans. Nakagawa).

This twofold movement of seeking and returning constitutes the dynamic movement of Eastern philosophy. This is not to say, however, that the "ordinary" consciousness that has reappeared in the returning mode is the same as the original pre-contemplative state (the first dimension), because it integrates all the dimensions of consciousness and thereby it is *radically transformed.* This resurrected consciousness is both ordinary and extraordinary in the sense that the infinite reality permeates the very ordinary state of consciousness.

In the seeking mode of contemplation, the ultimate Zero Point inevitably serves to deconstruct and negate all beings, phenomenal or

imaginal, into Non-Being. In the returning path, on the contrary, it reveals an all-generating, all-embracing, all-affirming, absolutely positive
aspect of Non-Being.

> The returning way of contemplation surely has its ontological aspect.
> In this aspect, the "Non-Being" as the starting point becomes the abso-
> lutely pre-phenomenal level, *Urgrund* [the primordial ground] for the
> entire phenomenal world, and the Metaphysical Unarticulated from
> which the world of beings emerges in temporal and spatial diversifica-
> tion. (1985, 37, trans. Nakagawa)

All beings in the phenomenal level here are no longer self-subsistent
separate entities but arise as "self-articulation," "self-evolvement," or
"self-manifestation" of "the Metaphysical Unarticulated." "In the eye of
those who have experienced this spiritual Awakening, all things ... manifest the presence of 'Something beyond.' And that 'Something beyond' is
ultimately ... the Absolute" (1983/1984, 481).

It is on this ontological ground that diverse appearances of all beings
are fundamentally unified. "Beneath everything in the empirical world
lies absolute unity in non-articulation, which permeates into all realms
of phenomenal beings" (1985, 37, trans. Nakagawa). There is no longer
division between the Absolute and the particular: "The only 'reality' (in
the true sense of the term) is the Absolute revealing itself as it really is in
the sensible forms which are nothing but the loci of its self-manifestation" (1983/1984, 480). Eastern philosophy regards this as the truly ultimate reality.

As mentioned before, the interconnectedness of all beings has appeared at the third stage of the "Chaos" in the seeking path of contemplation. In the returning path, the ontological Chaos emerges in the midst of
ordinary experiences of everyday life. Here "ordinary life as such is
'chaotified'; all things appear under the phase of limitless overlapping,
infinite mutual penetration, and mutual fusion by way of underlying
'Non-Being'" (1985, 38, trans. Nakagawa). The conscious states of those
who have experienced "Nothingness" are so radically transformed that
they perceive the phenomenal beings under the phases of
interpenetration as well as individuality. The individual phenomenal
being is in this state no longer a separate solid entity with a definite
boundary but emerges as an "ontological event," or a fluid "process."

Izutsu (1985) describes the "ontological landscape" thus realized as follows:

> As a whole, things that are supposed to exist in this [phenomenal] world are nothing but a multidimensional, multistratified extension of "events" that arise in the process whereby "Non-Being," or the Absolute Unarticulated, diversifies itself in various forms. What is more, each "event" is literally a momentary event. The Unarticulated turns into its self-articulated form in a moment and then returns into the original state of non-articulation. This self-evolvement into a being and reversion [into Non-Being] of the Unarticulated is ceaselessly repeated.... The world of Existence, therefore, is in an endless dynamic process, in the cosmic flux. All beings in this world are fundamentally marked by the ontological fluidity in this sense. This is the ontological landscape of Reality witnessed by those who have realized all levels of Consciousness, both surface and deeper levels, through their contemplation starting with "Being" and arriving at "Non-Being" and then returning from "Non-Being" to "Being." (p. 39, trans. Nakagawa)

To sum up, Izutsu's multidimensional ontology includes the dimensions of the phenomenal multiplicity of individual beings, the unconscious realm of imagination, or *mundus imaginalis,* the ontological Chaos, and the ultimate Zero Point of Non-Being. They are not static strata but dynamically interconnected. While in the seeking mode of contemplation they may be respectively experienced; in the returning mode they are simultaneously experienced in one and the same reality.

The critical concern of Eastern philosophers has been a spiritual seeking after the true "Self" and thereby the true Existence. The multidimensionality of the "Self" realized in contemplation reveals the corresponding multidimensionality of Existence. Izutsu (1985) remarks:

> The whole of the "Self," namely, Consciousness being thoroughly aware of its depth and span, can correctly perceive the whole picture of multiple realities of Existence with its infinite span and immense depth. The world of Existence is infinitely wide and bottomlessly profound, and so is the "Self." (p. 40, trans. Nakagawa)

Izutsu's reconstruction of Eastern philosophy as a multidimensional ontology, I believe, can best guide us to develop an Eastern philosophy of holistic education. Inspired by Izutsu as well as Suzuki, Nishida, and

Hisamatsu, in the next chapter I will delineate a multidimensional theory of holistic education.

NOTES

1. Sizuteru Ueda (1926–) is one of the most important contemporary Zen philosophers ever to appear in the Kyoto school of philosophy.

2. Masao Abe (1915–), a leading scholar of the Kyoto school of philosophy, is a translator of Nishida's *An Inquiry into the Good*.

3. Robert Carter (1997) provides a systematic introduction to Nishida's philosophy in English. See also Nishitani (1991).

4. A journal called *The Eastern Buddhist*, founded by D. T. Suzuki in 1921 and published by the Eastern Buddhist Society, has introduced the essential work of the Kyoto school to the world.

5. The idea of multidimensional reality as such has its counterparts in Western philosophy. Quite a few thinkers have provided various conceptions and models of multidimensional reality. However, Eastern philosophy is original in its emphasis on the deepest dimension that is absolutely nothing, empty, and infinitely open in its structure.

6. Among Western thinkers are some who are very close to the Eastern way of thinking. In this regard, Suzuki (1957), Hisamatsu, and Ueda (1982b, 1983a, 1983b, 1990, 1991a) highlight Meister Eckhart and his thought.

7. Izutsu first studied Western philosophy and wrote books on Greek mysticism and the Russian intellectuals. Later he became known worldwide as a prominent scholar of Islamic philosophy, especially Sufism. His work in this field includes the Japanese translations of *Qur'an* and the discourses of Jalal al-Din Rumi, and philosophical treaties such as *Ethico-Religious Concepts in the Qur'an* (1966) and *Sufism and Taoism* (1983/1984). He had been Professor at Keio University in Tokyo, at McGill University in Montreal and at the Imperial Iranian Academy of Philosophy in Teheran. Also, from the late '60s to the early '80s he was one of the main speakers at the Eranos conferences held in Switzerland where he addressed broad topics from Eastern philosophy, including Taoism, Neo-Confucianism, *I Ching*, Hua-yen Buddhism, and Zen. Essays on Zen based on his presentations were compiled in *Toward a Philosophy of Zen Buddhism* (1977/1982).

8. It is to be noted that like Lao Tzu's philosophy, the heart of Chuang Tzu's philosophy lies in the profound ideas of Non-Being.

9. The two terms "seeking" and "returning" correspond to Japanese words *oso* and *genso*, whose literal meanings are "going forth" and "coming back." Also, the same twofold movement has been called in Japanese *kojo* and *koge*, whose literal meanings are "going upward" and "coming down," or "ascending" and "descending."

The Multidimensional Theory of Holistic Education

THE FIVE DIMENSIONS OF REALITY

This chapter will present a multidimensional ontology as a basic framework for holistic education, a framework called *the five dimensions of reality*. The five dimensions include the objective reality, the social reality, the cosmic reality, the infinite reality, and the universal reality. An overview of the model is this:

Dimension I is *the objective reality*. It is *the phenomenal empirical world of objective beings* perceived by our ordinary sense cognition. This objective dimension is comprised of particular individual beings that appear to be sensible, tangible, physical, material, and substantial. It is the world of assembly or aggregation of these "objective" beings. This dimension is the realm of "naive realism" in which atomistic and mechanistic worldviews and subject-object dualism are predominant. This objective reality is marked by concepts such as fragmentation, diversification, separation, disconnection, and compartmentalization.

Dimension II is *the social reality*. It is the social world underlying the phenomenal objective world. This social world articulates the phenomenal distinctions of individual beings. It differentiates a thing into each discrete objective being in accordance with the pre-established structure of meaning. Every objective being is a "meaning unit" that is articulated, constructed, and maintained in an entire meaning structure produced by language. Therefore, this social dimension is a semantic linguistic foundation of the phenomenal objective reality. It is also the world of *interrelation* due to the nature of language. A meaning is not a label attached to an object but a construct articulated in relation to other meanings in a language system. This function of semantic articulation is not an individual fabrication but a collective, intersubjective, and *social* performance. This social reality has been explored in structuralism, semantics, hermeneutics, and other related fields.

Dimension III is *the cosmic reality*. It is the deeper dimension of *nature, life*, and *the universe* that embraces the preceding dimensions. This cosmic dimension is the realm of spatio-temporal *interconnection* in which everything is dynamically and organically interconnected. Everything is here no longer clearly differentiated or articulated. Nature, life, and the universe are organic wholes inseparably connected, and they form a cosmic world. The interconnections between things on this level are neither linear causal relations between objective beings nor the fixed codes of meaning of the social world but relationships that are perceived in synchronic mutual causality and interdependence. Also, the cosmic world is structured not in a static manner but in a fluid process of constant metamorphosis. In this sense, it is the world of *Becoming*, which includes both relative being and relative non-being taking place in the flux of self-organizing, self-renewing processes of the universe. Ceaseless processes of birth, growth, decay, and death—the cycle of being and non-being—are the essential aspect of Becoming (the evolutionary process of the universe). This is the realm of "cosmology" that involves not only various cosmological ideas of the past but now also ecology and systems theories. This cosmic reality has been described in mythic worldviews and now in scientific worldviews of ecology and systems theories. In the cosmological worldviews, the constitution of the human being correlates to the essential structure of the cosmos; that is, the human being is grasped as a microcosm of the macrocosm.[1]

Dimension IV is *the infinite reality*. It is the deepest dimension of reality. This fourth dimension is the ontological foundation of the cosmos. The traditions of Eastern philosophy have conceptualized this reality in such terms as *Brahman, nirvana, sunyata, wu, t'ai-chi,* and *li.* This dimension has also been called "Mind" (*h'sin*) in the Yogacara tradition of Buddhism, "essential nature" by Hui-neng, "the Unborn" (*fujyo*) by Bankei, and "the primordial state" in Dzogchen of Tibetan Buddhism. It is also the dimension of Suzuki's "Eastern Perspective" and "Cosmic Unconscious," Nishida's "pure experience" and "Absolute Nothingness," Ueda's "Infinite Openness," Hisamatsu's "Eastern Nothingness," and Izutsu's "Zero Point." This dimension is also what Ken Wilber calls "Mind," "Unity Consciousness," and "the Causal," John Welwood calls "the open ground," and Herbert Guenther calls the "open dimension." Among Eastern conceptions are two different types of thought: The concepts such as *Brahman* and *li* are *realistic* in their ethos, meaning Absolute Being. On the other hand, the concepts such as *nirvana, sunyata, wu* are *nihilistic,* meaning Absolute Non-Being. However, ontologically they all share the same aspect; they all represent the Absolute, or the Ultimate, beyond qualifications and conditions of any kind. So Huston Smith (1976/1992) uses the word "Infinite" (in the sense of not being finite) to denote such an aspect (pp. 54-55). In this sense, this deepest dimension of reality is called *the infinite reality.*

Dimension V is *the universal reality.* The infinite reality is the deepest dimension of reality, yet it is not the final phase of the multidimensional reality. As we have seen in Izutsu's exposition of Eastern philosophy, there is a twofold movement of seeking and returning in contemplation. In the seeking path, one starts with the phenomenal level, explores the deeper levels, and then attains the deepest level. The realization of the deepest, infinite reality is called *Enlightenment* or *Awakening.*[2] After Awakening, the returning movement begins. In the returning path, the whole dimensions (the objective reality, the social reality, and the cosmic reality) reappear in such a way that the infinite reality manifests itself into them. In this way, they are radically transformed by the infinite reality. *Dimension V* signifies this transformed reality, which is called *the universal reality.* The universal reality is *this* world that appears in Enlightenment. Eastern philosophy regards this universal dimension as the *truly* ultimate reality in which no dualistic separation between dimensions can be found. In other words, this non-dual universal reality is the world where every finite being reveals the infinite reality as it is. The mode of relationships on this dimension is called *interpenetration* (as distinct from interconnection of the cosmic reality). Interpenetration is the aspect of relationships to be emerged in Enlightenment.

This model of the five dimensions of reality is informed by both Eastern and Western ideas. Western theories of contemporary holistic education have so far attempted to enlarge the foundation of education from the objective and social realities to the cosmic reality. On the other hand, Eastern ideas of holistic education are mainly concerned with the infinite reality and the universal reality.

If we try to make a correlation between these dimensions and such major concepts as the body, the mind, the soul, and the spirit, we can say that the objective reality represents the aspect of the body, that the social reality is the production of the mind, that the cosmic reality is the place where the soul thrives, that the infinite reality is identical with the ultimate level of the spirit, and that the universal reality is the spirit-in-action manifest in the body, the mind, and the soul.

These five dimensions of reality do not form a static hierarchy or stratum in which discrete dimensions overlap one another, but they constitute *the wholeness of reality,* a particular aspect of which each dimension reveals.[3] According to the Eastern ideas, all dimensions are ultimately identical in a non-dualistic way, which the universal reality means. However, this fullest realization of wholeness arises in Enlightenment.

All dimensions are inseparably interwoven and ever present. However, the mind usually fails to recognize this wholeness of reality. Exclusive identification with the first two dimensions by the mind obstructs the recognition of the wholeness. Hence, the point is to *remember* what *is* always already by transforming the mind. Eastern philosophy is an effort to recover the wholeness of reality by the twofold movement of seeking and returning. The first four dimensions portray the gradual degrees of awakening towards the deeper dimensions of reality in the seeking path. And the universal reality discloses the "original face" of this wholeness in the returning path.

This multidimensional theory gives us a definition of holistic education; that is, *holistic education is an attempt to explore multidimensional real-*

ity in our own existence. Holistic education helps us attain the depth of our existence and thereby recover the wholeness of reality.

FROM SUBSTANTIALISM TO RELATIONALISM

Before we explore the five dimensions, we will consider an important thought factor called "relationalism." Relationalism is a philosophical position that intends to overcome substantialism, a form of thought that holds the primacy of substantial entities. Wataru Hiromatsu (1982), who presents a "relationalist worldview" (*koto-teki sekaikan*) in place of a "substantialist worldview" (*mono-teki sekaizo*), states: "In this [substantialist] worldview, the basic understanding is that in the first place there are self-independent beings (entities) and that these entities have various characteristics and relate to each other" (p. vi, trans. Nakagawa). Substantial beings are self-contained and self-subsistent entities, ranging from atoms to a physical thing to a living organism to a human individual. Substantialism takes actual existence of these entities for granted. This substantialist worldview is virtually predominant in our conventional, common-sense, everyday thinking.

In contrast, relationalism tries to deconstruct the substantialist conceptions by comprehending them in larger contexts where an individual substance is no longer seen as an independent entity but as a knot of various relations. Hiromatsu (1982) says:

> Relationalism sees what are supposed to be not only so-called "characteristics" but also "entities" as in reality nothing more than "knots" of relational determinants. In this view of being, the basic understanding is not that entities independently exist and secondarily relate to each other but that relational determinants are the primary being.... The primacy of relationships means ... that relationships as "events" (*koto*) are universal and fundamental determinants of being. (pp. vi-vii, trans. Nakagawa)

We are familiar with a variety of relationalist thought. For example, in 1849, in a prophetic voice, Soren Kierkegaard (1941/1954) already gave a relationalist definition of the "self" in his *The Sickness unto Death*. He said: "The self is a relation which relates itself to its own self, or it is that in the relation ... that the relation relates itself to its own self" (p. 146). In the early twentieth century Martin Buber (1970/1996) originated a dialogical philosophy that represents a relationalist philosophy. In his classic *I and Thou* (originally published in 1923), he claimed: "In the beginning is the relation" (p. 69). In Germany, a group of hermeneutic philosophers—Wilhelm Dilthey, Martin Heidegger, Hans-Georg Gadamer, and Otto Friedrich Bollnow—has attempted to understand the meanings of human existence embedded in cultural and historical contexts called "meaning-connections" (*Sinnzusammenhänge*). In France, structuralists have analyzed the underlying unconscious structure of culture that defines our belief systems and behaviors. In response to structuralists, post-structuralists have tried to deconstruct the fixed structure of culture into the flux of uncoded interactions.

In the field of education and pedagogy, there remains a predominant tendency to rely on substantial ideas such as intrinsic or innate nature, instincts, interests, motives, drives, needs, abilities, identity, individuality, the ego, and so forth, as if human beings were endowed with them from the beginning of life. This type of substantialist thinking has been evident among the naturalistic, organismic, child-centered, humanistic, and individualistic orientations of education. However, from a relationalist point of view, it is impossible to assume an independent entity of any sort within a person, simply because everything is related to each other. In this regard, Gregory Bateson (1979/1980), a proponent of relationalism, once remarked:

> Relationship is not internal to the single person. It is nonsense to talk about "dependency" or "aggressiveness" or "pride," and so on. All such words have their roots in what happens between persons, not in some something-or-other inside a person. (p. 147)

As he says, "the relationship comes first; it *precedes*" (p. 147). An important task of pedagogical thinking is to reinterpret substantial ideas in relationships. In this respect, the ideas of holistic education are definitely relationalist.

Relationalism in education, as we will see soon, refers to two different modes of relationships, which I call "communication" and "communion." Therefore, the relationalist pedagogy includes two major fields: "pedagogy of communication" and "pedagogy of communion." Among the five dimensions of reality as delineated before, the first and second dimensions (the objective reality and the social reality) correspond to the pedagogy of communication, and the third, the fourth, and the fifth dimensions (the cosmic reality, the infinite reality, and the universal reality) correspond to the pedagogy of communion.[4] In the following discussion, I will explore each dimension with regard to these two modes of relationships.

THE PEDAGOGY OF COMMUNICATION

FRAGMENTATION THROUGH COMMUNICATION

The objective reality and the social reality are always connected in the way that the phenomenal individual beings are constructed by the underlying social interrelation. The separate objective beings are always interrelated in the social world. It is the underlying social interrelation that produces and maintains the apparent distinctions (objectivity) of beings. Individual beings are implicitly interrelated in such a way that they appear to be explicitly separate and objective.

The pedagogy of communication explores this relationship between the first two dimensions. In other words, it focuses on formative interactions working through our everyday communicative relationships. The communicative interactions in our everyday life ceaselessly reproduce and maintain our social reality in which each objective being is formed. The primary function of education in communicative process is to form "individual" beings that seem to be separate from each other and in this sense objective.

To comprehend this, we need to see how a human society is constituted. To begin with, let us compare it with the biological world called by Jacob von Uexküll (1928/1973) the *Umwelt* (the environmental world). The *Umwelt* of a species forms a "functional circle" (*Funktionskreis*) by means of the animals' receptor and effector systems. It means that animals of different species do not live in the same one environment, that each species articulates its own biological world in accordance with its biological system and dwells in a different biological circumstance. This holds true for human beings as long as their biological conditions are concerned. However, humans are different from other species, for they dwell in a "symbolic world" as well. Ernst Cassirer (1944, 24) makes the point:

> Obviously this world [the human world] forms no exception to those
> biological rules which govern the life of all the other organisms. Yet in
> the human world we find a new characteristic which appears to be the
> distinctive mark of human life. The functional circle of man is not only
> quantitatively enlarged; it has also undergone a qualitative change.
> Man has, as it were, discovered a new method of adapting himself to
> his environment. Between the receptor system and the effector system
> … we find in man a third link which we may describe as the *symbolic
> system*. This new acquisition transforms the whole of human life.

Human beings live in a symbolic world as well as a biological world
by means of the "symbolic system" that articulates reality into the "symbolic" world in accordance with its own categories, independent of biological dispositions. In this way, human beings dwell in the
"double"—biological and symbolic—worlds.

Keizaburo Maruyama (1984) calls this system peculiar to human beings "double articulation" that contains "primary articulation" and
"secondary articulation." The primary, or biological, articulation corresponds to Uexküll's *Umwelt*, which Maruyama regards as "the structure
of somatic articulation" (*miwake-kozo*). In contrast, the "secondary articulation," called "the structure of linguistic articulation" (*kotowake-kozo*),
arises in the symbol-making function of language. On the relation between the two structures of articulation, he concludes: "'The structure of
linguistic articulation' has been created not because 'the structure of somatic articulation' was destroyed, but rather the rise of the unnatural
'structure of linguistic articulation' has caused the cogwheels of natural
instincts to become out of gear and swiftly destroyed 'the structure of somatic articulation'" (p. 127, trans. Nakagawa). The "unnatural" factor of
symbolic articulation, namely, human "culture," has become so dominant in human existence that the natural biological factors have deterio-
rated. Indeed, humans no longer live in a "pure" physical and biological
reality but in a symbolic reality. The "secondary articulation" is geneti-
cally "secondary" but factually and existentially "primary."

The symbolic articulation of the world through language that takes
place in the social world creates a realistic image of objective beings.
Toshihiko Izutsu (1985) summarizes the function of language to create a
symbolic world as follows:[5]

> Language, from a semantic point of view, is a system to articulate "reality," that is, a network of linguistic symbols projected onto the raw being in chaos. The raw being in chaos is divided, articulated, and ordered in different ways in accordance with the paradigmatic lines designated by the meanings of words which are semiotic units constituting a language (Saussure's *langue*). Through this process, there arises a culture and the "world." The "world" is a metamorphosis of "nature" semantically structured by the intermediation of linguistic symbols, and it is the whole of things and events meaningfully articulated. (p. 55, trans. Nakagawa)

The nature of language lies in its articulation and differentiation of a given reality according to the predetermined meanings. This is the semantic ground for separate objective beings to arise on the phenomenal level. According to Izutsu (1966, 10),

> upon the originally formless mass of existence, the human mind has drawn an infinite number of lines, and made divisions and segments, large and small; and the world of reality has in this way received the imprints of linguistic and conceptual formulation; and an order has been brought into the original chaos.

The objective reality (the objective distinctions of individual beings) is always mediated by the linguistic and semantic articulation. However, this mechanism is totally invisible, concealed from our everyday consciousness. It is this concealment that makes it possible for a thing to present itself as if it were an independent objective thing.

> Usually we are so accustomed to this middle screen, and it is something so natural, so transparent, that we are not even aware of its existence. We naively believe that we are experiencing directly and without any intermediary the objective world as it naturally is. (Izutsu 1966, 10)

Hermeneutic philosophy has grasped this tacit pre-conscious function of understanding in such conceptions as "pre-ontological understanding of being" (*das vor-ontologische Seinsverständnis*) (Heidegger 1996, 11) and "pre-understanding" (*Vorverständnis*) (Bollnow 1970/1981, 104). As Bollnow observes, the pre-understanding is powerful in its hidden *pre*-structure.

The symbolic world is an interrelational reality based on language, which can be sustained only through social interrelation, or communication (non-verbal behaviors, gestures, performance, conversation, fashion, customs, routines, rites, institutionalized social systems, and so forth). The primary function of communication is to fulfill the meanings of the symbolic system and thereby to reproduce and perpetuate the symbolic articulation. In doing so, communicative relationships maintain the social reality as a whole, which is nothing but a symbolic system. Not only does society sustain individuals therein but also *individuals through their everyday communication and interactions sustain society*. For example, ethnomethodology observes that people construct social reality through their social interactions. As Kenneth Leiter (1980, 20) says, "social reality is constituted through meaning and people's meaning-endowing activities." The social reality is a socially constructed reality by people's sense-making activities.

THE COMMUNICATIVE FORMATION OF SELF-IDENTITY

Human beings articulate and maintain the phenomenal objective reality of individual beings by constituting the deeper, social reality through communication. In the same way, the formation of a "self-identity" of a human being takes place. Self-identity is a socially constructed unit in accordance with the symbolic articulation. The self is not a substantial entity but a relational self determined by social interrelation. Communicative social interrelation articulates and maintains the social self in the entire context of the social reality.

The formation of self-identity involves a twofold aspect of "identification" and "differentiation." Identification is to identify and define the self with a certain meaning, and differentiation is to differentiate others from the self by defining them as having different but complementary meanings. Every self-identity needs simultaneously both identification and differentiation for it to emerge, because the self is always defined in relation to others. In this regard, R. D. Laing (1961/1971, 82) introduced the concept of "complementary identity": "By complementarity I denote that function of personal relations whereby the other fulfills or completes self." For example, a person needs a student for her or him to be a teacher. In a social setting, every self-identity needs its complementary

identity for it to take a specific form. "Every relationship implies a definition of self by other and other by self" (p. 86). Self and other reciprocally
contribute to the completion of each other's identity. They cooperate together to build their distinctive identities on the phenomenal level
through their communicative interrelation.

Karl Löwith (1928), a German philosopher, described this process of
self-formation in his *Das Individuum in der Rolle des Mitmenschen* as follows:

> Because a human "*Dasein*" (being-there) is always already "be-
> ing-with," the "as," which characterizes it in itself, means simulta-
> neously the "as" in keeping sight of others, that is, the "as different
> from." (p. 50, trans. Nakagawa)

The "as" (*als*) corresponds to identification and the "as different from"
(*anders-als*) to differentiation. The "as" that is the structural moment of
the self is always coupled with the "as different from." The self-under-
standing made by "as" simultaneously contains an understanding of the
other "as being different from" the self. This structure of self-under-
standing reveals underlying relationships that diversify self and others.
Löwith (1928) says: "In the 'as' of the 'as different from' is revealed a dif-
ferentiating connection" (p. 50, trans. Nakagawa). Based on the underlying connection, articulation (identification-differentiation) of self and
others takes place. In this sense, a human being (*Dasein*) is always a "be-
ing-with" (*Mitdasein*).

The formation of self-identity in identification-differentiation does
not occur in an arbitrary way but normally follows the pre-given or
pre-imposed meaning structure of the social system. Self-identity (or the
social self) that appears in the phenomenal world is a socially constructed meaning in the social world. The meaning of self-identity is initially imposed by others who have already embodied the social world.
As Laing (1961/1971, 95) says, "one's first social identity is conferred on
one. We learn to be whom we are told we are." In other words, a person is
given a certain "position," or "place," by significant others in their social
"world." Peter Berger and Thomas Luckmann (1966/1967), who define
"socialization" as "the comprehensive and consistent induction of an individual into the objective world of a society or a sector of it" (p. 130), see
the formation of self-identity as follows:

Indeed, identity is objectively defined as location in a certain world
and can be subjectively appropriated only *along with* that world. Put
differently, all identifications take place within horizons that imply a
specific social world. The child learns that he *is* what he is called. (p.
132)

Self-identity is given together with the social world as a whole wherein it
has to be meaningfully placed. Berger and Luckmann say:

To be given an identity involves being assigned a specific place in the
world. As this identity is subjectively appropriated by the child ... so is
the world to which this identity points. Subjective appropriation of
identity and subjective appropriation of the social world are merely
different aspects of the *same* process of internalization, mediated by
the *same* significant others. (p. 132)

Self-identity thus constructed, however, cannot be seen as an "authentic self" as conceived by existential philosophy. For example,
Heidegger (1996) called the social self *das Man* ("the they"): "The self of
everyday Da-sein is the *they-self* which we distinguish from the *authentic
self*, the self which has explicitly grasped itself" (p. 121). The mode of "the
they" determines and molds everyday self:

Initially, "I" "am" not in the sense of my own self, but I am the others in
the mode of the they. In terms of the they, and as the they, I am initially
"given" to "myself." Initially, Da-sein is the they and for the most part
it remains so. (p. 121)

As Heidegger states here, the self is given as "the others" who are the embodiment of the social world. After Laing (1967, 62), "The others have become installed in our hearts, and we call them ourselves." Here lies an
existential alienation from authenticity.

Self-identity is maintained through social communicative interrelations, because it is an intersubjective symbolic reality. Every human behavior in everyday life basically serves to fulfill this function. S. I.
Hayakawa (1950/1963, 37) remarks: "The basic purpose of all human activity is the protection, the maintenance, and the enhancement not of the
self, but of the self-concept, or symbolic self." Human behaviors fulfill
the symbolic meanings of the self in communicative interrelations with
others. According to Berger and Luckmann (1966/1967, 154-55), "One
can maintain one's self-identification as a man of importance only in a

milieu that confirms this identity." Every situation contributes to the confirmation of self-identity, no matter how trivial it appears to be.

> In an important way all, or at least most, of the others encountered by the individual in everyday life serve to reaffirm his subjective reality. This occurs even in a situation as "non-significant" as riding on a commuter train. The individual may not know anyone on the train and may speak to no one. (p. 149)

In our communicative social reality, consciously or unconsciously, it becomes the most important concern for everyone to fulfill her or his self-identity. Therefore, a sense of the self becomes so intensified as if it were an independent agency. However, ironically enough, by reinforcing self-identity we strongly depend upon communicative interrelation. In other words, it is in reinforcing self-identify that we reinforce communicative social reality. The stronger the self-identity becomes, the firmer and the more stable becomes a society. The social reality does not easily change in spite of its being a relational world, for the maintenance of individual self-identities correlates with the maintenance of society.

Here we reach a basic aspect of communicative education. From the viewpoint of the pedagogy of communication, *education is a ceaseless process of constructing both the individual self and the social reality in the same process of symbolic articulation of reality.* The communicative interactions form and maintain the structures of both the individual selves and the social world. The pedagogy of communication focuses on the aspect of everyday life that is formative, definitive, communicative, and, in these senses, educative. The definition of education by Heinrich Rombach (1979), a German phenomenological philosopher, is important here.

> "Education" is possible only in the pre-given life-worlds (social structures)—and these [life-worlds] are, as something genetic, already in a profound sense educationally (namely, in the way of molding human nature) functioning in each individual. This *ground process* of education ... is the authentic pedagogical phenomenon.... (p. 148, trans. Nakagawa)

Likewise, John Dewey (1916/1966) was already aware of the pedagogical aspect of communication. He recognized that society can exist only by the "transmission" and "communication" of socio-cultural systems from the older generation to the younger generation. In addition, he remarked: "Society not only continues to exist *by* transmission, *by* communication, but it may fairly be said to exist *in* transmission, *in* communication" (p. 4). As communication constitutes society, it is "educative"; "all communication ... is educative" (p. 5).

> This education consists primarily in transmission through communication. Communication is a process of sharing experience till it becomes a common possession. It modifies the disposition of both the parties who partake in it. (p. 9)

Just as Dewey says that "the very process of living together educates" (p. 6), so the pedagogy of communication is concerned with the communicative process of "living together" that is fundamentally educative.

THE PEDAGOGY OF COMMUNICATION: EAST AND WEST

It is worthwhile examining and comparing the pedagogies of communication in the East and the West. The pedagogy of communication concerns both the objective reality and the social reality. As general tendencies, Eastern ideas emphasize the aspect of social interrelation, whereas Western ideas stress the objective distinction of the individual self.

Western "individualistic" ideas of education tend to prevent us from perceiving implicit relations between the individuals and the social world. The Western system of education seems to embody the paradox that society forces children to become "individuals" independent of society, although this is impossible simply because they are basically conditioned by society. Alan Watts (1966/1989) captures this complexity when he says: "The community of which he [the child] is necessarily a dependent member defines him as an independent member" (p. 72). Using a Batesonian terminology, Watts describes this contradiction as a "social double-bind": "Our society—that is, we ourselves, all of us—is defining the individual with a double-bind, commanding him to be free and separate from the world, which he is not " (pp. 79-80). Western society tends to enforce "separation" among people, which is usually initiated by others through communicative interrelation. Watts remarks:

> When we are children, our other selves, our families, friends, and teachers, do everything possible to confirm us in the illusion of sepa-

rateness—to help us to be genuine fakes, which is precisely what is meant by "being a real person." (p. 40)

What results is the formation of the isolated "ego," which is easily regarded as a substantial entity. In Erich Fromm's (1976/1981, 59) words, "the ego is felt as a thing we each possess," and "this 'thing' is the basis of our sense of identity." But no matter how strong a sense of the ego is, it is a social identity produced in a social process. Accordingly, the strongest identification with one's ego means a total determination of the self by society. Here arises a pervasive situation. As Fromm says, "most people believe they are following their own will and are unaware that their will itself is conditioned and manipulated" (p. 66). Likewise, Laing (1967, 61) states:

> Having at one and the same time lost our *selves,* and developed the illusion that we are autonomous *egos,* we are expected to comply by inner consent with external constraints, to an almost unbelievable extent.

This is what Herbert Marcuse (1969, 13) called "voluntary servitude." Due to the inseparable relation between the ego and the underlying society, the very act of forming the separate ego simultaneously serves to reinforce social stability.

On the other hand, we find the opposite case in Eastern societies where the idea of a separate individual had never flourished. The Eastern system of education has totally attuned itself to social reality. Take a Japanese way of thinking, for example. In Japanese society, social relationships have always had priority over individuality. According to Hajime Nakamura (1964/1971, 409),

> Due to the stress on social proprieties in Japan another characteristic of its culture appears—the tendency of social relationships to supersede or take precedence over the individual. To lay stress upon human relationships is to place heavy stress upon the relations among many individuals rather than upon individual as an independent entity.

Japanese society has embodied this to the fullest extent in the systems of language, social organizations, family-system, morals, and religions, in which the existence of a person has been relational, contextual, and ambiguous in its boundary. Nakamura (1984, 144) says:

> The relatedness of existence penetrates so deeply that it is difficult to
> isolate any one person or one thing in the total existential sphere. This
> is the reason why in Japanese the term for human being is *ningen*
> which literally means "between or among men."

A person is not an independent individual but an "interrelational existence." On the basis of this fact, a number of Japanese thinkers have developed their relationalist theories in different fields. Among others, Tetsuro Watsuji's idea of ethics as "the study of *ningen*" and Bin Kimura's (1981) psychiatric studies in "betweenness" (*aida*) stand out. We will look at Watsuji's idea of *ningen*, which, as Steve Odin (1996, 19) suggests, represents "the classic analysis of the social self in modern Japanese philosophy."

Tetsuro Watsuji (1889-1960) begins his masterpiece *Rinrigaku* [Ethics] (the original work dividedly published in 1937, 1942, 1949) with the following statements:

> The essential significance of the attempt to describe ethics as the study
> of *ningen* consists in getting away from the misconception, prevalent
> in the modern world, that conceives of ethics as a problem of individual consciousness *only*. This misconception is based on the individualistic conception of a human being inherent in the modern world.
> (Watsuji 1996, 9)

Watsuji criticizes Western ideas of independent individuals and instead posits "human relations" (*aidagara*) as the foundation of ethics: "The locus of ethical problems lies not in the consciousness of the isolated individual, but precisely in the in-betweenness of person and person" (p. 10). Here appears the significance of the Japanese concept of *ningen*, which signifies a personhood embedded in betweenness among people. It has a "dual characteristic" in itself; namely, "*ningen* is the public and, at the same time, the individual human beings living within it" (p. 15). It refers to a "dialectical unity" of the two aspects or dimensions, in which an individual human being (*hito*) is never separable from the social nexus. To be a human means to exist in "betweenness." In our scheme, "betweenness" is the social dimension from which a person as an individual being emerges on the objective dimension. The concept of *ningen* involves both dimensions. Robert Carter (1992, 102) describes this concept:

> [T]he Japanese assumption is that we are always already related *as well*
> *as* individual, and that unless that were so, we would not know that
> we are individuals. Individuals are individuals necessarily against a
> background of social relatedness.

The underlying social interrelations are always pre-given as social codes (norms). In East Asian countries, Confucianism had provided the system of norms called *li* (J. *rei*), or "ritual propriety." In Odin's (1996) account, on this Confucian basis Watsuji established a "communitarian ethics" (p. 66). Carter (1992, 101) also comments on this aspect:

> "Between" can refer to the various sorts of contacts, encounters, du-
> ties, obligations, co-operation, struggles, enmity, and so on between
> one individual and another. This sense of between is the relational
> sense, and in the Orient it automatically draws to the surface the net-
> work of relational duties emerging from the Confucian heritage.

In contrast to the Western social system that prohibits one to perceive the underlying social construction of a personhood in order to preserve separateness of the ego-identity, the Eastern system enforces one to recognize the underlying social interrelations to always remain a social being.

THE POLITICS OF COMMUNICATIVE EDUCATION

This comparison between Eastern and Western views of education does not argue that Eastern ideas are superior to Western ideas in terms of relationalist thinking,[6] but simply means that they represent two different patterns of communicative education—individualistic and collectivist patterns.

In both cases, the process of communicative education forms a socialization process through which the normalization of a person takes place. The communicative process of everyday life molds a person in accordance with the pre-given codes of society. However, the "successful" completion of this process tends to cause "micro-political" problems of education: people are so heavily conditioned by the socialization process that they become identified with the social self, excluding and ignoring the deeper dimensions of the self. In this respect, Laing (1967, 24) defines "normalness" as follows: "Society highly values its normal man. It educates children to lose themselves and to become absurd, and thus to be normal." To become normal means to be alienated from the deeper dimensions of reality.

This criticism holds true for the Eastern system of education as well. Eastern relationalist society is far from an ideal relationalist world, for the social relationships have in practice caused sufferings on the side of individual persons. Joseph Campbell (1972/1993, 68) observes this:

> [In the East] the only thought is that one should become identical absolutely with the assigned mask or role of one's social place.... For there ... the focus of concern is not the person but ... the established social order: not the unique, creative individual ... but his subjugation through identification with some local social archetype, and his inward quelling, simultaneously, of every impulse to an individual life.

Identifying "education" in the East with "indoctrination," Campbell goes on to say, "The ideal student in such a society is the one who accepts instruction without question" (p. 69). In this way, we need to critically look at communicative education in both Western and Eastern societies, focusing on their restricting effects on personal existence in the very process of communication.

The question we need to ask is whether or not communicative reality is the sole ground of education. For instance, those who hold to the position of social criticism tend to regard social reality as the sole reality in critically analyzing how the power structure of the educational process causes social injustice and trying to construct a more righteous democratic society. This critical orientation itself is undoubtedly important, and I do not deny its value; however, from the viewpoint of multidimensional theory, it is still a limited view because of exclusion of the other deeper dimensions of reality. The multidimensional theory regards social reality as an intermediate dimension. The point here is not to reform society but to transform it to find the deeper dimensions of reality (for further discussion, see Chapter 7).

Jidu Krishnamurti (1964/1970) calls for "revolt" that can break through social conditionings. He describes "education at present" as follows:

> Ultimately, education at present is aimed at making you conform, fit into and adjust yourself to this acquisitive society.... You are educated

> to fit into society; but that is not education, it is merely a process which
> conditions you to conform to a pattern. (p. 22)

In opposition to this, Krishnamurti addresses a real function of education:

> The function of education is not to make you fit into the social pattern;
> on the contrary, it is to help you to understand completely, deeply,
> fully and thereby break away from the social pattern, so that you are
> an individual without that arrogance of the self; but you have confi-
> dence because you are really innocent. (p. 95)

For Krishnamurti, education as "revolt" does not mean the external
change of social institutions but the transformation of the self-structure
in which we can break away from the social conditionings imposed
upon us.

> Society influences all of us, it constantly shapes our thinking, and this
> pressure of society from the outside is gradually translated as the in-
> ner; but, however deeply it penetrates, it is still from the outside, and
> there is no such thing as the inner as long as you do not break through
> this conditioning. (p. 85)

As Krishnamurti always emphasizes, it is through a radical understanding of the socially conditioned self that it becomes possible for us to liberate ourselves from its bondage and to enter the deeper dimensions of
reality.

Finally, a few words are to be added on holistic education in terms of
communicative education. It is a common understanding among proponents of contemporary holistic education that there are dimensions of reality embracing the social reality, but the problem is that holistic
education tends to underestimate how powerful the social
conditionings are. As Ron Miller (1990/1997, 84) says, this is "the least
developed aspect of holistic education." In other words, it tends to overlook the social dimension when it tries to overcome fragmentation in the
objective world by reclaiming the cosmic reality; however, this is impossible because it is the social system that gives rise to fragmentation. To
overcome fragmentation, it is necessary to transform the social reality.

THE PEDAGOGY OF COMMUNION

The pedagogy of communication is concerned with structural dynamics between the phenomenal objective reality and the underlying social reality. The social dimension is the ground for the phenomenal separation of objective beings by articulation and differentiation through communicative interrelation. The pedagogy of communion, on the other hand, concerns the communal modes of relationships that take place in the deeper dimensions of reality. In communal relationships, all beings are interconnected, unified, and interpenetrate one another without obstruction. Unlike communication, communion does not reproduce pre-established social distinctions, but it is open to novel experiences coming from deeper dimensions. In a communal reality, it becomes possible for the self to disidentify with the social self to become *a communal self*.

The relationship between communication and communion is *initially* defined in such way that *a communicative mode is (has to be) transformed into a communal mode.* As *initially* human beings find themselves in the communicative mode of existence, a communal mode arises only when the pre-given communicative mode dissolves away. For instance, Heidegger (1996) regards an "authentic being one's self" as an "existential modification of the they" (p. 122, original in italics). Laing (1967) also refers to the "true sanity" which appears in the "dissolution" of a pre-existent "normality": "True sanity entails in one way or another the dissolution of the normal ego, that false self competently adjusted to our alienated social reality" (p. 119). These suggest a movement from communication to communion. Theories of holistic education have to take this shift into their framework. Kathleen Kesson (1993) seems to be aware of this when she says:

> A truly transformative education could be a mutual and collective effort to unveil the hidden codes embedded in the everyday experience of the students which explicate the underlying paradigm that frames their present reality. Beyond this decoding of the common reality structures, educators could then work with students to enable them to actively participate in the reconstruction of their social reality. (p. 108)

Various Concepts on "Communion"

The concept of "communion" is not commonly circulated yet, but similar ideas have been put forth—ideas such as Buber's "I and You relation," Fromm's "being" mode, Illich's "conviviality," Turner's "communitas," Grof's "holotropic mode of consciousness," and Bateson's "Learning III." To explicate "communion," I will provide the following overview of these concepts.

Buber (1970/1996) discerns two fundamentally different modes of relation: "I-It" relation and "I-You [Thou]" relation. The "I-It" relation describes a dualistic opposition between subject and object in which the subject "I" "experiences" and "uses" objects. It belongs to communicative relationships in its function of separation. On the other hand, the "I-You" relation means a primordial connectedness. Buber says:

> Whoever says You does not have something for his object. For wher-
> ever there is something there is also another something; every It bor-
> ders on other Its; It is only by virtue of bordering on others. But where
> You is said there is no something. You has no borders. (p. 55)

"You" has "no borders," and the "I-You" stands "in relation." "The basic word I-You establishes the world of relation" (p. 56). Whereas the experiences of I-It dominate our everyday life, the I-You relation discloses a deeper, communal reality.

Fromm (1976/1981) discerns "two fundamental modes of existence": the "having mode" and the "being mode." They are basically relational concepts because they represent "two different kinds of orientation toward self and the world" (p. 12). "In the having mode of existence my relationship to the world is one of possessing and owing" (p. 12). This "having mode" changes a thing into a lifeless object to be possessed: "In the having mode, there is no alive relationship between me and what I have. It and I have become things, and I have *it*" (p. 65). The having mode is a predominant "social character" in our industrialized society. On the other hand, the "being mode of existence" is a mode in which one is "joyous, employs one's faculties productively, is *oned* to the world" (p. 6). The being mode is marked by a communal relation to the world, an "authentic relatedness to the world" (p. 12). This mode is realized by transforming the having mode of existence. "Only to the extent that we decrease the mode of having...can the mode of being emerge" (p. 77).

In his socio-political philosophy, Ivan Illich (1973/1980) provides a significant concept of "conviviality" as an alternative concept for the "industrial productivity" dominating our society. Industrial productivity is a communicative mode of relationships, for it is composed of "the conditioned responses of persons to the demands made upon them by others, and by a man-made environment" (p. 11). On the other hand, conviviality is "autonomous and creative intercourse among persons, and the intercourse of persons with their environment" (p. 11). Those who are "autonomous," liberated from conditioned responses, can interact with one another to create "primary groups." In this manner, conviviality denotes a transformed mode of relationships.

Victor Turner (1974) describes a dialectical relation between what he calls "structure" and "anti-structure" from his anthropological studies. The "structure" means a "social structure" which "holds people apart, defines their differences, and constrains their actions" (p. 274). Relationships in the "structure" separate people in accordance with a pre-organized, institutionalized social order. On the contrary, the "anti-structure" that emerges in "liminality" between structures brings about a fundamentally different mode of relationships called "communitas":

> The bonds of communitas are anti-structural in the sense that they are undifferentiated, equalitarian, direct, extant, nonrational, existential, I-Thou (in Feuerbach's and Buber's sense) relationships. Communitas is spontaneous, immediate, concrete—it is not shaped by norms, it is not institutionalized, it is not abstract. (p. 274)

"Communitas" deconstructs structured relationships to create authentic, spontaneous, unmediated, unbound encounters in which "men confront one another not as role players but as 'human totals,' integral beings" (p. 269). The anti-structure thus realized in communitas is not a negative state but "something positive, a generative center" (p. 273). Turner sees that both structure and communitas are essential for a society to meaningfully exist, because "man is both a structural and an anti-structural entity, who *grows* through anti-structure and *conserves* through structure" (p. 298). Communitas as anti-structure serves as creative, revitalizing forces to a structural society.

Stanislav Grof (1985, 1998), a renowned transpersonal psychiatrist, discerns two different modes of consciousness: the "hylotropic" and "holotropic" modes of consciousness. The hylotropic mode denotes our ordinary state of consciousness. The word "hylotropic" means "oriented toward the world of matter (from the Greek *hyle* = matter, and *trepein* = moving in the direction of something)" (1998, 78). The hylotropic, or matter-oriented, mode of consciousness "involves the experience of oneself as a solid physical entity with definite boundaries and a limited sensory range" (1985, 345). On the other hand, the word "holotropic" means "[being] 'oriented toward wholeness' or 'moving in the direction of wholeness'" (1998, 5). (The word *holos* means "whole.") The holotropic consciousness "involves identification with a field of consciousness with no definite boundaries which has unlimited experiential access to different aspects of reality without the mediation of the senses" (1985, 346). According to Grof, those who are functioning exclusively in the hylotropic mode are seen as having "lower sanity," even though they seem to have no psychopathological symptoms. On the other hand:

> The experience of holotropic consciousness should be treated as a manifestation of a potential intrinsic to human nature and does not in itself constitute psychopathology. When it occurs in a pure form and under the proper circumstances, it can be healing, evolutionary, and transformative. (1985, 400)

The "higher sanity" is, in his view, possible when both the hylotropic and holotropic modes of consciousness are integrated in balance.

Gregory Bateson (1972) discerns levels or "logical types" of learning. Among the four types, "Learning II" and "Learning III" are relevant to our concern. Learning II corresponds to the communicative mode of learning, because it has to do with the formation of the "selfhood":

> If I stop at the level of Learning II, "I" am the aggregate of those characteristics which I call my "character." "I" am my habits of acting in context and shaping and perceiving the contexts in which I act. Selfhood is a product or aggregate of Learning II. (p. 304)

Learning III illuminates a higher level of learning that transcends the level of the selfhood and attains a communal mode of existence.

> To the degree that a man achieves Learning III, and learns to perceive
> and act in terms of the contexts of contexts, his "self" will take on a sort
> of irrelevance. The concept of "self" will no longer function as a nodal
> argument in the punctuation of experience. (p. 304)

Learning III gives rise to a communal self in which "personal identity
merges into all the processes of relationship in some vast ecology or aesthetics of cosmic interaction" (p. 306). These definitions of Learning II
and III by Bateson would be very useful in the discussions of holistic education as well.

Finally, I want to introduce Krishnamurti's (1991a, 1992a, 1992b,
1992c) ideas, for he often referred to the very concepts of "communication" and "communion" in his talks. For example, he said:

> There is, I think, a great deal of difference between communication
> and communion. In communication there is a sharing of ideas through
> words ... through symbols, through gestures.... But in communion I
> think there is something quite different taking place. In communion
> there is no sharing or interpretation of ideas.... [Y]ou are directly in re-
> lationship with that which you are observing.... (1992a, 180)

Although communication concerns transmission made possible by the
mind functions, in communion the mind ceases to function and silence
arises. In his words, "To be in communion with someone or something,
demands space, silence; your body, your nerves, your mind, your heart,
your whole being must be quiet, completely still" (1992a, 185). As Rohit
Mehta (1973/1979, 283) accounts, "communion comes into being only in
a condition of non-verbalization." In the state of silence, communion becomes a "direct relationship" (Krishnamurti 1992c, 222) with "no hindrance," "no interference," and "no barrier" (1992a, 281) between one
and that which is experienced. There is "no division" between subject
and object, for in communion the subjective self no longer exists: "Communion exists only when the center is not" (1992b, 127); "There is no
'you' as an observer apart from the thing observed; there is only that
state of complete communion" (1992a, 189). As Mehta (1973/1979, 262)
says, "Communion is a non-dual experience."

Communion is a relationship in which people encounter each other
with the same "intensity." Krishnamurti states: "Communion can take
place only when you and I are at the same intensity, at the same level, at

the same time, when we both feel these things strongly, vitally, at the same depth and at the same moment" (1992b, 163). As "intensity" means "attention," communion is a state of "intense attention" shared by those involved therein. It is in this intensity that a total involvement or "partaking" of one's whole existence with what is becomes possible, in which the totality of what is becomes manifest. Mehta (1973/1979, 312) says, "To commune with anything is to perceive the Whole." Communion can disclose the deeper levels of reality. Krishnamurti recognizes "a form of communion which comprehends not only the conscious but also the unconscious level, and also goes further, beyond that" (1991a, 155). Regarding education, Krishnamurti (1974, 123) says, "I think learning can exist only in that state of communion between the teacher and the student."[7]

These concepts from Buber's "I-You relation" to Krishnamurti's "communion" disclose an essential aspect of communal relationships—non-articulation and non-differentiation (or connectedness and unification). Moreover, they all suggest that the communal reality is deeper than the communicative reality.

The pedagogy of communion attempts to explore the communal modes of being. In accordance with the five dimensions of reality, it embraces the deeper three dimensions (the cosmic reality, the infinite reality, and the universal reality). The remainder of this chapter will focus on the pedagogy of communion realized by pioneers of Western holistic education and then on some aspects of Eastern holistic education. (Chapter 3 will discuss contemporary holistic education, and Chapters 4 to 7 will detail Eastern holistic education.)

MACROCOSM AND MICROCOSM

The educational philosophies of Western thinkers such as Froebel, Montessori, Emerson, and Steiner represent the pedagogy of communion that has emerged in the West. These thinkers celebrated the cosmic reality in which harmonious correspondence between the human being as microcosm and the cosmic world as macrocosm can be attained through education. Furthermore, Froebel, Emerson, and Steiner referred to the perennial philosophy that has illuminated the human beings' fundamental unity with the deepest dimension of reality.

Friedrich Froebel (Fröbel) (1782-1852) developed a typical, mystical philosophy of education based on Christian mysticism. In his system "God" is the metaphysical ground of what exists. God is also called "Unity," "an all-pervading, energetic, living, self-conscious, and hence eternal Unity" (1887/1900/1974, 1). He states, "All things have come from the Divine Unity, from God, and have their origin in the Divine Unity, in God alone. God is the sole source of all things" (pp. 1-2). God is not only transcendent but also immanent in all beings. "In all things there lives and reigns the Divine Unity, God" (p. 2). So the ultimate cause of existence is this: "It is the destiny and life-work of all things to unfold their essence, hence their divine being, and, therefore, the Divine Unity itself—to reveal God in their external and transient being" (p. 2).

According to Froebel, education is designed for the actualization of the "Divine Unity": "By education ... the divine essence of man should be unfolded, brought out, lifted into consciousness" (p. 4). His definition of education is as follows:

> Education consists in leading man, as a thinking, intelligent being, growing into self-consciousness, to a pure and unsullied, conscious and free representation of the inner law of Divine Unity, and in teaching him ways and means thereto. (p. 2, original in italics)

Education should attain unity between nature and the human being, because both are manifestations of the divine essence, ruled by the same divine law.

> Education, in instruction, should lead man to see and know the divine, spiritual, and eternal principle which animates surrounding nature, constitutes the essence of nature, and is permanently manifested in nature. (p. 5)

In this way, Froebel's philosophy of education highlights an inseparable continuum of human-nature-God. The following definition still represents the ideas of Western holistic education.

> *Education should lead and guide man to clearness concerning himself and in himself, to peace with nature, and to unity with God;* hence, it should lift him to a knowledge of himself and of mankind, to a knowledge of God and of nature, and to the pure and holy life to which such knowledge leads. (p. 5)

Ralph Waldo Emerson (1803-1882) conceived a similar view of education. His entire philosophy of education is based on the idea of "nature," which includes not only both external natural environment and internal human nature but also the infinite reality called "Spirit." In its essence, Emerson's "nature" signifies the manifestations of the universal "Spirit." In his essay *Nature*, Emerson (1981) describes the immanence of the Spirit ("the Universal Spirit") in nature as follows:

> Through all its kingdoms, to the suburbs and outskirts of things, it [nature] is faithful to the cause whence it had its origin. It always speaks of Spirit. It suggests the absolute. It is a perpetual effect. (p. 34)

He holds that "behind nature, throughout nature, spirit is present" (p. 35). His ontology takes reality as a multidimensional one comprised of nature and the Spirit. Then nature can serve to mediate the Spirit to the human being: "Nature is made to conspire with spirit to emancipate us" (p. 28); "It [nature] is the organ through which the universal spirit speaks to the individual, and strives to lead back the individual to it" (p. 34). Here is a continuum of human-nature-Spirit. Richard Geldard (1993, 80) comments on this:

> Spirit is present to the human soul as a totality of aspects, including wisdom, love, beauty, and power. Spirit creates and is present within each person as the force of life itself, just as we witness the same force in nature. It is through this connection—the life-force evident in nature and humanity—that spirit can be witnessed by the human mind in matter.

For Emerson, returning to nature means not only union with physical nature but also a return to the metaphysical dimension of the Spirit by the experience of nature. He sees that the ultimate aim of education is to awaken in us the spiritual dimension and for this purpose nature becomes a fundamental organ.

In his essay *Education,* Emerson (1966, 210) says, "Education should be as broad as man," and he celebrates "the Vast" in the human being. As the "broad" and the "Vast" imply "the spiritual," he adds: "If the vast and the spiritual are omitted, so are the practical and the moral" (pp. 210-11). He refers to the object of education as follows:

> The great object of Education should be commensurate with the object of life. It should be a moral one; to teach self-trust: to inspire the youth-

> ful man with an interest in himself; with a curiosity touching his own
> nature; to acquaint him with the resources of his mind, and to teach
> him that there is all his strength, and to inflame him with a piety to-
> wards the Great Mind in which he lives. Thus would education con-
> spire with the Divine Providence. (p. 211)

As a critical point, education should be oriented towards the "Great
Mind" as the universal spirit. "Nature" or the "world" is integral to this
education; that is, "the world is only his teacher, and the nature of sun
and moon, plant and animal only means of arousing his interior activity"
(pp. 205-206). Geldard (1993, 30) witnesses that "Emerson taught again
and again that nature was a teacher."

Education can safely draw on nature as a manifestation of the Spirit.
For the same reason, Emerson (1966) respects the innate nature of the
child. He says, "the secret of Education lies in respecting the pupil" (p.
216); "Respect the child. Wait and see the new product of Nature" (p.
217). The imperative of education is to keep the "nature" of the child (p.
217). Emerson advocates "natural methods" as opposed to "mechanical
or military methods."

> [T]his function of opening and feeding the human mind is not to be
> fulfilled by any mechanical or military method; is not to be trusted to
> any skill less large than Nature itself.... Whilst we all know in our own
> experience and apply natural methods in our own business—in edu-
> cation our common sense fails us, and we are continually trying costly
> machinery against nature, in patent schools and academies and in
> great colleges and universities. (pp. 219-20)

His emphasis on respect for the child is not a mere child-centered Romantic view, because, believing in the spirit's immanence in every child,
he demands that we "respect the child" and follow the "pace of Nature."

Rudolf Steiner (1861-1925) developed a holistic philosophy of education based on "anthroposophy," an esoteric philosophy deeply rooted in
the traditions of Western mysticism. Anthroposophy is a multidimensional theory of the human being, integrating the three basic dimensions
of the spirit, the soul, and the body, and, correspondingly, it has a magnificent view of the cosmos composed of the physical, psychic, and spiritual worlds. Steiner (1996) recognized inseparable connections between
the human being as microcosm and the cosmos as a whole when he said

that: "the essence of the human being can be understood only in connection with the cosmos" (p. 58); "The human being is directly coupled to the cosmos" (p. 75). Here the point is to recognize that the cosmos is within the human being: "We are really a whole universe" (p. 164); "the human being is the world stage upon which the great cosmic events play again and again" (p. 77). Therefore, Steiner declared as follows:

> We are in the classroom, and within every child lies a center of the universe. The classroom is a center, yes, even many centers for the macrocosm. Think to yourselves how alive this feels and what it means! Think about how the idea of the cosmos and its connection to the human being becomes a feeling that makes each act of teaching holy (p. 171)

Maria Montessori (1870-1952) developed the idea of "cosmic education."[8] She recognized the "Cosmic Plan" in which "all, consciously or unconsciously, serve the great Purpose of Life" (1948, 1). The universe is an organic whole in which all beings are interconnected: "The universe is an imposing reality, and an answer to all questions. We shall walk together on this path of life, for all things are part of the universe, and are connected with each other to form one whole unity" (p. 9). The cosmic education attempts to provide children with the grand view of the evolution of the universe, or the "story of the universe," so that they can acknowledge the wholeness of the universe and their unique places in the universe.

In this way, Froebel, Emerson, Steiner, and Montessori conceived cosmological views of holistic education, views of harmonious correspondence between microcosm and macrocosm.[9] What is more, the perennial philosophies of Froebel and Emerson definitely involve the infinite reality. This second point is important when we examine notions of contemporary holistic education, for they tend to highlight the cosmic reality rather than the infinite reality (see Chapter 3).

THE CONFUCIAN VIEW OF THE UNIVERSE

Eastern philosophy has developed various ideas of the cosmic reality. Confucian cosmology may well represent an Eastern view of macrocosmic and microcosmic correspondence (e.g., Yuasa 1994; Tucker and Berthrong 1998). Confucius (correctly, K'ung Ch'iu) expressed a course of life in the *Analects* (2:4):

> He said: At fifteen I wanted to learn. / At thirty I had a foundation. / At forty, a certitude. / At fifty, knew the orders of heaven. / At sixty was ready to listen to them. / At seventy could follow my own heart's desire without overstepping the t-square. (Pound 1951/1969, 198)

Confucius here traced a course of life from the intellectual to the social and moral to the spiritual stages, which culminates in the matured stage in perfect accordance with the will of "Heaven." "Heaven" (*t'ien*) represented the divine reality of the cosmos in ancient China. As Julia Ching (1993, 55) points out, "K'ung was a believer in Heaven as personal deity, as higher power, order and law." The perfection of the human being in accordance with Heaven has been called in Confucianism "the superior person" (*chün-tzu*).

Later on, Confucian thinkers in the Han period (206 B.C.–A.D. 220) developed cosmological ideas that celebrated the continuity and correlation of the human being (*jen*) and Heaven (*t'ien*) and Earth (*ti*). In doing so, they incorporated the ancient thought of the *I Ching* (Wilhem, 1950/1977)[10] and the naturalistic philosophies of the Yin-Yang and Five Agents schools, which later became fused with the central teachings of Confucianism. *Yin* and *yang* mean the two complementary forces or energies which rule the movement of all phenomena, and the Five Agents mean the five basic elements that compose the cosmic world through their cyclic transformation. Confucian cosmology saw that both the human being and the cosmos were composed of the dynamic interactions of *yin-yang* and the Five Agents. Therefore, Ching says: "Together with *yin* and *yang*, they [the Five Agents] formed a system of correlation which integrated life and the universe" (1993, 155).

The development of Neo-Confucian ontology in the Sung period (960-1279), however, deepened the Confucian worldview from the cosmic to the infinite reality. Chou Tun-i (1017-1073) reinterpreted the so-called "T'ai Chi Diagram" (originally developed in Taoism) in accordance with the *I Ching* to give a foundation to the Neo-Confucian metaphysics. The *I Ching* regards *t'ai chi* (the Great Ultimate or the Great Primal Beginning) as the deepest dimension of reality. The *Ta Chuan*, or the Great Treatise, one of the ten philosophical commentaries (the *Ten*

Wings) of the *I Ching*, reads: "there is in the Changes the Great Primal Beginning. This generates the two primary forces" (Wilhelm 1950/1977, 318). The "two primary forces" were later referred to as *yin* and *yang*. According to Chou's *An Explanation of the Diagram of the Great Ultimate* (Chan 1963, 463), the Great Ultimate through its movement generates *yang* (the active force) and *yin* (the passive force), through whose alternation arise the Five Agents. And then through their cyclic movement arise the world of nature and the animal world of the male and the female. Finally the interaction of these two forces engenders the physical world of myriad things.

Chou also incorporated the Taoist idea of "Non-Being" (*wu*) as the deepest infinite reality: "The Ultimate of Non-being [*wu-chi*] and also the Great Ultimate (*T'ai-chi*)" (Chan 1963, 463). Izutsu (1980, 397) comments on this: "Metaphysically the *wu chi* is a complete Void, the state of Nothingness. It is the absolutely undifferentiated state of the ultimate Reality. It is the Undifferentiated." The relation of *wu chi* to *t'ai chi* is explained by Izutsu as follows:

> [T]he undifferentiated conceals within itself an ontological proclivity toward self-differentiation or self-determination. In reference to this positive aspect of it the same absolute Reality is called *t'ai chi*, the ultimate Principle of Being, meaning the metaphysical Ground of all things and the ultimate origin from which all things emanate. (pp. 394-95)

Chu Hsi (1130-1200), drawing on Chou's ideas, elaborated the Neo-Confucian metaphysics and cosmology as a philosophy of *li* (principle) and *ch'i* (material force).[11] He identified *t'ai chi* with *li*, or principle: "The Great Ultimate is nothing other than principle" (Chan 1963, 638). *Li* or *t'ai chi* is the metaphysical principle, yet at the same time it is immanent in each phenomenal being: "Fundamentally there is only one Great Ultimate, yet each of the myriad things has been endowed with it and each in itself possesses the Great Ultimate in its entirety" (p. 638). *Li* has aspects of both the absolute and the particular. Izutsu (1980, 398) makes this point:

> The *t'ai chi* is the primal source of all things, the metaphysical Ground of being.... [I]t is the absolute *li*, the eternal unchanging Essence prior to being articulated into the particular *li* (the particular essences) of the

individual things. Thus these individual essences are all particular-
ized forms of the one absolute *li*. The *t'ai chi* in this sense is the metaphysical Unity of all things.

The Neo-Confucian way of education, namely, the way of the
"sagehood," aims to help us attain an in-depth insight into *li* by spiritual
cultivation, including such methods as "quiet sitting" and "investigation of the *li* of all things" (e.g., Taylor 1988).

THE EASTERN SELF

Eastern views of holistic education involve the infinite reality as well
as the cosmic reality. The realization of the infinite reality in the seeking
path is called Awakening (or Enlightenment). The whole notion of Eastern holistic education is centered around Awakening. *Eastern holistic education is none other than an education for Awakening.* Its primary aim is to
help us attain Awakening.

Enlightenment (or Awakening), however, does not remain in a mere
transcendental realm distanced from other dimensions, but it reveals itself in the other dimensions in the returning movement. In the returning
phase of Enlightenment, all worlds (the objective world, the social
world, and the cosmic world), which were once abnegated in the infinite
reality, reappear as the *universal reality.* As Aldous Huxley (1946/1968,
342) says, "For the fully enlightened, totally liberated person, *samsara*
and *nirvana,* time and eternity, the phenomenal and the Real, are essentially one." The infinite reality reveals itself in the world and turns it into
the universal reality. In accordance with this transformation, the education for Awakening comes to term with the universal reality.

Eastern philosophy has a variety of names for those who have realized this final phase of the universal reality: Buddhism's "buddha" and
"bodhisattva," Lao Tzu's "the wise," Chuang Tzu's "the True Man" or
"the Perfect Man," Lin-chi's "the True Man with no rank," and so forth.
Take Lin-chi's concept, for example. Lin-chi, a great Ch'an/Zen master,
addressed the state of his Enlightenment to disciples as follows: "Here in
this lump of red flesh there is a True Man with no rank" (Watson 1993,
13). This phrase means that the infinite depth ("True Man with no rank")
is realized in this finite embodied existence ("this lump of red flesh").
Lin-chi also referred to "the person" in the sense of the True Man; "the

person here listening to the Dharma has no form, no characteristics, no root, no beginning, no place to abide, yet he is vibrantly alive" (p. 36). His statements address the true Selfhood grasped in Eastern philosophy, which can be called in our context the *Eastern Self*.

The Eastern Self is the Self who has realized the infinite reality in her or his Awakening and then has embodied the universal reality in her or his existence. The Eastern Self is a finite embodied existence which has realized an infinite depth in its "selfless" openness. That is why the Ch'an Master Bodhidarma replied to the Emperor Wu of Liang that "I don't know," when he was asked, "Who is facing me?" (Cleary and Cleary 1977/1992, 1). This phrase "I don't know" implies that Bodhidarma's existence reaches an infinite depth or the mystery of Existence. Kierkegaard's definition (1941/1954) might be suitable for the Eastern Self; that is, "Man is a synthesis of the infinite and the finite, of the temporal and the eternal, of freedom and necessity, in short it is a synthesis" (p. 146).

The selfless structure of the Eastern Self has been explored by modern concepts such as Izutsu's "Eastern Philosopher," Suziki's "supra-individual Person," Nishida's "contradictory self-identity," Hisamatsu's "Formless Self," Ueda's "Selfless Self," and Hayashi's "trans-existential consciousness." These concepts attempt to grasp the essential aspects of the Eastern Self, which seem to be too difficult to be described in a logical fashion.

Izutsu (1983) describes the "Eastern Philosophers" as follows:

> The so-called Eastern Philosophers are ones who have opened up the deeper realms of their consciousness and have settled themselves there. They are able to replace things and events that arise in the dimension of surface consciousness into the levels of deeper consciousness and to see them from a deeper perspective. The metaphysical and physical horizons of their consciousness embrace both surface and deeper realms where "Being" in the dimension of the absolutely Unarticulated and "beings" articulated into pieces appear simultaneously as they are. (p. 12, trans. Nakagawa)

The Eastern Philosopher is the Self who has fully cultivated the multidimensions of consciousness from the surface to the deepest levels, in which the metaphysical "Being" and the physical "beings" arise in a simultaneous, non-dualistic way.

Suzuki (1972) grasps a contradictory aspect of the Eastern Self—an aspect of co-existence of selfness (personhood) and selflessness, an identity between "the individual self" and "the supra-individual Person." He says:

> Because the supra-individual Person transcends individuality, it is not within the realm of the individual self. Thus, even though I speak of *Person*, it is not a person functioning in the individual self. And yet neither is it a person that remains excluded from the things of the world, for such a person would still be the person of the individual self.
>
> The supra-individual Person is not without a relation to the individual self; there is a deep, in fact inseparable, relation between them. Though we cannot say that the Person *is* the individual self, still the Person cannot exist apart from it. (p. 76)

The supra-individual Person appears as the "real" individual person; the real individual person is an actual individual being who has realized the supra-individual Person, and who has immediately embodied both the surface and the deepest dimensions of the self. Suzuki remarks: "The individual spirit begins a relation straightforward to the supra-individual spirit. In no case does it allow intermediaries. In this insight the supra-individual spirit is transformed into the individual" (p. 115).

Likewise, in defining *kensho*, Kitaro Nishida (1987, 108) says: "*Kensho*, seeing one's nature, means to penetrate to the roots of one's own self. The self exists as the absolute's own self-negation." This account includes the twofold movement of seeking and returning; that is, one realizes one's roots, or "the absolute," by self-negation in the seeking path, and then in the returning path the absolute manifests itself as the self through its own self-negation. The self that arises through double negation is a contradictory existence. Nishida states:

> Therefore the self has a radically self-contradictory existence.... Hence we always possess ourselves in something that transcends ourselves in our own bottomless depths; we affirm ourselves through our own self-negation. *Kensho* means to penetrate to the bottomlessly contradictory existence of one's own self. (p. 108)

The self is selfless in its "bottomless depths," opened up to the absolute, and arising as a definite being through the self-negation of the absolute. This double mode of the self—identity between the infinite and the finite—is called by Nishida "contradictory self-identity":

> On the one hand, there is that which transcends the self and yet establishes it in being—that is, what is transcendent and yet the fundamental ground of the self—and, on the other hand, there is the unique, sheerly individual, volitional self. Religion consists in this contradictory identity of transcendence and immanence. (p. 98)

Shizuteru Ueda (1973/1993, 1992) calls the Eastern Self the "Selfless Self." If a person truly leaps into Absolute Nothingness, or what he calls "Infinite Openness," in the seeking path, the selfhood of the self completely falls away, and the self becomes completely "selfless." In this selflessness, the person is an infinitely open being. Here comes the real turning point: Absolute Nothingness (the infinite reality) turns into Absolute Being (the universal reality). This is a resurrection of the self. The resurrected self is no longer identified with a particular selfhood on the surface level but in its fundamental selflessness is opened up to the infinite reality (see Chapters 3 and 5).

The Eastern Self arises in the fullest realization of multidimensional reality, which results in a contradictory realization of phases of the individual as well as the universal states of being. Nobuhiro Hayashi (1993) captures this aspect in terms of the "trans-existential consciousness," which is distinct from the two other modes of consciousness: the "pre-existential consciousness" and the "existential consciousness." He defines the "trans-existential consciousness" as follows:

> This trans-existential consciousness negates and at the same time affirms the is-ness of a being. In other words, this trans-existential consciousness is an intuitive awareness that a being does not exist and simultaneously exist, and that it exists and simultaneously does not exist; or that, it might be said, a being exists because it does not exist, and that it does not exist because it exists. Therefore, in this consciousness ... all that exists is totally affirmed in its total negation and totally negated in its total affirmation. (p. 99, trans. Nakagawa)

The "pre-existential consciousness" is the collective state of "ontological indifference," or fusion of subject and object. The "existential consciousness" is the individual self-consciousness marked by an "ontological gap" between subject and object. On the other hand, the "trans-existential consciousness" is marked by "the unity of subject and object in opposition." Here, while oppositions between individual beings remain as they are, they are at the same time immediately united. Hayashi grasps contradictory identity between opposition and union, between difference and unity, in the Eastern Self.

To comprehend a contradictory and dynamic structure of the Eastern Self, it is essential to understand the dynamic aspect of *sunyata* (Emptiness) and *mu* (Nothingness) elaborated in Mahayana Buddhist philosophy. Emptiness (or Nothingness) does not imply a transcendental, static realm separated from other dimensions of Being, but it implies a *dynamic movement*. True Emptiness is *a dynamic activity of emptying and negating itself*. If Emptiness were viewed as a static realm, it would retain its own substantial entity. The Zen philosophers Keiji Nishitani (1982) and Masao Abe (1985, 1997) regard such a substantialized Emptiness (Nothingness or "nihility") as "relative" Emptiness (Nothingness). Nishitani remarks:

> [T]he nihility seen to lie at the ground of existence is still looked upon
> as something outside of existence; it is still being viewed from the side
> of existence. It is a nothingness represented from the side of being, a
> nothingness set in opposition to being, a *relative nothingness.* (p. 123)

On the other hand, the "absolute" Emptiness does not arise in a dualistic opposition between a relative Being and a relative Emptiness. The true absolute Emptiness is not a static relative realm but *a dynamic activity of emptying itself*. Nishitani states: "Emptiness in the sense of sunyata is emptiness only when it empties itself even of the standpoint that represents it as some 'thing' that is emptiness. It is, in its original Form, self-emptying" (p. 96). Likewise, Abe remarks: "In order to attain true Emptiness, Emptiness must 'empty' itself" (1985, 128); "True Emptiness is not a static state of everything's non-substantiality, but rather a dynamic function of emptying everything, including itself" (1997, 49). Abe calls this function "double negation" or "absolute negation" which is "negation of negation."

Therefore, *it is in the endless movement of emptying itself that the absolute Emptiness becomes one with Being.* Nishitani remarks that "true emptiness is not to be posited as something outside of and other than 'being.' Rather, it is to be realized as something united to and self-identical with being" (1982, 96-97). According to Abe (1985, 127), "an absolute negation is nothing but an absolute affirmation." In this sense, Nishitani sees "absolute nothingness" disclosed in the very existence of Being as "the absolute near side" (1982, 95). In Abe's (1985, 130) words: "True Emptiness and wondrous Being are completely non-dualistic: absolute *Mu* [Nothingness] and ultimate Reality are totally identical."

In the ceaseless activity of. Emptiness (Nothingness), Being is transformed into the "wondrous Being." This is the heart of Mahayana understanding of reality. As Abe (1985, 128) says, "true Emptiness is wondrous Being, absolute *U* [Being], the fullness and suchness of everything, or *tathata* [Suchness]." In the emptying movement of Emptiness, a relative finite reality of this world comes to appear as the absolute "wondrous Being" (the universal reality), in which a finite being realizes and embodies absolute Emptiness or, in other words, Emptiness manifests itself in the "form" of a being. True Emptiness (Absolute Nothingness) is what turns the relative Being into the absolute Being. In this regard, it is a radically positive movement, for it brings about a "Great Affirmation" of all beings. Nishitani remarks:

> On the field of sunyata each thing becomes manifest in its suchness in its very act of affirming itself, according to its own particular potential and *virtus* and in its own particular shape.... The field of sunyata is nothing other than the field of the Great Affirmation. (1982, 131)

In this way, the Eastern Self arises in accordance with the dynamic movement of Emptiness. It is the Self who has been radically emptied in the all-negating activity of Emptiness and then has reemerged as an absolute wondrous Being in the all-affirmative activity of Emptiness. Like others, Nishitani identifies the essence of the Eastern Self with contradictory identity between "being self" and "not being self."

> On the field of sunyata, our selfness goes beyond the so-called subject. Our selfness is the point at which all modes of being of the self—personal, conscious, corporeal, and so forth—have all been cast off. There "being" is a mode of being that can no longer be called self. There the self is what is *not* the self. This mode of being, however, pervades the various modes of being of the self—personal, conscious, corporeal,

and so on—and constitutes, together with them, one "being," one "position." (pp. 156-57).

The "not being self" does not exist apart from "being self," and these two
contradictory modes of being constitute a non-dual identity. Nishitani
concludes: "We have no choice but to express our self in itself as 'that
which is not self in being self' and as 'that which is self in not being self'"
(p. 157).

The Eastern Self is surely able to provide a totally different model of
the human being from all the others developed in the history of pedagogy and education. As Joan Stambaugh (1999) says in her discussions
of the "Formless Self" in Dogen, Hisamatsu, and Nishitani, "if selfhood
is not to be conceived egotistically as a separate self opposed and hostile
to everything other than itself, formlessness offers an eminent possibility of rethinking selfhood" (p. 165). The education for Awakening is ultimately aimed at realizing the Formless Self.

NOTES

1. In terms of transpersonal theories, the cosmic reality includes the dimension of the
   "transpersonal"; for example, what John Welwood (1979, 166) calls "the transpersonal
   ground" is "a sense of oneness and relatedness between self and world." Thomas
   Armstrong (1985, 45) regards it as "the larger sense we have of our own interrelatedness
   to all living things, of our place within the biosphere." However, the cosmic reality, I
   think, maybe contain not only the "transpersonal" but also the "prepersonal" realms.
   Ken Wilber clearly discerns these two levels to reject what he calls the "pre/trans fallacy," a false equation between the pre- and trans-personal levels. I admit this discernment, yet I am also inclined to characterize the cosmic reality as the dimension
   encompassing both levels, because it constitutes an all-embracing matrix from which
   the "personal" can arise. In this respect, the cosmic reality may be close to what Michael
   Washburn (1995) calls "the Dynamic Ground." But this characterization of the cosmic
   reality does not necessarily commit the pre/trans fallacy, but it only means that the cosmic reality may involve various levels within itself, from prepersonal to transpersonal.
   In my view, the levels of "the psychic" and "the subtle" in Wilber's model may belong
   to the cosmic reality, and "the causal" corresponds to the infinite reality, and "the
   nondual" corresponds to the universal reality.

2. Enlightenment or Awakening in the sense of the realization of the infinite reality has
   been diversely called *bodhi* in Early Buddhism, *mahaprajna* in Mahayana Buddhism,
   kensho and *satori* in Japanese Zen Buddhism, *rig-pa* in Dzogchen (Great Perfection) of Tibetan Buddhism, and *fana* in Sufism.

3. For example, the Yogacara philosophy presented a similar view in "the three-nature theory," a theory that sees reality under three phases. According to Gadjin Nagao (1991,182), "[t]he three-nature theory demonstrates that the world has three natures (*tri-svabhava*) or three aspects or three characteristics. The three natures refer to the 'imagined or conceptualized' (*parikalpita*) nature, the 'other dependent' (*paratantra*) nature, and the 'consummated' (*parinispanna*) nature. These three do not represent three distinct territories of the world. They refer to the fact that the world is characterized as being completely 'imagined' at one time, as an 'other-dependent' existence at another time, and as a 'consummated' world at still another time. The former situation constitutes the world of bewilderment/affliction, and the latter one, the world of enlightenment, and there is the world of the 'other-dependent' that mediates between the two." This three-nature theory refers to the dimension of differentiation by conception (the objective reality, the social reality), the dimension of interconnection (the cosmic reality), and the dimension of unity (the infinite reality, the universal reality).

4. To underscore the importance of relationalism, I want to add a few words on how my studies in holistic education have developed in connection with relationalism. I had encountered the idea of relationalism before I came across holistic education. I had devoted myself to rethinking the fundamental framework of pedagogy from a relationalist point of view. A series of my studies (1985, 1986a, 1987b, 1988, 1989a, 1989b) had led me to develop a "relationalist pedagogy." In doing so, I had figured out two different fields: the "pedagogy of communication" and the "pedagogy of communion." Since my studies in holistic education and Eastern philosophy began, I realized that the ideas of relationalist pedagogy are very close to them. The interactions among them have greatly enriched my ideas. Indeed, the model of the five dimensions of reality has arisen from my studies in relationalism, holistic education, and Eastern philosophy.

5. Izutsu's concept of the "symbolic images" discussed in the previous chapter is not the same as the "symbolic world" in this context, for the symbolic world represents the social world but the symbolic images refers to a deeper dimension.

6. For example, Watsuji's (1996) ethics, in the final analysis, rasped into a totalitarian, nationalistic, and conservative thought that required one to subordinate to the socio-ethical whole (family, friends, a company, or a state) through her or his self-negation, despite that he heavily relied on the idea of *sunyata* in Zen philosophy. Watsuji used the logic of self-negation in *sunyata* to support his nationalistic attitude. But, as the subordination to the socio-ethical whole does not bring about Enlightenment, this is a manifest reductionism of *sunyata* to the social dimension.

7. A similar idea on communication and communion was put forth by Thomas Merton (see Del Prete 1990, chap. 6).

8. It is worth mentioning that Montessori's ideas of cosmic education matured during her stay in India from 1939 to 1946, which was made possible by the invitation of the Theo-

sophical Society. In this period, her ideas might have involved Eastern thought. Also, for her ideas of spiritual education, see Wolf (1996).

9. It is important to consider that Emerson and Steiner were fairly familiar with Eastern thought as well as Western philosophy.

10. See Wilhelm and Wilhelm (1960/1979/1988/1995) and Izutsu (1980).

11. Chu Hsi also sees *ch'i* as a material force that belongs to the material realm but is not equated with a sensible material form itself. *Ch'i* is a subtle energy that manifests itself in all material forms starting from the dimension of *yin-yang*. As Yasuo Yuasa (1994) states, "*ch'i* is a dynamic movement which connects the transcendental dimension with the empirical dimension and acts behind material forms to vitalize them" (p. 188, trans. Nakagawa). Furthermore, Chu Hsi underlines connection between *li* and *ch'i*: "Principle has never been separated from material force" (Chan 1963, 634). This means that *ch'i* is as fundamental as *li*. "Fundamentally principle and material force cannot be spoken of as prior or posterior. But if we must trace their origin, we are obliged to say that principle is prior. However, principle is not a separate entity. It exists right in material force" (p. 634). To grasp this relation has been a difficult question in Neo-Confucianism; in our scheme this equation of *li* and *ch'i* might imply an aspect of the universal reality.

Contemporary Holistic Education

This chapter will examine theories of contemporary holistic education from the vantage point of the multidimensional theory of holistic education delineated in the previous chapter. If we define "holistic education" as an approach to the wholeness of the human being in education, we can count diverse forms of holistic education appearing from ancient times until now. What differentiates the contemporary movements of holistic education of the past decade from the other forms of holistic education?

Contemporary holistic education fundamentally deals with underlying worldviews or paradigms in an attempt to transform the foundations of education as such. As Ron Miller (1992, 21) observes, "'Holistic education' is *not* to be defined as a particular method or technique; it must be seen as a *paradigm*, a set of basic assumptions and principles that can be applied in diverse ways."

Contemporary holistic education attempts to provide alternative worldviews to the dominant worldview of modern education. As a whole, the postmodern holistic worldviews have emerged in response to the modernist worldview often referred to as the "mechanistic" or "atomistic" worldview. Fritjof Capra (1982/1983) saw our worldview shifting from the "mechanistic" or "Cartesian-Newtonian" worldview to "the systems view of life" that recognizes "the essential interrelatedness and interdependence of all phenomena" (p. 265). More recently, Capra (1996, 6) restated "a new perception of reality": "The new paradigm may be called a holistic worldview, seeing the world as an integrated whole rather than a dissociated collection of parts."

Contemporary holistic education totally agrees with this shift. For Ron Miller (1991b), the fundamental turn in education is a moving from "an industrial-age culture" to a "post-industrial" age. He describes the worldview of industrial-age culture as materialistic, reductionistic, economic-centered, and discriminating and states that "[c]onventional education serves to perpetuate this worldview" (p. 1). He portrays the "holistic worldview" of the post-industrial age, on the other hand, in terms of its reverence for life, ecological perspective, spiritual understanding of human beings, and global perspective (p. 2). As he says, "Holistic education is not any one technique or curriculum; it is the application of this post-industrial worldview to the challenges of raising children" (p. 2).

The basic assumption of contemporary holistic education is a relationalist worldview that everything is interconnected. Ron Miller (1990/1997, 81) states: "A holistic perspective is rooted in an epistemology of wholeness, context, and interconnectedness." Likewise, John Miller (1988/1996, 8) says, "Holistic education ... involves exploring and making connections. It attempts to move away from fragmentation to connectedness." We can safely mark contemporary holistic education as a *connection-oriented education*.

In our concepts, this orientation towards connection stands for *a shift from communication to communion*. Therefore, the connectionist view of holistic education involves an assumption of multidimensionality. The interconnectedness of all beings signifies the "deeper" communal reality of the cosmic world from which surface fragmentation arises in the forms of alienation. As Aldous Huxley (1946/1968, 261) says, "The capacity to suffer arises where there is imperfection, disunity and separation from an embracing totality." To cure this suffering, education has to attune itself to the interconnectedness of the cosmic world. John Miller (1988/1996, 3) states:

> If nature is dynamic and interconnected and our education system is static and fragmented, then we only promote alienation and suffering.

But if we can align the institutions with this interconnection and dynamism, then the possibilities for human fulfillment increase greatly.

In the following I would like to give an overview of representative
theories of contemporary holistic education to further clarify their structures and then through critical observations to discuss fundamental
problems therein. In my view, among a variety of currents in contemporary holistic education, at least six major orientations may be discerned:
perennial philosophy, indigenous worldviews, Life philosophy, ecological worldview, systems theory, and feminist thought.

Six Orientations of Contemporary Holistic Education

Perennial Philosophy

The first orientation attempts to build a theory of holistic education
on the ideas of "perennial philosophy." It includes the work of James
Moffett, John Miller, Parker Palmer, Richard Brown, Aostre Johnson,
Huston Smith, Thomas Moore, and Thomas Armstrong.[1]

The perennial philosophy usually acknowledges multiple dimensions of reality. In his classic *The Perennial Philosophy*, Huxley (1946/1968,
2) gives a definition: "The Perennial Philosophy is primarily concerned
with the one, divine Reality substantial to the manifold world of things
and lives and minds." Likewise, based on a theosophical understanding,
Anna Lemkow (1990, 38) says, "All existence is rooted in, pervaded and
transcended by the boundless, ineffable Oneness or Godhead or Reality
or the Absolute." This fundamental dimension is the ontological ground
for the evolution of the whole of existence. Huxley (1946/1968, 42) says,
"there is a hierarchy of the real. The manifold world of our everyday experience is real with a relative reality ... but this relative reality has its being within and because of the absolute Reality." "The absolute Reality"
manifests itself into the multidimensional strata of the cosmos. The creation of the cosmos has been grasped in perennial philosophy as manifestation, flowing-out, or descent of the Absolute. Lemkow explains this:

> It [the universe] issues from and is both pervaded and transcended by
> the ineffable Oneness. Thus the universe must be a unity. But it is also
> multi-dimensional, and so organized that each dimension or level of

being produces the next, less inclusive level, from the most unitive to
the most particular. (1990, 38)

The perennial philosophy also holds that the human being is composed of multidimensional levels that correspond to the constitution of reality. According to Huston Smith (1976/1992), "the levels of reality," or the four-folded levels—"the terrestrial sphere," "the intermediate sphere," "the celestial sphere," and "the Infinite"—correlate with the "levels of selfhood": "body," "mind," "soul," and "Spirit" (see chaps. 3 and 4). Huxley (1946/1968) refers to the "trinity of body, psyche and spirit" of the human being and says that the "spirit" is "akin to, or even identical with, the divine Spirit that is the Ground of all being" (p. 48). Due to this identity of the human spirit with the "divine Ground," "the ultimate reason for human existence" is to attain "unitive knowledge of the divine Ground" (p. 29). In terms of education, Huxley (1992) gives a clear definition based on the perennial philosophy:

> Education ... aims at reconciling the individual with himself, with his
> fellows, with society as a whole, with the nature of which he and his
> society are but a part, and with the immanent and transcendent spirit
> within which nature has its being. (p. 101)

Now we turn to essential ideas presented by John Miller and Parker Palmer. Their educational refinements of the perennial philosophy are strongly connection-centered. Miller (1988/1996) regards the perennial philosophy (or holism) as "the philosophic context of holistic education" and sees its essential aspect in the worldview of connectedness. "The perennial philosophy holds that all life is connected in an interdependent universe. Stated differently, we experience relatedness through a fundamental ground of being" (p. 12). Though he does not explicate a framework of multidimensional reality, his ideas of interconnectedness imply the deeper dimensions of reality. He says, "There is an interconnectedness of reality and a fundamental unity in the universe" (p. 20). In our scheme, this "interconnectedness" may imply the cosmic reality, and "fundamental unity" may imply the infinite reality. Indeed, Miller (1994) restates the deepest realm as "the invisible world": "The invisible world is the primary reality" (p. 48). For Palmer (1983/1993) as well, a true reality is an interconnected whole. "Reality's ultimate structure is that of an organic, interrelated, mutually responsive community of being" (p. 53).

The "holistic curriculum" is an effort to make connections. Miller articulates six major domains of connections or relationships, that is, ones between linear thinking and intuition, mind and body, among domains of knowledge, between self and community, to the earth, between self and the Self (1988/1996, chaps. 6-11). Palmer (1983/1993) also calls for a revision of education as "a communal enterprise," saying that "education would be more truthful if our schools themselves became more reflective of the communal nature of realities we teach in school" (p. xiv). The practice of education here becomes an attempt to enter the reality of "community"; "reality is a web of communal relationships, and we can know reality only by being in community with it" (Palmer 1998, 95, original in italics). So Palmer (1983/1993) gives a definition of teaching as follows: "To teach is to create a space in which the community of truth is practiced" (p. xii).

Both Miller and Palmer see the recovery of connection or community as the very core of educational implementation in which the teaching, learning, and living of teacher and students are woven into a communal relationship. Palmer regards this as a "spiritual" education. By "spiritual" he means "the diverse ways we answer the heart's longing to be connected with the largeness of life" (1998, 5). With regard to spirituality,

> I mean the ancient and abiding human quest for connectedness with something larger and more trustworthy than our egos—with our own souls, with one another, with the worlds of history and nature, with the invisible winds of the spirit, with the mystery of being alive. (Palmer 1998/1999, 6)

The quest for connectedness means, in our context, an inquiry into the deeper dimensions of reality.

The correspondence between the human being and the cosmos plays an essential role in their thought. Miller (1988/1996, 20) remarks, "There is an intimate connection between the individual's inner or higher self and this [fundamental] unity." To realize the fundamental unity, self-inquiry is the basic path. "Holistic education can be traced back to the Greek statement 'know thyself'.... It also involves an inward journey to realize the Self" (1993a, 22). As a practical way of self-inquiry, Miller highlights "contemplation and meditation": "The way to access the invisible world is not through reason and analysis, but through various forms of contemplation" (1994, 48). Contemplation is an attempt not to escape from the world but to recover deeper connections.

In this regard, Palmer celebrates the importance of "solitude." Through detachment from the social life, solitude allows us to know ourselves as we are. "Solitude calls us to confront ourselves with a directness impossible in everyday life, to learn who we really are and what we can rely on" (1983/1993, 121). And this self-knowing in solitude opens avenues to communal relations in deeper levels. "Solitude opens us to the heart of love which makes community possible.... Community requires solitude to renew its bonds" (p. 122).

Miller and Palmer focus on the importance of the teacher whose work comes from the deeper dimensions of the Self. With Emerson, Miller (1993a, viii) says: "Ultimately, holistic education ... flows from what Emerson calls our 'depth' and 'presence.'" He discerns two levels of being a teacher—the "ego-based" and the "Self-based" teachers. The ego-based teacher plays the social role of the teacher in the social world; on the other hand, the Self-based teacher is connected with the student in the deeper levels of the Self. In the depth of the Self, there is a "centre-to-centre" encounter in which there is no longer any boundary distancing the teacher from the student, which could ultimately lead to the awakening of the student to her or his Self. Miller (1994, 122) says, "when we teach from the Self, we gradually experience more moments of communion with our students." Palmer also stresses that "the transformation of teaching must begin in the transformed heart of the teacher" (1983/1993, 107), for "we teach who we are" (1998, 2). Therefore, it is imperative for the teacher to know who he or she is. "Whatever self-knowledge we attain as teachers will serve our students and our scholarship well. Good teaching requires self-knowledge: it is a secret hidden in plain sight" (Palmer 1998, 3)

INDIGENOUS WORLDVIEWS

Indigenous (or aboriginal or native) worldviews from all over the world are filled with reverence for nature, the earth, the universe, and the Spirit. They emphasize the organic interconnectedness of all beings, which Native Americans call *mitakuye oyasin* (We are all related), for instance. They also contain spiritual perception of the world; the world is "sacred" because it is permeated with spiritual force, which has been called *wakan-tanka,* or the Great Spirit, in the Lakota tradition. A description is given by Mircea Eliade (1967, 11-12) as follows:

> Every object in the world has a spirit and that spirit is *wakan.... Wakan* comes from the *wakan* beings. These *wakan* beings are greater than mankind.... They are never born and never die. They can do many things that mankind cannot do.... The word *Wakan Tanka* means all of the *wakan* beings because they are all as if one.

The indigenous worldviews are multidimensional in character. According to Black Elk's account, *wakan-tanka* stands for the infinite as well as the finite dimensions; it is "everything, and yet above everything," "the source and end of everything," and "the One who watches over and sustains all life" (Brown 1953/1989, 13-14).

Furthermore, indigenous peoples have developed spiritual practices in the forms of rituals, rites, ceremonies, art, and shamanic healing as well as humble ways of everyday life so as to align themselves harmoniously with the sacred nature of things.

These indigenous worldviews and practices have gradually become influential in contemporary holistic education. Gregory Cajete, a Native American philosopher of holistic education, has enriched holistic education through his *Look to the Mountain: An Ecology of Indigenous Education* (1994), which intends not only to recall the traditional native education but also to provide "the 'new' kinds of educational thought that can address the tremendous challenges of the twenty-first century" (p. 27). Cajete also believes that the crisis of education is caused by disconnection, and that indigenous worldviews can give us a clue to deal with this.

> Understanding the depth of relationships and the significance of participation in all aspects of life are the key to traditional American Indian education. *Mitakuye Oyasin* (we are all related) is a Lakota phrase that captures an essence of Tribal education because it reflects the understanding that our lives are truly and profoundly connected to other people and the physical world. (p. 26)

Cajete celebrates the idea that "we are all related," saying that "it is a deeply spiritual, ecological, and epistemological principle of profound significance" (p. 74). Indigenous education is thus defined in terms of connections-making activities: "Education is, at its essence, learning

about life through participation and relationship in community, including not only people, but plants, animals, and the whole of Nature"
(p. 26).

At the same time, the spiritual dimension has a central place in indigenous education: "Indigenous education, at its innermost core, is education about the life and nature of the spirit that moves us.... The ultimate
goal of Indigenous education was to be fully knowledgeable about one's
innate spirituality" (p. 42).

Acknowledging these two aspects of the indigenous worldview,
namely, the interconnectedness and the sacredness of reality, Cajete
takes "spiritual ecology" for the essential foundation of indigenous education. "The *Spiritual Ecology* of Tribal education is both a foundational
process and field through which traditional American Indian education
occurs" (p. 39). Centered around "spiritual ecology," a framework of indigenous education is presented which is divided into the sacred "seven
directions," or the seven "foundations," including mythic, visionary, artistic, environmental, affective, communal foundations as well as spiritual ecology.

Interestingly, educators are beginning to incorporate indigenous
ways such as vision quest, council, and storytelling into their educational practices (e.g., Kessler 1997, 2000). In particular, rites of passage,
which the modern world has mostly lost, can be utilized to offer oppor-
tunities in which both youth and adults can transform their lives at critical moments of transition through their reintegration with nature and
the Spirit (e.g., Mahdi, Christopher, and Meade 1996).

LIFE PHILOSOPHY

The concept of "Life" has a central importance for many holistic educators. Ron Miller (1990/1997) introduced the term "life-centered" to describe "a spiritually rooted [holistic] education" (p. 88). Generally
speaking, the "philosophy of Life" or "Life philosophy" assumes that
there exists a fundamental Life force, or a universal Life process, such as
Bergson's *élan vital* or Nietzsche's *Macht*.[2] The Life in this sense is both a
transcendental and immanent principle of the cosmic world. This orientation of holistic education conceives education as an integral part of the
greater Life process; that is, education is a manifestation of Life and at the

same time a vehicle in the service of reconnecting human life with the fundamental Life.

In Japan, the ideas of Life philosophy have attracted many holistic educators. "Life" is called *inochi* or *seimei* in Japanese. Atsu'hiko Yoshida (1995b), a leading scholar of holistic education in Japan, maintains: "Should holistic education be defined in one word, it could be defined as an education into *inochi*" (p. 139, trans. Nakagawa). The concept of *inochi* plays a central role in his conception of holistic education:

> When we reflect upon the harmony of an ecosystem as a whole, and the creative evolution of all life ... we can assume a dynamic *working* as such that has connected the great chain of all life, maintained the harmony, renewed the whole system with gradual increases of its multiplicity and complexity. Such a fundamental dynamic working can be called *inochi*. Each individual life form is a manifestation of *inochi* on the phenomenal plane.
>
> Education can be viewed as a practice that participates in the great tide of *inochi* and then meets and consciously takes part in a focused situation where *inochi* arises as a form of the human being. (p. 142, trans. Nakagawa)

Inochi means a holistic principle of the cosmos, an all-embracing fundamental force that generates and organizes all beings in the cosmos. All beings are manifold manifestations of the fundamental *inochi*. Therefore, the primary purpose of education is to invite us to the deeper processes of *inochi*.

Historically speaking, as Sadami Suzuki (1996) demonstrates, throughout Japanese intellectual history since the beginning of modern times, Life-centered philosophy has been one of the most influential currents among others. Suzuki calls this intellectual movement *seimei shugi*, or Life-ism, and makes the following points among others (pp. 266-68):

- Life-ism sees Life as the fundamental and universal principle of being.
- Life-ism encourages us for action because, it feels, Life is in danger.
- Life-ism seeks to express Life in unlimited, creative ways.

- Life-ism avoids reductionism and moves towards holism of any kind.

Suzuki's research tells us that Life philosophy in Japan remarkably flourished as a *Zeitgeist* in the short period called the *Taisho* era (1912-1926) and has survived as a powerful undercurrent to be revived in contemporary holistic thought in the last two decades of the twentieth century. Indeed, throughout the 1980s, we have witnessed a growing interest in the idea of Life among many holistic educators as exemplified in the work of Yoshida. Life-centered holistic education may be an authentic contribution to holistic education from contemporary Japanese thought.

ECOLOGICAL WORLDVIEW

The ecological perspective is so integral in contemporary holistic education that the term "holistic" is often interchangeably used with "ecological." A large part of holistic education can be seen as *ecological holistic education.* For example, David Hutchison (1998, 52) remarks that "the holistic philosophy would seem to forward an ecologically sensitive view of the educational process." This makes sense because ecology focuses on the principle of interconnectedness of all beings in nature, life, and the universe. The basic assumption of ecology is that everything hangs together; every living organism is connected with and dependent upon each other to grow and maintain itself; a living phenomenon is understood only in relation to other phenomena and in larger ecosystems. For ecological holistic education, Gregory Bateson's thought and deep ecology are especially important.[3]

Bateson (1972) located the concept of "mind" in an ecological context and transferred it from a substantialist connotation to an interconnection in the ecosystem. Drawing on the findings of cybernetics, he focused on the "message pathways" that extend outside the skin boundary, and regarded them as "the mental system" at large. Therefore, "mind" spreads over a total circuit of pathways through which a series of messages are running; the individual and her or his circumstances form a unit of "mind," which forms a subsystem for a more inclusive larger system. In this way, orbits of minds extend subsequently to a boundless extent. In Batesonian philosophy, there is no substantial, autonomous self but only the nexus of minds that is identical with the entire ecosystem. The "Mind" is "immanent in the large biological system—the ecosystem" (p. 460).

The work of Bateson contains insights for such diverse fields as communication, psychiatry, epistemology, learning, and so forth. His thought has attracted holistic thinkers who consider it a representative post-Cartesian worldview (e.g., Berman 1981/1984). In particular, C. A. Bowers has explored the educational implications of his ecological thought. Bowers (1993b, 42) remarks, "the use of Bateson's conceptual framework helps us understand humans as part of an ecology (as opposed to the Cartesian view that man must dominate nature through rationally based techniques)." In his successive works, Bowers has provided us with ecological views of education.[4]

At present, deep ecology is also forming a strong alliance with ecological holistic education. Arne Naess,[5] a Norwegian philosopher, first put forth this concept in the early 1970s to clarify the "biocentric" idea of ecology as opposed to the "anthropocentric" idea of what he called "shallow" ecology. This involved principles such as "rejection of the man-in-environment image in favor of *the relational, total-field image*" and "organism as knots in the biospherical net or field of intrinsic relations" (Naess 1973/1995, 151). Deep ecological thinking does not separate substantial subject ("man") from object ("environment"), but it sees that the fundamental ground of "the relational, total field" constitutes each phenomenal A and B as "knots" of relations. Deep ecology recognizes the primacy of interdependent reality, or the web of life (ecosystem), in which all life forms are embedded.

Naess (1986/1995) elaborated the idea of "self-actualization," which is also significant in the discussion of education. The conventional, individualistic meaning of the self is untenably narrow because it leaves out the essential dimension of its identification with "Nature." If the self were confused with "the narrow ego," self-realization would only imply "ego-trips." Instead, he introduced the concept of "ecological self" to encompass the entire extension of the self: "We may be said to be in, and of, Nature from the very beginning of our selves" (p. 226). An "ecological self" requires the individual self to be "widened and deepened" so as to realize the primordial identification with all living beings. Thus the self-

realization turns into a realization of the ecological self, which is an inclusive actualization of the potentialities of all living beings. Naess remarks: "We 'see ourselves in others.' Our self-realization is hindered if
the self-realization of others, with whom we identify, is hindered" (p.
226).

As far as I am aware, ecological holistic education has two basic orientations: one is concerned with teaching and learning about ecological
principles called "ecological literacy," and the other is more concerned
with cultivating the "ecological self."

David Orr (1992) provides the idea of "Earth-centered education"
that seeks to foster "ecological literacy" in terms of integrated approaches to environmental issues, dialogues with nature, participatory
and experiential learning in natural settings, and practical competence
with natural systems. In his definition,

> The ecologically literate person has the knowledge necessary to com-
> prehend interrelatedness, and an attitude of care or stewardship. Such
> a person would also have the practical competence required to act on
> the basis of knowledge and feeling. (p. 92)

The program of "ecological literacy" stresses intellectual understanding:
"The basis for ecological literacy ... is the comprehension of the interrelatedness of life grounded in the study of natural history, ecology, and
thermodynamics" (p. 93). Ecological literacy projects also attempt to
know about the environmental crisis and its human causes, the modern
world's domination of nature, reasons for human destructiveness, definitions of nature, development of ecological consciousness, designs of
sustainable society, environmental literature, and environmental
thought.

Capra and his collaborators (1993) have put forth a similar project
called "Ecoliteracy" (originally coined by Clark in 1981). Capra (1993, 8)
says: "Ecoliteracy is both a context and a process designed to help students to become ecologically literate—to understand the 'connectedness
of things' and to live and act in ways which reflect this understanding."
He underlines the importance of learning the basic principles of ecology.
"Being ecologically literate, or 'ecoliterate,' means understanding the
principles of organization of ecological communities (ecosystems) and
using those principles for creating sustainable human communities"

(Capra 1996, 297). They include interdependence, sustainability, ecological cycles, energy flow, partnership, flexibility, diversity, and coevolution. The Ecoliteracy project incorporates these ecological principles into both curriculum and the formation of learning communities. According to Edward Clark Jr. (1993, 30), "The mission of an Ecoliteracy curriculum is to help students become ecologically literate by designing and creating schools as collaborative learning communities."

The second orientation of ecological holistic education has two distinctive stages in cultivating the ecological self; the first stage takes a "reflective approach," and the second a "contemplative approach." Mitchell Thomashow's (1995) program of "ecological identity" concerns the first stage. "Ecological identity" is a sense of ecological self that can be cultivated through identification processes with nature—cognitive, affective, and intuitive perception of ecosystems, direct experiences of nature, and personal connection to special places. "Ecological identity refers to all the different ways people construe themselves in relationship to the earth as manifested in personality, values, actions, and sense of self" (p. 3). "Ecological identity work" attempts to associate the learning of ecology especially with personal transformation. Central to this work are the aspects of "reflective learning" and "reflective environmental practice."

At this point, we need to consider John Miller's (1994) revision of Donald Schön's (1983) idea of "the reflective practitioner"; that is, reflection needs contemplation for it to reach a "holistic experience." It is true that Thomashow's ecological identity work includes meditations, but the emphasis seems to be on the part of reflection. According to Miller,

> Simply put, reflection is still rooted in a dualistic view of reality in that there is a subject that reflects on an object. If we stay with a dualistic view of reality, we ultimately end up with a fragmented and compartmentalized approach to life. Yes, there is a need for analysis and reflection, but there is also a need for synthesis and contemplation. Contemplation is characterized by a merging of subject and object... It is through contemplation that we can see, or envision, the Whole. (p. vii)

In this regard, Joanna Macy's (1991b) effort of "the greening of the self" provides an outstanding example of the contemplative approach, which seeks a transformation of the "ego-self" to "the ecological self or the eco-self, co-existensive with other beings and the life of our planet" (p. 183). The greening of the self intends to expand and deepen our sense of the self to the extent that it becomes merged and embedded in nature. She states: "The awakening to our true self is the awakening to that entirety, breaking out of the prison-self of separate ego.... We are profoundly interconnected and therefore we are all able to recognize and act upon our deep, intricate, and intimate inter-existence with each other and all beings" (p. 190). In particular, in collaboration with John Seed, Macy has developed an educational program that has a variety of contemplative practice (e.g., Seed et al. 1988).

In this way, ecological holistic education has developed a variety of approaches—ranging from intellectual to reflective and contemplative—to realize the interconnectedness of the natural world.

SYSTEMS THEORY

Systems theory is a theoretical attempt to explore comprehensive, cosmological models of the cosmic world, in most cases drawing on evolutionist ideas that can give systemic explanations of the dynamic structure of the universe. Cosmological models of *systemic holistic education* are found in Ron Miller's "coherent holistic theory," Edward Clark's theory of "integrated curriculum," Thomas Berry's ideas on "earth education," and Atsu'hiko Yoshida's ideas on education in the self-organizing universe. The first two are structural models, and the last two are evolutionist dynamic models.

Each theory of systemic holistic education tries to provide a comprehensive view that understands the function of education in the structure and evolution of the universe as a whole. In general, it assumes several major subsystems within the entire universe such as the inanimate physical realm, primordial life forms, the biological realm of plants and animals, the mental field (symbolic and linguistic systems) produced by the human mind, and socio-cultural systems. In short, to use Wilber's (1995) terms, it deals with the physiosphere, the biosphere, and the noosphere. The systems views not only describe these subsystems in detail but also underline their structural connections. Therefore, systemic holistic education takes the entire universe as the relevant field of education.

Ron Miller (1991a, 24) says that "the key is for holistic theory to describe *multiple levels of wholeness*." His "coherent holistic theory" describes "five levels of wholeness": the whole person, the community, the society, the whole planet, and the cosmos (pp. 25-29). More recently, he has reconsidered it as four levels: the whole person, community, culture (the unconscious structure), and spirituality (1990/1997, 81-89). Although his ideas remain preliminary models, they are significant in their conceptions of multidimensional reality.

Clark (1997), who is the main contributor to the above-mentioned Ecoliteracy project, relies on "systems thinking," that is, a connection-centered "contextual thinking." Systems thinking sees everything in the phases of continuum, relationship, and wholeness. It sees human intelligence, thinking, and learning in an inseparable organic connection; "intelligence/thinking/learning is a single, dynamic, multi-faceted, functional capacity that is inherent in human consciousness" (p. 29, original in italics). Likewise, Clark sees knowledge as "contextual knowledge": "The essence of contextual knowledge is knowing how to identify, create, and explore contexts of meaning" (p. 31). All facets of intelligence, thinking, learning, and knowledge form a "systemic process." Therefore, curriculum requires a systemic design to meet their systemic nature, which he calls "integrated curriculum."

> Curriculum must be organized systematically to reflect the natural process of intelligence/thinking/learning, to demonstrate the interrelationships among subjects, and to allow students to construct their own meaning. (p. 35, original in italics)

Integrated curriculum helps the students explore their personal "meaning" by providing them with "contexts of meaning" that serve as frames of reference. The objective is to cultivate a "functional literacy" that includes such qualities and competencies as flexibility, problem-solving, decision-making, cooperation, self-direction, personal discipline, envisioning and realization of the desirable future, and so forth (pp. 51-52). Those who are functionally literate, according to Clark, are prepared "to respond deliberately and creatively to the demands of economic necessity, enlightened and informed social responsibility, and qualified planetary citizenship" (p. 51).

There are two significant evolutionist approaches to systemic holistic education. Thomas Berry (1988), inspired by Teilhard de Chardin, provided one of the most magnificent visions of education that has ever emerged. Education, in his view, is not a human enterprise but rather an ongoing process of the universe itself. He identifies three developmental stages of education: "universe education," "earth education," and "human education." Human education is seen as "a continuation, at the human level, of the self-education processes of the earth itself" (p. 89). Universe education is "the education which identifies with the emergent universe in its variety of manifestations from the beginning until now" (p. 89). In earth education, Earth is "the immediate self-educating community of those living and nonliving beings that constitute the earth" (p. 89). In this way, Berry holds that the evolutionary process of the universe and the earth *is* the process of education, for the process of self-organization of the universe is "education." "The earth's evolutionary process is planetary self-education" (p. 92).

Hence, human education must be placed in this continuous evolutionary process. As the human part of the evolution is its creation of human culture, "Human education can be defined, then, as a process whereby the cultural coding is handed on from one generation to another" (p. 93). This definition itself is rather commonplace, yet his whole idea of education is extraordinary. Education is no longer isolated from the unfolding process of the universe and the earth that gave rise to human beings.

Berry identifies five basic phases of the development of human culture—the Paleolithic, the Neolithic, the classical-traditional, the scientific-technological, and the ecological phases (p. 93). The emerging period we witness is the ecological phase in which human education needs a "new cultural coding" suitable for the ecological age. The task of human education in this particular stage of evolution is to help students understand themselves in the context of the evolution by providing them with the "universe story."

> At such crisis moments we need to return to the story of the universe. The entire college project can be seen as that of enabling the student to understand the immense story of the universe and the role of the student in creating the next phase of the story. (p. 98)

Brian Swimme and Thomas Berry (1992) describe a form of the "universe story." In this story, the coming ecological age is called "the Ecozoic era," an era when the planetary organic community of the earth becomes a central concern as opposed to the preceding Cenozoic era when the human component claimed its superiority over other nonhuman components and treated them as objects for exploitation. A new cultural coding of the Ecozoic era calls for the reintegration of the human process into the earth process to restore the lost communion. "What the Ecozoic era seeks ultimately is to bring human activities on the Earth into alignment with the other forces functioning throughout the planet so that a creative balance will be achieved" (p. 260).[6]

Yoshida (1996a), who appeared in the discussion of Japanese Life philosophy, has tried to develop his model of holistic education through his extensive studies in postmodern "non-mechanistic, non-reductionistic" systemic sciences, including Jantsch's theory of the self-organizing universe. He understands education in terms of the evolutionist context and develops a "holistic, anthropological, ground model" of human beings (p. 415, trans. Nakagawa) and thereupon a "holistic, pedagogical anthropology" (p. 416, trans. Nakagawa). He highlights systemic theories that deal with "the holarchical becoming of self-organizing systems" (p. 400, trans. Nakagawa) and at the same time accepts an ancient Confucian idea, *tenchi no kaiku*,[7] as a basic guideline for his theoretical effort.

> The wisdom of the ancient East was holistically aware of the work of education as the process of celebrating *tenchi no kaiku*. What I would like to describe is a perspective or a vision that enables us to understand "the process of evolution and growth" (*kaiku*) of the "human being" in "the multidimensionally self-organizing universe" (*tenchi*) with reference to post-mechanistic modern sciences. (p. 403, trans. Nakagawa)

The evolution of human beings is interwoven with the multidimensionally self-organizing evolution of the universe; that is, the universe has given rise to multistratified dimensions from microscopic to macroscopic levels, to which human beings belong in how they organize themselves in multidimensional ways through co-evolution with other subsystems of the universe. The evolution of human beings involves dimensions from the physical-chemical, to the biological, to the socio-cultural, and to conscious evolution. A human being as a micro-cosm is always subject to this open-ended "becoming" of the universe. In this regard, Yoshida rejects static structural models to emphasize the process nature of "becoming." Therefore, his definition of education reads: "[Education is] a work which [participates] in the process of evo-lution of the multidimensionally self-organizing universe, especially a work which constructively helps the formation of human beings who can consciously take part in the process" (p. 416, trans. Nakagawa).

In his recent work, Yoshida (1999) has become more concerned with the holistic thought of Jan Christian Smuts (1926/1961), the originator of the very concept of "holism." Indeed, Yoshida's ideas on holistic educa-tion, including tendencies of Life philosophy and systemic evolutionist thought, look very similar to Smuts' ideas on evolution. Like Yoshida's *inochi*, Smuts' "Holism" refers to the fundamental force behind the evo-lutionary process of the universe: "Holism is the term here coined ... to designate this fundamental factor operative towards the making or cre-ation of wholes in the universe" (p. 98). For Smuts, "Holism" is "the cre-ative principle" and "the motive force behind Evolution" (p. 99). He continues: "We thus have behind Evolution ... something quite definite. Holism is a specific tendency, with a definite character, and creative of all characters in the universe" (pp. 99-100). On his penetrating study in this forgotten yet all-important thinker, Yoshida has tried to develop a phi-losophy of holistic education.[8]

FEMINIST THOUGHT

Finally, consideration is given to feminist thought, which becomes relevant to contemporary holistic education for it shares a similar connectionist view. Nel Noddings (1984, 1992) proposed ideas of caring-centered education, a representative feminist approach to contemporary holistic education. Caring is a relational concept. Influenced by Buber's dialogical philosophy, Noddings regards caring as an encounter be-tween a carer and a cared-for. Her proposal of caring-centered education calls for cultivating caring relations in children, that is, caring for self, for intimate others, for distant others, for nonhuman animals, for plants, for the natural environment, for the human-made world, and for ideas. Ed-ucation should be organized around these "centers of care." Education for caring enables children to make intimate connections with those centers chiefly through caring relationships between them and the teacher (see Chapter 7).

Riane Eisler (2000) has also designed a model of holistic education called "partnership education." It is based on an alternative relationship to the "dominator model." The dominator model is marked by authoritarian structure; ranking of males over females; institutionalization of fear, violence, and abuse; high social investment in "masculine" traits and activities such as control and conquest; and myths and stories sacralizing domination (p. 11). On the other hand, the "partnership model" involves core elements such as these: democratic and egalitarian structure; equal valuing of females and males; institutionalization of mutual honoring, respect, and peaceful conflict resolution; social investment in "female" traits and activities such as empathy, caring, nonviolence, and caretaking; myths and stories sacralizing partnership (p. 11). Providing "the partnership-dominator continuum," Eisler refers to partnership education as follows:

> At the core of partnership education is learning, both intellectually and experientially, that the partnership and dominator models are two underlying alternatives for human relations. Relations based on fear, violence, and domination are a possibility. However, what distinguishes us as a species is not our cruelty and violence but our enormous capacity for caring and creativity. Constructing relations and institutions that more closely approximate the partnership model helps us actualize these capacities. (pp. 9-10)

Education based on the partnership model is strongly connection-oriented. As distinct from the dominator model of education that is teacher-centered, male-centered, and subject-centered, partnership education is more democratic, gender balanced, and integrated. It also emphasizes our interconnection with other people and Earth, and celebrates mutual responsibility, empathy, and caring (p. 23).

Some eco-feminist thinkers pay special attention to connections with nature, Earth, the body, and the emotions in opposition to the masculine and patriarchal emphasis on the spirit and transcendence dissociated from nature and bodily experiences, though they do not mention education as such. Embodied experiences associated with nature and the body have been subordinated under the spiritual and transcendental dimensions, and furthermore they have been associated with "female" experiences. Naomi Goldenberg (1990/1993, 211) says:

> What I am calling body stands in contrast to the notion of transcendence in traditional theology. Transcendence is a wish for something beyond body, beyond time, and beyond specific relationships to life. Such a notion of perfect safety involves negation of this world and is probably motivated by a characteristically (but not exclusively) male fear of being merged with matter.

Goldenberg requires "transcendence" to be connected with the body. "A transcendence with body, a transcendence that is life-oriented, would involve feelings of connection instead of separation" (pp. 211-12).

Furthermore, spiritual feminist thought involves ideas of "feminine spirituality," a celebration of immanent spirituality. Andrew Harvey (1996) celebrates "the sacred feminine," or "the motherhood of God," to correct imbalance between the feminine and the masculine.

> What a recovery of the wisdom of the Mother brings to all of us is the knowledge of inseparable connection with the entire creation and the wise, active love that is born from the knowledge.... The Mother's knowledge of unity, her powers of sensitivity, humility, and balance, and her infinite respect for the miracle of all life have now to be invoked by each of us and practiced if the "masculine" rational imbalance of our civilization is to be righted before it is too late. (pp. xii-xiii)

Charlene Spretnak (1991) also calls feminine spirituality "contemporary Goddess spirituality," whose common threads are "the desire to honor the Earthbody and one's personal body via an ongoing birthing process of cosmological unfolding" (p. 134). Goddess spirituality sees the divine as immanent in both the Earthbody and the human being as an "embodied Earthbeing." It enables us to experience "empowerment" through realizing the "cosmological self" embedded in a larger reality. Goddess spirituality evokes a "perceptual shift" from the "death-based sense of existence" of patriarchal culture to a "regeneration-based awareness" which is "an embrace of life as a cycle of creative rebirths" (p. 137). In this way, there is a strong tendency in feminine spirituality to identify the divine with the cosmic world.

FUNDAMENTAL PROBLEMS OF
CONTEMPORARY HOLISTIC EDUCATION

I have given an overview of the six philosophic orientations of contemporary holistic education—perennial philosophy, indigenous worldviews, Life philosophy, ecological worldview, systems theory, and feminist thought. From the viewpoint of multidimensional theory, the first three orientations seem to involve the infinite reality as well as the cosmic reality, while the last three are chiefly concerned with the cosmic reality. Roughly speaking, in this regard, the first three are closer to the position of Eastern philosophy than the last three orientations.

However, the problem is that even the first three orientations are not totally clear in discerning the infinite reality from the cosmic reality and tend to confuse them. This confusion may be caused by the logic of interconnection, because this logic has a tendency to overlook dimensional differences in emphasizing the opposite quality of continuity of all things. The point is that *there are multiple dimensions of relationships,* not a one-dimensional continuum.

In the remainder of this chapter, I will focus on theoretical and practical problems especially found in the ecological and systemic orientations, because they are concerned with essential differences between Eastern and Western approaches to holistic education.

ECO-SPIRITUALISM

Ontological questions arise in the ecological theories of contemporary holistic education that tend to assume that the ecosystems of the earth and the universe (the cosmic reality) are the all-embracing ultimate reality, reflecting an ecological mysticism, or *eco-spiritualism*. Eco-spiritualism here means a belief that the natural world, or the entire ecosystem, is the supreme spiritual reality. For example, Bateson (1972) regards "God" as "immanent" in the ecosystem:

> The individual mind is immanent but not only in the body. It is immanent also in pathways and messages outside the body; and there is a larger Mind of which the individual mind is only a subsystem. This larger Mind is comparable to God and is perhaps what some people

mean by "God," but it is still immanent in the total interconnected social system and planetary ecology. (p. 161)

He also interprets "Enlightenment" in terms of biological context: "I
think it important ... to notice how often Enlightenment is a sudden realization of the biological nature of the world in which we live. It is a sudden discovery or realization of *life*" (Bateson and Bateson 1987/1988, 74).
Capra (1996) also shows an eco-spiritualist view of deep ecology:

> Ultimately, deep ecological awareness is spiritual or religious aware-
> ness. When the concept of the human spirit is understood as the mode
> of consciousness in which the individual feels a sense of belonging, of
> connectedness, to the cosmos as a whole, it becomes clear that ecologi-
> cal awareness is spiritual in its deepest essence. (p. 7)

It is important to recognize the twofold aspect of the eco-spiritualist
position. On the one hand, it breaks a new horizon of naturalistic, ecological spirituality, a horizon that has been overlooked for many years. It re-
minds us of the "sacredness" of the natural world, and it would be
effective in preventing us from further planetary destruction. However,
on the other hand, there emerges a problem rarely expressed by eco-
spiritualists; that is, all dimensions of spirituality may easily be reduced
to the one dimension of ecosystem. This may be called *ecological
reductionism.*

In his recent work, Ken Wilber (1995, 1996, 1998) has made a similar
point: the modern and even postmodern worldviews are dominated by
the "flatland" view of "empirical nature" or "mononature" that claims
itself as the sole reality in denial of the deeper dimension of "Spirit." As
this empirical worldview has been strongly supported by the progress of
science and technology, Wilber (1996, 274) calls it "the industrial ontology"; "with the modern industrial ontology, nature is the ultimate reality, nature alone is real." In his view, ecological thinkers and
ecophilosophers, or what he calls "the Eco-Romantics," are caught up by
this industrial ontology, despite their apparent opposition to industrial-
ization. "The belief that empirical nature is the ultimate reality—that *is*
the industrial ontology. The Eco-Romantics rejected the industry but
kept the ontology" (1996, 275).

The eco-spiritual view of the Eco-Romantics tends to ignore or deny
the dimension of Spirit, to reduce it to empirical nature, and instead to el-

evate and worship nature, or the ecosystem. While Spirit is reduced to "spirit," nature is converted into "Nature." In Wilber's (1995, 610) words:

> Many ecophilosophers want to use *Nature*, with a capital *N*, to mean the same thing as God or Goddess or Spirit, except without the "other-worldly" connotation. For them, Nature is spirit-in-this-world, and we don't need any *transcendental* aspect to it.

This view eventually veils and represses the truly *deeper* dimensions by its erroneous identification of nature with the ultimate reality:

> But as long as I am locked into the flatland world of empirical mononature, as long as I *interpret* nature as the *source* of the Divine, then to just that extent I am locked out of any deeper or truer spiritual illuminations and intuitions.... (Wilber 1995, 471)

From the viewpoint of multidimensional ontology, however, nature is seen as a manifestation of the infinite reality. With Wilber, "nature is not Spirit but an expression of Spirit" (1995, 286). As mentioned before, Emerson's appreciation of nature comes from this understanding: "It [nature] always speaks of Spirit. It suggests the absolute" (1981, 34). For Emerson, nature is "sacred," for it is a manifestation of the infinite reality (Spirit), but not *vice versa*. (In my view, Wilber's and Emerson's Spirit denotes the infinite reality as the deepest, ontological ground of reality. Therefore, it is not a transcendental realm separated from the other dimensions of reality.)

In the field of Eastern philosophy, Zen master Dogen (1200-1253)[9] gives us an example in terms of "Buddha-nature." In his *Shobogenzo*, Dogen (1975) quotes a passage from the *Nirvana Sutra*: "All sentient beings without exception have the Buddha-nature" (p. 96). Tathagata-garbha thought in Mahayana Buddhism assumed that all sentient beings contain the Buddha-nature (the infinite reality) as a potential nature like an embryo or a seed hidden within themselves. In opposition to this, Dogen rejects the substantialist concept of the Buddha-nature and intentionally reads the passage as follows: "All" means sentient beings and all beings, and "*whole being* is the Buddha-nature" (p. 97). Here the Buddha-nature is no longer a potential core hidden within sentient beings. Tetsuro Watsuji (1926/1992) comments on this:

> Therefore, that "whole being is the Buddha-nature" must mean the
> omnipresence of the Buddha-nature.... Here it is impossible to raise
> such a notion that there is the Buddha-nature only in sentient beings as
> a potentiality. On the contrary, it is *in the Buddha-nature* that all sentient
> beings exist. (pp. 325-26, trans. Nakagawa)

The Buddha-nature embraces all sentient beings. Furthermore, as the
whole being includes non-sentient as well as sentient beings, Dogen
(1975, 105) says that "these mountains, rivers, and earth are all the Buddha-nature Sea." In this way, the whole of nature (the cosmic reality) is
the Buddha-nature. This does not mean an eco-spiritual view but refers
to the universal reality that takes place after Awakening. As Dogen
(1976a, 88) says, "Buddha-nature is not incorporated prior to attaining
Buddhahood; it is incorporated upon the attainment of Buddhahood.
The Buddha-nature is always manifested simultaneously with the attainment of Buddhahood."

Malcolm David Eckel (1997) examines the concept of "nature" in Buddhist philosophy as follows:

> The natural world functions as a locus and an example of the imper-
> manence and unsatisfactoriness of death and rebirth. The goal to be
> cultivated is not wilderness in its own right but a state of awareness in
> which a practitioner can let go of the "natural"—of all that is imperma-
> nent and unsatisfactory—and achieve the sense of peace and freedom
> that is represented by the state of *nirvana*. One might say that nature is
> not to be dominated but to be relinquished in order to become free.
> (pp. 337-38)

According to Mahayana understanding, after *nirvana* is realized (or one
is enlightened), the entire world including the natural world will revive
as the universal reality. As Eckel says, "The earth is not, as it were, a mere
illusion. It is the body of an enlightened sage, and it is as worthy of reverence as the throne of the Buddha.... [I]t [the natural world] is the place
made holy by the quest for enlightenment. Enlightenment is made present in this body and this earth" (p. 346). In this way, the natural world becomes a sacred reality (the universal reality) only in Enlightenment.

COSMOS AND ANTI-COSMOS

The problem of eco-spiritualism is closely related to the second point that concerns the systemic views of contemporary holistic education. When the systemic approaches attempt to develop cosmological models of education, they usually involve the aspects of *Being* and *Becoming* (the cosmic reality) yet ignore the aspects of *Non-Being* (the infinite reality). Eastern philosophy, on the other hand, has definitely concerned itself with *Non-Being*.

Toshihiko Izutsu (1989) remarks that Existence has dimensions of both the cosmos and the "anti-cosmos." The anti-cosmos signifies the infinite reality (Emptiness and Non-Being). Eastern ontology, he says, has involved this anti-cosmological reality as the deepest dimension:

> The mainstream of Eastern philosophy ... has traditionally taken the position of anti-cosmos (Being-destructive position). In other words, it attempts to radically destroy the cosmos by introducing the fundamentally negative concepts like "Emptiness" and "Non-Being" into the structure of the world of Being and placing them at the bottom of the cosmos. (p. 230, trans. Nakagawa)

Eastern philosophy has taken the anti-cosmological Non-Being for the ontological ground of the cosmos. On the contrary, cosmological theories fail to grasp the aspect of the anti-cosmos, for they have no ideas and no frameworks for this dimension. However, from the Eastern perspective, the dimension of the anti-cosmos is crucial, for it not only deconstructs the world of Being into Non-Being but also serves as the creative ground for it to reappear as the universal reality. Izutsu (1989) states:

> It is more important to see that the thought of Eastern philosophy not only realizes "Non-Being" at the deepest dimension of Being but also proceeds to step forward in a positive way: It regards "Non-Being" emerging at the end in the destruction of the world of Being as an origin or a new starting point of "Being." (p. 240, trans. Nakagawa)

Likewise, Keiji Nishitani (1982) acknowledges that "a system of being" is ultimately grounded in the level of "emptiness":

> [A] system of being becomes genuinely possible, not on a field where the system of being is seen only as a system of being, but on a field of

emptiness where being is seen as being-*sive*-nothingness, nothing-
ness-*sive*-being. (p. 147)

Shizuteru Ueda (1992) characterizes this double mode of Being and
Non-Being ("being-*sive*-nothingness") as "the double-being-in-the-
world-in-Emptiness," relying on Heidegger's concept of the "being-in-
the-world" (*In-der-Welt-sein*). In Heidegger's "being-in-the-world," the
"world" does not involve the dimension of Emptiness. But, according to
Ueda, the human being dwells in "Emptiness" as well as in the "world";
therefore, human existence is defined as "the double-being-in-the-
world-in-Emptiness." "The world 'in' which we are, is as a world 'in'
Emptiness. We as 'being-in-the-world' are simultaneously 'in' Emptiness, 'in' which the world is, through our being-in-the-world" (p. 13,
trans. Nakagawa). Or, he says, "The world as a world is 'in' Infinite
Openness" (p. 29, trans. Nakagawa).

This double-ness of the world and Emptiness gives the same double
quality to the "self" therein. Ueda defines the self as the "Selfless Self" or
"the Self as No-self." The self exists as a self in the world and simultaneously as a No-self in Emptiness. Ueda (1994b, 23) states:

We are in the world, yet at the same time we somehow remain in the infinite openness that both envelops and transcends the world.... This is
not to say that there are two worlds—the world is just as it is, and yet is
imbued with an infinite openness. This imparts a decisive quality to
our existence in the world, leading to a way of being in which one lives
within and yet transcends (or, perhaps, penetrates) the world. The "actor" exists as a self within the world and at the same time penetrates to
the infinite openness in which there is no self; this actor might thus be
called "a self that is not a self."

In this way, Ueda's conception of the double-being-in-the-world-in-
Emptiness involves both the cosmos and the anti-cosmos in a non-
dualistic way.

Haridas Chaudhuri (1977), a modern Indian philosopher inspired by
Sri Aurobindo's Integral Philosophy, gives another account of the anti-
cosmos. His idea of "Being" involves both the cosmos and the anti-
cosmos:

Being is reality in its multidimensional fullness. Broadly speaking
there are two dimensions of Being. First, Being is revealed as time, as

cosmic energy, as the evolutionary process. Secondly, Being is revealed as the timeless ground of the cosmic manifold, as the indeter-
minable silence or void. (p. 25)

"Being" has two dimensions: the "temporal," "evolutionary" dimension (the cosmic reality) and the "nontemporal," "ontological" dimension (the infinite reality). In the temporal dimension emerges the
evolution of the universe. "From the temporal perspective, Being appears as an evolutionary hierarchy of increasingly marvelous spheres of
existence such as the material, the vital, the mental, the rational, and the
spiritual" (p. 23). In his view, the temporal evolution includes the cosmic
energy, the universal life force, the sentient consciousness, the universal
reason or logos, and the consciousness. On the other hand, the non-
temporal dimension of Being is "the ultimate ground of the universe beyond space, time and causation" (p. 23). On this dimension, "Being is no
particular mode of existence, no determinate structure. It is the formless
ground of all particular forms and modes of existence" (p. 34).

The problems arise when these two dimensions are confused, which
Chaudhuri calls "the fallacy of false equation." For example, it is likely
that some philosophers identify Being with cosmic energy or the universal life force and see it as the ultimate ground of all beings; however, it is a
manifest error to equate it with the non-temporal, formless Being.

In addition to these notions given by Eastern philosophers, I would
like to refer to the "phenomenological" descriptions of two contemporary mystics, Jidu Krishnamurti and Bernadette Roberts, who seem to
give us glimpses of the anti-cosmos. Krishnamurti left in his *Notebook*
(1976) descriptions of what happened to him. What he calls "vastness,"
"immensity," "benediction," or "otherness" seems to flow from the infinite depth. For example, when he climbed up a mountain with a friend, it
happened:

> We were going up the path of a steep wooded side of a mountain and
> presently sat on a bench. Suddenly, most unexpectedly that sacred
> benediction came upon us, the other felt it too, without our saying
> anything. As it several times filled a room, this time it seemed to cover
> the mountainside across the wide, extending valley and beyond the
> mountains. It was everywhere. All space seemed to disappear; what
> was far, the wide gap, the distant snow-covered peaks and the person

sitting on the bench faded away. There was not one or two or many but
only this immensity. (p. 25)

What he calls "it" seems to imply infinite depth from which the world of
beings appears as it is. Indeed, Krishnamurti says, "The essence of being
is non-being, and to 'see' the depth of non-being, there must be freedom
from becoming" (pp. 57-58).

What happened to Roberts (1984/1993, 1989) is also worth mentioning, for her background was the Christian contemplative tradition yet
what really happened was surprisingly coincident with the Eastern way
of contemplation. For years she followed the Christian contemplative
path and came to have experiences of "the unitive state," experiences of
the "true self" being in union with "the divine" and the fullness of "life"
and "being." She says, "the basic sense of the true self is a wholistic sense
of unity and oneness that results from realization (or disclosure) of the
divine center of ourselves" (1989, 23). However, quite unexpectedly, one
day she found herself in a completely different phase. She called it "the
experience of no-self" in which the true self together with the divine fell
away and dissolved into "nothingness." In her words, *the definitive no-
self experience is the sudden falling away (or "drop") of the divine center of consciousness along* with its profound mysterious experience of life and being" (1989, 48). The no-self experience may be a similar experience to the
"Great Death" in Zen and "Death before death" in Sufism. "It is as if the
Ground of Being had been pulled out from under the entire self-
experience" (1989, 48).

One remarkable aspect of the no-self experience is that it opens up an
immense deeper dimension in which the experience of divine life and
being in the unitive state falls away. Thus Roberts entered the all-
negating "nothingness" or "void." It frightened her, as she was not prepared for such an experience. Particularly, "life" disappeared in nothingness.

Suddenly I was aware that all life around me had come to a complete
standstill. Everywhere I looked, instead of life, I saw a hideous nothingness invading and strangling the life out of every object and vista in
sight. (1984/1993, 46)

She remarks that "the no-self event is first and foremost the *falling away of the divine center, the source and ground of the experience of "life," "being," energy and a great deal more"* (1989, 72).

However, as time went on, the nothingness turned into an all-embracing positive ground; "the usual void was replaced by something else, something that was not localized as a presence, but something more pervasive and intense" (1984/1993, 74). She called this something "what Is." For her, "what Is never comes and goes," and it "can be intense at times, even though it is not something ecstatic, ineffable, or transcendent. On the contrary, it is obvious, natural, and somewhat ordinary, for it is what we see everywhere we look" (p. 76). She at last learned to find that "what Is" is "Truth"; "only when I had finally to accept what is, did I suddenly realize that what is *Is* Truth itself and all that Is" (p. 84). After a while, having been in accord with what Is, "another new way of life" emerged to her, in which "doing" became possible. However, this "doing" was not an ordinary doing evoked by willing and maintained by conscious effort.

> Doing is an energyless, non-reflective, effortless activity that must be distinguished from a deliberate, self-aware type of activity that needs constant effort and maintenance. For this reason, doing is nothing we can bring about by our own efforts and energies because doing is what follows automatically when all personal efforts and energies have ceased. (p. 77)

"Doing" is a sheer manifestation of what Is; "what Is can only be known because it is identical with its acts (or doing)" (p. 77).

The stages of Roberts' contemplative path illustrate all the dimensions the Eastern way has; that is, they have shifted from the unitive state (the cosmic reality) to the state of no-self and nothingness (the anti-cosmos, or the infinite reality), and then to what Is and finally to doing (the universal reality).

THE TRANSFORMATION OF THE SELF

Now we turn to the practical and methodological aspect of contemporary holistic education. One of the primary purposes of its practices is to help students realize the interconnectedness of all beings. To attain this, many theories of contemporary holistic education adopt intellectual, reflective, and experiential methods, which may come under what John Miller (1988/1996) calls the "transaction position." No matter how innovative they are in comparison with conventional methods (the "transmission position"), they seem to fall short of bringing about a real transformation.

To use Wilber's (1999) terms, many methods in contemporary holistic education can be marked by "translation" mode rather than "transformation" mode. In his definitions: "With typical *translation*, the self (or subject) is given a new way to think about the world (or objects); but with radical *transformation*, the self itself is inquired into, looked into" (p. 28). With "translation," the student may be given a new holistic belief or worldview and then learn to "translate" the world in accord with this new perspective. This is what most contemporary holistic education practices intend to do. However, it does not necessarily require a deep transformation penetrating to the very ground of the self. "Authentic transformation," on the other hand, concerns itself not with the "horizontal" translation of our belief system but directly with the "vertical" exploration into the deeper dimensions of the self. (Wilber himself proposes not to choose one of them but to have "an integral approach" that combines both ways in an optimal manner.)

With this in mind, we need to pay more attention to the transformation of the self by contemplation. Here we need to understand the nature of fragmentation; in short, fragmentation is concerned not only with our worldviews but also with the very ground of our own existence, so that it is really difficult for us to realize interconnectedness in our knowing and being. David Bohm (1980/1995) refers to this deep-rooted fragmentation: "Our fragmentary way of thinking, looking, and acting, evidently has implications in every aspect of human life.... This comes about because the roots of fragmentation are very deep and pervasive" (p. 16). The "fragmentary way" of thinking is a strong "habit" of the modern mind that brings about the fragmentation of the world. "Since our thought is pervaded with differences and distinctions, it follows that such a habit leads us to look on these as real divisions, so that the world is then seen and experienced as actually broken up into fragments" (p. 3). Divisions created in our minds are projected onto the "undivided" world.

The existential root of this fragmentation is in the nature of language, as discussed in the previous chapter. Language serves to articulate and differentiate the undivided world into the objective world of individual beings. *The articulation of language is a primary root of fragmentation.* Therefore, a holistic perception of undivided connection is not an ordinary but rather a non-ordinary mode of perception, which can be actualized only if we "transform" the built-in habit of articulation. Eastern philosophy has been aware of this, so it has developed the way of contemplation to transcend the working of the mind and to realize a "no-mind" state of being.

For example, Zen master Takuan (1573-1645) left a famous letter called *The Mysterious Record of Immovable Wisdom* to the great master swordsman Yagyu Tajimanokami Munenori, in which Takuan (1986) clearly described the difference between the mind and the no-mind. The basic nature of the mind is to "stop in one place," a tendency to attach to one object of thought. Takuan called it "the Confused Mind" (*maushin*) or "the Existent Mind" (*ushin*):

> The Existent Mind is the same as the Confused Mind and is literally read as the "mind that exists." It is the mind that thinks in one direction, regardless of subject. When there is an object of thought in the mind, discrimination and thoughts will arise. Thus it is known as the Existent Mind. (p. 33)

This Confused or Existent Mind is the ordinary state of the mind. In contrast, he celebrated the "Right Mind" (*honshin*) or the "No-Mind" (*mushin*) that stops nowhere and identifies nothing.

> The No-Mind is the same as the Right Mind. It neither congeals nor fixes itself in one place. It is called No-Mind when the mind has neither discrimination nor thought but wanders about the entire body and extends throughout the entire self.
> The No-Mind is placed nowhere.... Where there is no stopping place, it is called No-Mind. (p. 33)

It is in the No-Mind state of consciousness that fragmentation disappears. To attain the No-Mind, however, it is necessary to practice contemplation. The No-Mind with no fixed focal point is the same as what has been called "awareness," "mindfulness," and "witness" in meditation practices.

Self-identity as delineated in the previous chapter is another aspect of fragmentation that penetrates deep into our being. Wilber (1977/1993, 1979/1985) has explored this issue in light of the "spectrum of consciousness." In his notion, self-identity is created by drawing "boundary" lines between self and not-self. There is no entity such as the self prior to drawing boundaries, but it is in the very act of drawing them that the self and the not-self (or the world) are bounded. The fundamental process of boundary formation is comprised of "dualism-repression-projection." In his words, "a dualism 'severs' a process, *represses* its non-dual or 'unitary' character, and *projects* that process as two apparently antagonistic opposites" (1977/1993, 107). This threefold operation makes a boundary appear as if it were a "real" division; however, it is not a solid barrier but a mental construct. "Boundaries are illusions, products not of reality but of the way we map and edit reality" (1979/1985, 31). At the bottom of consciousness, there is "no boundary," but "we progressively limit our world and turn from our true nature in order to embrace boundaries" (1979/1985, 3-4). Wilber delineates a successive formation of boundaries, or the "spectrum of consciousness," with three major boundaries that divide organism from environment, ego from the body, and persona from shadow. Therefore, the "levels of self-identity" are gradually narrowed from organism to ego to persona. This is a fragmentation in the formation of self-identity. As Wilber significantly suggests, education takes part in this fragmentation of the self. "To receive an education is to learn where and how to draw boundaries and then what to do with the bounded aspects" (1979/1985, 18).

Therefore, a holistic consciousness can be realized only if boundaries dissolve away, which needs a radical transformation of self-identity. If contemporary holistic education seeks to overcome fragmentation, it has to reverse the process of boundary formation. Importantly enough, Wilber sees the dissolution of boundaries as "growth": "Growth is re-apportionment; re-zoning; re-mapping; an acknowledgment, and then enrichment, of ever deeper and more encompassing levels of one's own self" (1979/1985, 13). "Growth" in this sense reverses the process of "dualism-repression-projection" and reintegrates the fragmented parts of the self, "heals" them into a wholeness (1977/1993, 267). The process of becoming whole ("healing") runs through a "spectrum" of intermediate "levels" to attain "unity consciousness."

According to Phiroz Mehta (1989, 141), "Whilst functioning in holistic consciousness, no awareness of separate selfhood is possible. Holistic consciousness is not yours, not mine. It is the One Unitary Consciousness of the One Unitary Whole." To realize holistic consciousness, it would be imperative to incorporate the way of contemplation into the practice of holistic education in a more authentic manner.

As the fundamental problems of contemporary holistic education we have discussed the theoretical limitations of ecological and systemic worldviews and the methodological limitations of holistic education practices. From the multidimensional theory, many ideas of contemporary holistic education seem to settle down in the third dimension of the cosmic reality. Therefore, theoretically they need to involve the deeper dimensions of reality, and methodologically they need to include contemplative practice to bring about the transformation of the self (see Chapter 6). If they fail to take these aspects seriously into account, they seem to fall short of their original expectations.

NOTES

1. The orientation of perennial philosophy also includes the work of Plato, Froebel, Emerson, Steiner, Alice Bailey, Gurdjieff, Ouspensky, J. G. Bennet, Aldous Huxley, Thomas Merton, and E. F. Schumacher. In reality, it is not a new trend but one of the oldest trends of thought found in both Western and Eastern mysticism. For the most part, Eastern philosophy is seen as the perennial philosophy developed in the East, and in this sense the perennial philosophic orientation in contemporary holistic education is best akin to the Eastern views of holistic education.

2. The philosophy of Life or Life philosophy has its historical origin in the *Lebensphilosophie* of Friedrich Nietzsche, Wilhelm Dilthey, Georg Simmel, Henri Bergson and others. But in this context, I include a broad tendency of thought that celebrates Life as the fundamental principle.

3. Besides these, "ecopsychology" conceived by Theodore Roszak (1992) and others (Roszak, Gomes, and Kanner 1995) and "transpersonal ecology" developed by Warwick Fox (1990) may be also important for ecological holistic education.

4. Satoji Yano (1996) at the Kyoto University, Japan, has also provided an in-depth exploration of Bateson's philosophy as a theory of education.

5. For his philosophical ideas on "ecosophy," see Naess (1989).

6. In his recent work on transformative education, Edmund O'Sullivan (1999) has made a major contribution to Berry's cosmological ideas of education.

7. The literal translation of *tenchi no kaiku* is "the transformation of Heaven and Earth"; however, Yoshida interprets this phrase as the human process of evolution and growth in accordance with the evolution of the universe and the earth.

8. Beukes (1989/1991) provides an introduction to Smuts and his thought.

9. Dogen is now looked upon not only as a great Zen master, the founder of the Soto school of Zen in Japan, but also as an authentic thinker whose profound thought has unlimited potentiality as postmodern thought. His masterpiece is *Shobogenzo*, the complete English translations of which are found in Nishiyama (1975-1983) and Nishijima and Cross (1994-1998). Also, Tanahashi (1985, 1999) provides excellent selections to Dogen's writings. For an introduction to his thought, see Abe (1992).

Buddhist Views of Relationships

A fundamental assumption of contemporary holistic education is interconnection of everything. However, despite this being an all-important concept, as far as I see, this concept as such seems to have been less explored and examined, and instead it has been assumed as the unquestionable ontological foundation of holistic education.

On the other hand, Eastern philosophy is able to enrich the idea of relationships. It has refined multidimensional ideas of relationships, which the logic of interconnection tends to overlook. In particular, Buddhist views of relationships are important as they provide profound insights into the multidimensional nature of relationships.

The following discussion will focus on various conceptions of "dependent-arising" or "dependent co-arising" (Pali, *paticca samuppada*; Sanskrit, *pratitya-samutpada*; Japanese, *engi*) which appeared in Early Buddhism (the Buddha's teachings, or Theravada Buddhism) and Mahayana Buddhism (Prajna-paramita thought, Nagarjuna's Madhyamika philosophy, and Hua-yen ontology).

THE RELEVANT TEACHINGS OF THE BUDDHA

THE BUDDHA'S PROCESS PHILOSOPHY

The Buddha's philosophy has a strong tendency to deconstruct substantialist ideas and to reveal the relational and process-oriented nature of reality, which is seen in his key ideas such as "impermanence," "selflessness," and "dependent-arising." "Impermanence" (P. *anicca*; Skt. *anityah*) is what the Buddha always emphasized in his teachings. It refers to a basic fact of life; namely, every being arises and passes away, and nothing is permanent. This means that reality is not a static structure composed of permanent substances but is constantly changing. S. Radhakrishnan (1923/1996) described the Buddha's philosophy as a "wonderful philosophy of dynamism" and said:

> Impressed by the transitoriness of objects, the ceaseless mutation and transformation of things, Buddha formulated a philosophy of change. He reduces substances, souls, monads, things to forces, movements, sequences and processes, and adopts a dynamic conception of reality. (p. 367)

Impermanence means that there is no entity that can endure in its own being without change. The whole existence of the universe is in a ceaseless process of becoming. The Buddha observes that "sufferings" (P. *dukkha*; Skt. *duhkha*) for humans arise when they confuse what is impermanent with permanent things. So he taught people to release attachment to anything that is impermanent.

Impermanence implies that every being has no permanent, substantial, independent self in its essence. This is called "selflessness" (or no self, not-self) (P. *anatta*; Skt. *anatman*). This holds true to our self-identity; the human self is no-self. It may be what the Buddha himself realized when he attained the great enlightenment. The *Dhammapada*, a classic in Early Buddhism, includes the following phrases (No. 154):

> Now are you seen, O builder of the house, you will not build the house again. All your rafters are broken, your ridgepole is destroyed. The mind, set on the attainment of *nirvana*, has attained the extinction of desires. (Radhakrishnan 1950/1996, 110)

As the "builder of the house" means the root of self-structure, the Buddha ultimately had an insight into the selfless nature of the self.

One of the strongest attachments is that to our own self-identities, and the fundamental sufferings arise when we believe in the existence of substantial self-identities. Early Buddhism challenged this deep-rooted belief by raising the idea of "the five aggregates" (P. *khandhas*; Skt. *skandhas*) (see Harvey 1990, 49-50; Cheetham 1994, 157). They include:

- *rupa*—material shape or form, physical and bodily faculties
- *vedana*—feelings
- *sanna* or *samjna*—perception, cognition
- *sankhara* or *samskaras*—volition, constructing activities
- *vinnana* or *vijnana*—discriminative consciousness.

The idea of the five aggregates means that any phenomenon ascribed to "self" is composed of these five aggregates, and that the self dissolves itself into these components. Here, the Buddha did not fall into a naive elementalistic view, for the five aggregates are not atomistic elements but impermanent factors in themselves. As Peter Harvey (1990, 52) comments, "None of the *khandhas* is a 'being' or 'self,' but these are simply conventional terms used to denote the collection of functioning *khandhas*." The "self" is none other than a contingent system that is fundamentally empty of any selfhood.

The Buddha's View of Interdependence

The idea of selflessness is related to the third doctrine of dependent-arising,[1] a doctrine that can explain how impermanent selfless being arises. According to Joanna Macy (1991a, xi), "The contingent nature of the self … is … grounded in the radical interdependence of *all* phenomena, set forth in the Buddha's central doctrine of causality, *paticca samuppada*, or dependent co-arising." When Gautama attained the highest enlightenment under the Bodhi Tree, it is said that he realized this in the deepest state of *samadhi*. This doctrine in Early Buddhism has hundreds of patterns in its orderly formulation called *nidanas*. Among them, the most standard is the twelve *nidanas*, which run as follows (*Vinaya-pitaka I*, 1, in Conze 1995, 66; see also Macy 1991a, 37; Cheetham 1994, 207):

- *avijja* or *avidya*—ignorance
- *samkhara* or *samskara*—volitional or karmic formation
- *vinnana* or *vijnana*—consciousness or cognition
- *nama-rupa*—name and form, or mind-and-body
- *salayatana* or *sadayatana*—the six senses-fields
- *phassa* or *sparsa*—impression

- *vedana*—feeling
- *tanha* or *trsna*—craving
- *upadana*—grasping
- *bhava*—becoming
- *jati*—birth
- *jaramarana*—aging, dying, grief, sorrow, suffering.

This is a causal process starting from "ignorance" and leading up to "suffering." The basic structural moment is this: "If this is that comes to be; from the arising of this that arises" (*Samyutta-nikaya II*, 64-65, in Conze 1995, 66). When a preceding condition is present, a succeeding condition arises; or, conditioned by A, B arises; or, depending on A, B is. In this way, Early Buddhism provided an explanation of how a phenomenal being emerges through causal relations. This causal process implies that all events in the phenomenal world are in the deeper levels interdependent and mutually conditioning for them to arise and pass away.

As each component of dependent-arising has no permanent self-identity, this interrelational causation process is not an interaction between preexistent substances. But from an inseparable process of relations, each phenomenon emerges. At this point, Macy marks dependent-arising as "'the interdependent structure' of reality" (1991a, 63) and finds a similarity between the Buddha's view and contemporary systems theory. "The systems view of causal process ... reveals striking convergence with the Buddha's teaching of causality" (p. 1). In her effort of "mutual hermeneutic" of both fields, Macy found that:

> Systems concepts provide explanations and analogies which can illuminate Buddhist ideas that are less accessible from a linear causal point of view. Systems theory also offers a broad range of data showing the operation throughout the phenomenal universe of the causal principle the Buddha taught. For its part, Buddhism reveals the existential, religious, and ethical implications of the systems view of process. (pp. 1-2)

Macy's attempt is significant in inaugurating a dialogue between Early Buddhism and systems theory to articulate a "Dharma of Natural Systems" as a basis for "the ecological worldview." However, the emphasis on dependent-arising as a systemic principle of the universe seems to underestimate another aspect of dependent-arising, namely, the reverse movement to *nirvana* (P. *nibbana*). As systems theory primarily deals with the natural progression of the universe and the formation of human life in the universe, it is difficult to take the reverse movement into account. But the Buddha's primary concern was with the liberation from sufferings caused by dependent-arising.

THE DIMENSION OF NIRVANA

Dependent-arising involves two opposite directions. According to Musashi Tachikawa (1998), one is "the dependent-arising that tells the formation of the delusive world," and the other is "the dependent-arising that tells the cessation of the delusive world" (p. 158, trans. Nakagawa). This twofold movement of dependent-arising was what Gautama himself realized in his highest enlightenment. Sherab Chodzin Kohn (1994, 35) portrays this:

> In the third and last watch of the night, he applied himself to the task of rooting out this suffering once and for all. He had clearly understood the wheel of dependent arising in which each stage follows from a preceding cause, beginning with ignorance.... Now his divine eye sought the means of liberation. He saw that through the cessation of birth, old age and death would not exist; through the cessation of becoming, there would be no birth; through the cessation of grasping, no becoming—and so back through the sequence of causation to ignorance. He saw suffering, the cause of suffering, the cessation of suffering, and at last also the path to cessation.... Thus he attained complete and utter enlightenment and became the Buddha.

By recognizing and then abnegating dependent-arising, the Buddha liberated himself from its bondage. The structural moment of this phase is this: "if this is not that does not come to be; from the stopping of this that is stopped" (Conze 1995, 66). Cheetham (1994, 213) comments on this:

> If the prior condition is removed or de-activated, then its successor cannot come into being. This is the key to the stopping process known as the breaking of the links, or, the formula put into reverse. And that was one of the great secrets that the Buddha discovered on his Enlightenment.

The progressive stages of dependent-arising leading to suffering must be reversed and successively cease to be in order to attain *nirvana*.

To attain *nirvana*, we need to realize how our existence is unconsciously conditioned by causal relations. By practicing contemplation, we learn to raise awareness of the conditions and to disidentify with them. However, this enhanced awareness as such is not the state of *nirvana* but a stepping stone to it. In the final analysis, *nirvana* is a release from dependent-arising. The cessation of ignorance may imply the complete stopping of the unconscious driving force of life and an entry into the infinite reality.

Shin'ichi Tsuda (1987) captures the multidimensional structure regarding *nirvana* in the concept of "twofold Dharmadhatu" (*niju hokkai*). In his scheme, *nirvana* is called "the inner Dharmadhatu" (the inner realm of Buddhist reality), which is dimensionally distinct from "the outer Dharmadhatu" (the outer realm of Buddhist reality) where Buddhist practitioners are engaged in Buddhist contemplation to attain *nirvana*.

Nirvana is a radically transformed state of consciousness. Rune Johansson (1969) refers to the "transformation sphere" of *nirvana* (*nibbana*) as follows: "Nibbana is never described as the natural state of a human being but always as the result of a dramatic change. It is something that has to be achieved, by means of practical training and intellectual effort" (p. 131).

Nirvana was looked upon as the ultimate reality in Early Buddhism. Harvey (1990) underlines this aspect in terms of dependent-arising:

> As the cessation of *dukkha* [suffering] involves the stopping of each of the *nidanas* and *khandhas*, *Nibbana* lies beyond the occurrence of such states. One must therefore see *Nibbana* during life as a specific experience, in which the defilements are destroyed forever…. Such a destruction-of-defilements is clearly a transcendent, timeless experience. (pp. 61-62)

The Buddha describes *nirvana* as follows: "The stopping of becoming is Nirvana" (Conze 1995, 92); "I say that there is no coming or going or remaining or deceasing or uprising, for this is itself without support, without continuance, without mental object—this is itself the end of suffering. / There is, monks, an unborn, not become, not made, uncompounded" (pp. 94-95). These words including "the stopping of becoming" and "no coming or going" and "unborn" suggest that *nirvana* is the deepest dimension of reality that can arise only when the ongoing processes of the cosmic reality are broken through. In this respect, Radhakrishnan (1923/1996) remarks: "However much Buddha tried to refuse to reply to the question of the ultimate reality which lay beyond the categories of the phenomenal world, he did not seem to have had any doubt about it" (p. 379); "Buddha believed in an ontological reality that endures beneath the shifting appearances of the visible world" (p. 380). In addition, Radhakrishnan goes so far as to say:

> Nirvana ... is a positive blessedness. It is the goal of perfection and not the abyss of annihilation.... Perfection is then the sense of oneness with all that is, has ever been and can ever be. The horizon of being is extended to the limits of reality. (p. 448)

During the development of Early Buddhism, Buddhist philosophy reached a high level of refinement in the schools of *Abhidharma* Buddhism. The term *Abhidharma* means "studies in dharma." The "dharma" in this context implies elements composing the phenomenal world (physical and mental). Relying on ideas such as the five aggregates and twelvefold dependent-arising, Buddhist thinkers refined systematic explanations of the Buddhist worldview. For example, the most prominent school known as the Vaibhasikas saw each element as having its "self-nature" (*svabhava*). This school acknowledged seventy-five elements and saw the formation of the world in association or dissociation of these components according to the law of dependent-arising.[2]

Abhidharma philosophy, however, modified the original teachings of the Buddha. To be sure, it shared the fundamental idea of the selflessness of a person, but it regarded each element as an indivisible, independent, substantial, and permanent entity. As a result, it lapsed into a realistic substantialism of a finite number of atomistic elements. It lost sight of the selflessness of any dharma. Mahayana Buddhism appeared in its confrontation with this aspect of Abhidharma Buddhism.

MADHYAMIKA PHILOSOPHY OF NAGARJUNA

PRAJNA-PARAMITA THOUGHT

The earliest literature of Mahayana Buddhism includes collections of the *Prajna-paramita Sutras* (the *Perfection of Wisdom* texts). Prajna-paramita thought countered Abhidharma Buddhism by introducing the idea of *sunyata* (Emptiness), which means that everything is selfless. In a word, it was a philosophy of Emptiness, and its practical goal was to attain Enlightenment through the perfect "wisdom" (*prajna*) of Emptiness and to express "compassion" (*karuna*) as the manifestation of Enlightenment.

The *Prajna-paramita-hridaya Sutra,* known as the *Heart Sutra,* includes phrases such as these:

> [H]e [the Bodhisattva Avalokitesvara] perceived that there are the five Skandhas; and these he saw in their self-nature to be empty.
>
> "O Sariputra, form is here emptiness, emptiness is form; form is no other than emptiness, emptiness is no other than form…. The same can be said of sensation, thought, confection, and consciousness….
>
> Therefore, O Sariputra, in emptiness there is no form, no sensation, no thought, no confection, no consciousness; no eye, ear, nose, tongue, body, mind; no form, sound, color, taste, touch, objects…. (Suzuki 1960, 26-27)

In this way, Prajna-paramita thought thoroughly deconstructs the substantialist ideas assumed in the Abhidharma schools. The text declares that the five skandhas and the eighteen realms of elements are empty of their self-nature. As there is no substantial entity, nothing is independent but everything is interdependent, which Form-is-Emptiness implies.

Thich Nhat Hanh (1988) illuminates this relationalist aspect of Emptiness by introducing the term "interbeing." Taking a sheet of paper as an example, he says:

> When Avalokita says that our sheet of paper is empty, he means it is empty of a separate, independent existence. It cannot just be by itself.
> It has to inter-be with the sunshine, the cloud, the forest, the logger, the

> mind, and everything else. It is empty of a separate self. But, empty of
> a separate self means full of everything. (p. 10)

Emptiness means to be empty of separate self; therefore, it positively means that everything is inter-being with each other. In this respect, Emptiness implies interdependence of all beings. Emptiness in this sense seems to correspond to the interconnection of everything in the cosmic reality.

However, Emptiness not only means the interdependent nature of the cosmic reality but also refers to the infinite reality. As Masao Abe (1997, 42) remarks, "The ultimate reality in Buddhism is not God, or Being, or Substance, it is *Sunyata* [Emptiness]." D. T. Suzuki (1953/1970) examined eighteen forms of Emptiness found in the *Maha-prajna-paramita Sutra* and identified that although many of them imply the interdependent nature of things, some refer to the "ultimate" and "absolute" dimension or *nirvana* (pp. 255-63):[3] "Emptiness beyond every possible qualification, beyond an infinite chain of dependence—this is Nirvana" (p. 260). He also explains the difference between "relativity" and "emptiness" as follows:

> It is true that the *Prajnaparamita* teaches that things exist mutually re-
> lated as results of causal combinations and therefore they are empty.
> But for this reason we cannot state that relativity and emptiness are
> synonymous. In fact, it is one thing to say that things are relative, but
> quite another to say that they are empty. (p. 263)

Suzuki (1960, 29) says, "Emptiness does not mean 'relativity,' or 'phenomenality,' or 'nothingness,' but rather means the Absolute, or something of transcendental nature." In this way, Emptiness implies the deepest dimension of reality.

However, as we have seen in Chapter 2, Emptiness cannot be represented as a discrete, transcendental realm but arises only in a ceaseless movement of emptying substantial forms of any kind including itself. If it were posited as a transcendental realm, it would come to have a definite "form." At this point, Prajna-paramita thought arrived at a striking insight into the nature of Emptiness. For example, the *Diamond Sutra* says, "A bodhisattva should develop a mind that alights upon nothing whatsoever" (Price and Wong 1990, 28). The Yogacara philosophy called this aspect *apratisthita-nirvana*, which means "nirvana that is not dwelled in" or simply "not dwelling in nirvana" (Nagao 1991, 222). Emptiness or *apratisthita nirvana* refers to ceaseless process of disidentification with anything, or non-identifcation. One should not hold on to anything, because, as the *Diamond Sutra* says, "no bodhisattva who is a real bodhisattva cherishes the idea of an ego entity, a personality, a being, or a separated individuality" (Price and Wong 1990, 19). Even the ideas of the "Buddha," the "Dharma," and "enlightenment" should not be valued as objects to be attained. Lin-chi makes the point in his famous words:

> Whether you're facing inward or facing outward, whatever you meet
> up with, just kill it! If you meet a buddha, kill the buddha.... Then for
> the first time you will gain emancipation, will not be entangled with
> things, will pass freely anywhere you wish to go. (Watson 1993, 52)

For Lin-chi, "the true Buddha is without form, the true Dharma is without characteristics" (p. 49).

Emptiness can be realized only in the ceaseless movement of emtptying itself. Therefore, there can be no form of Emptiness. And, in the final analysis, there is no dualistic division between Emptiness and Being (Form), or *nirvana* and *samsara*. With Milarepa, "He who sees the world and Voidness as the same, / Has reached the realm of the True View" (Chang 1962/1989, 229). This non-dual identity between Emptiness and Form is the final attainment of Prajna-paramita thought. This is the aspect of Emptiness-is-Form.

Emptiness is identical with Being or Form; however, Being in this sense is transformed by Emptiness and becomes the universal reality. Herbert Guenther, who calls *sunyata* "open dimension," describes this as follows: "This openness is present in and actually presupposed by every determinate form. Every determinate entity evolves out of something indeterminate and to a certain extent also maintains its connection with this indeterminacy" (Guenther and Trungpa 1975/1988, 27). One of the remarkable features of Mahayana philosophy is in this emphasis on Emptiness-is-Being, a non-dual identity between *nirvana* and *samsara*.

Emptiness is itself a multidimensional concept that includes the relative and the absolute dimensions—the relative Emptiness and the absolute Emptiness; the relative Emptiness implies the interdependent nature of the cosmic reality, and the absolute Emptiness signifies the infinite reality that will turn into the universal reality.

NAGARJUNA'S PHILOSOPHY

Nagarjuna (A.D. 150-250 or 100-200) laid a philosophical foundation of Mahayana Buddhism by providing logical expositions of the Prajna-paramita scriptures. His philosophy has been called Madhyamika philosophy.[4] Nagarjuna was the first Buddhist philosopher who identified dependent-arising with Emptiness. He developed a philosophy of Emptiness; however, it is not easy to comprehend his ideas. According to Izutsu (1981b), Nagarjuna's thought has "semantic ambiguity or ambivalence" (p. 373); that is, on the one hand, Emptiness means the negation of substantial selfhood of beings and "the universal interdependence of all things" (p. 369), or "the network of ontological relations" (p. 370), but, on the other hand, "he ... characterizes the very same *sunyata* as the ultimate reality which is absolutely non-articulated and non-differentiated, which is, in short, 'nothing' or 'nothingness'" (p. 373). Nagarjuna's concept of Emptiness contains "[m]etaphysical non-diversification, i.e., the absolute oneness of Reality, on the one side, and on the other, the endless interrelation of empirical things" (p. 374).

This question raised by Izutsu suggests that Emptiness is multidimensional. It also implies that dependent-arising is multidimensional. Musashi Tachikawa (1997) and Gadjin Nagao (1989) have penetrated into the multidimensional structure of dependent-arising (dependent co-arising). According to Tachikawa,

> Dependent co-arising in the *Middle Stanzas* ... has an extremely structured and multifaceted character. And by interpreting dependent co-arising in this manner, Nagarjuna linked the concept of dependent co-arising with that of emptiness. (1997, 131)

Tachikawa discerns three dimensions of dependent co-arising. Associated with our conceptions, *Dependent co-arising A* denotes the social reality; *Dependent co-arising B* suggests the absolute Emptiness or the infinite reality; and *Dependent co-arising C* refers to the universal reality. According to Nagao, Dependent co-arising A includes "the one-dimensional, dependently co-arising birth-death cycle" (1989, 15), or the cosmic reality, and Dependent co-arising B is Emptiness as the ultimate reality, and Dependent co-arising C is the "restored and purified second dimension of dependent co-arising" (p. 19). (Therefore, Dependent co-arising A contains the cosmic reality as well as the social reality.)

This three-dimensional structure of Dependent co-arising is realized in the twofold movement of seeking and returning; the seeking path concerns the movement from Dependent co-arising A to B, and the returning path is the movement from Dependent co-arising B to C. To illuminate the dynamic structure of dependent co-arising, Tachikawa introduces the two poles of "the sacred" and "the profane" and refers to the two "vectors," namely, one from the profane to the sacred and another from the sacred to the profane.

THREE DIMENSIONS OF DEPENDENT CO-ARISING

Dependent co-arising A refers to the profane level of life. In particular, Nagarjuna highlights the function of "linguistic proliferation" (*prapanca*), the underlying function of language to articulate objective beings on the phenomenal reality. Here Nagarjuna comes very close to the findings of modern linguistic theories, for *prapanca* is the semantic articulation of manifold things. According to Izutsu, who uses the term "semantic diversification" for *prapanca*,

> it [*prapanca*] indicates primarily the articulation of reality into diverse
> entities in conformity with the meanings of words. It is, according to
> him, the very source of our ontological delusion, i.e., our perverted
> cognition of variously articulated things in the external world. (1981b,
> 372)

In our scheme, this function of linguistic proliferation corresponds to the linguistic interrelation of the social world that articulates the phenomenal world.

To attain the sacred pole, or the absolute Emptiness, one has to extinguish the root of the profane world, namely, "linguistic proliferation." According to Tachikawa,

> [T]he aim of Nagarjuna's *Middle Stanzas* is to make possible the experi-
> ence leading to the sacred under its aspect of "emptiness" (*sunyata*) by
> putting an end to the profane world in the form of linguistic prolifera-
> tion (*prapanca*), held to be the root of karma and mental defilements.
> (1997, 14)

The *Middle Stanzas* reads:

Action and misery having ceased, there is nirvana.

Action and misery comes from conceptual thought.

This comes from mental fabrication [linguistic proliferation].

Fabrication ceases through emptiness. (XVIII. 5, Garfield 1995, 48)

The sacred pole is *nirvana*, or the absolute Emptiness, which can be attained by the cessation of the "linguistic proliferation." Although Nagarjuna does not explicitly refer to Emptiness as the absolute reality, as Radhakrishnan (1923/1996, 701) admits, "It will be very difficult to account for Nagarjuna's metaphysics … if we do not admit the absolutist implications of his doctrine of sunya." In one place in the *Middle Stanzas*, Nagarjuna suggests this:

Not dependent on another, peaceful and

Not fabricated by mental fabrication,

Not thought, without distinctions,

That is the character of real*ity* (that-ness). (XVIII. 9, p. 49)

This is the absolute Emptiness, or what Izutsu (1981b, 373) calls "the metaphysical 'emptiness'" which is "the pre-linguistic state of reality, i.e., reality before it is semantically diversified into different independent entities."

Nagarjuna equates this metaphysical Emptiness with dependent co-arising. In the "salutation" verse placed at the beginning of the *Middle Stanzas*, he states:

I offer salutation to the Enlightened One, the best of preachers, who taught dependent co-arising, which has no ceasing, no arising, no nullification, no eternalness, no unity, no plurality, no coming, and no going, is quiescent of linguistic proliferation, and is auspicious. (cited in Tachikawa 1997, 25)

Dependent co-arising marked by "no ceasing, no arising" and "no coming and no going" is Dependent co-arising B that is identical with the absolute Emptiness, or *nirvana*. Nagao (1989, 11) remarks:

A one-dimensional view of dependent co-arising as the birth-death cycle [Dependent co-arising A], even if it includes a dynamic tendency toward non-being and is conceived as transcendent and ascendant in orientation, is not a true understanding of dependent co-arising unless it is identified with emptiness.

This equation between the absolute Emptiness and Dependent co-arising B is important, because it suggests the deepest dimension of relationships, which is distinct from both the social interrelation and the cosmic interconnection. According to Tachikawa,

> Although Nagarjuna relentlessly denied the existence of all dependently co-arisen things, the ultimate truth to which he finally attained was also designated "dependent co-arising," and there is no doubting the fact that this dependent co-arising was something positive. (1997, 26)

Dependent co-arising B marks the turning point from the seeking to the returning path. As Jay Garfield (1995, 101) comments on this phrase, "this insight contains within it the seeds of the eventual equation of the phenomenal world with emptiness, of samsara with nirvana, and of the conventional and the ultimate." Dependent co-arising B thus turns into Dependent co-arising C.

Nagarjuna attains the final position that does not recognize any difference between the absolute Emptiness and the phenomenal world, or the sacred and the profane.

> There is not the slightest difference
> Between cyclic existence [samsara] and nirvana.
> There is not the slightest difference
> Between nirvana and cyclic existence. (XXV. 19, Garfield 1995, 75)

The non-dual identity between the absolute Emptiness and the phenomenal world—the ultimate and the conventional—is the final attainment of Mahayana thought in which the conventional world turns into the "conventional truth" (the universal reality). Tachikawa remarks:

> Ultimate truth is not a goal where one can abide forever, but is like a flash of light, and after one has come in contact with it, the conventional becomes something that has been sanctioned; its continuing existence is, namely, acknowledged as conventional truth. (1997, 32)

Nagarjuna is ultimately concerned with the sacralization of the profane, the conventional truth, and the manifest Emptiness. He suggests this (XXIV. 18): "Whatever is dependent co-arising, that we declare to be emptiness. / It is provisional designation" (cited in Tachikawa, p. 31). This is the dimension of Dependent co-arising C, that is, the profane reborn in the sacred, Dependent co-arising A radically transformed in the absolute Emptiness. Tachikawa comments on this:

> Nagarjuna's goal was not emptiness itself in which linguistic prolifer-
> ation had ceased; rather, he aspired to the redemption of all existence
> as it is through the actualization of linguistic proliferation that had
> been reborn by the power of emptiness and thereby sacralized. (p. 22)

Dependent co-arising C is none other than this conventional world where we live; however, it is no longer the same as Dependent co-arising A, because the latter is negated and emptied in the absolute Emptiness. As Nagao puts it, it becomes a "phantom-like" being in which every being is transparent with each other. The phantom-like feature of Dependent co-arising C is marked by Nagarjuna as "provisional designation."

We have seen the three-dimensional dynamic structure of dependent co-arising in Nagarjuna's philosophy: Dependent co-arising A is the linguistic interrelation of the profane social world; Dependent co-arising B *is* the absolute Emptiness as the infinite reality; Dependent co-arising C is the manifest Emptiness, or the universal reality. This structure is important as it suggests the multidimensions of relationships and Emptiness: Dependent co-arising A (interrelation, interconnection) is the relative Emptiness, Dependent co-arising B is the unmanifest metaphysical Emptiness, and Dependent co-arising C (interpenetration) is the manifest physical Emptiness.

However, as a whole, Nagarjuna's philosophy did not well elaborate the reconstructive aspect of Dependent co-arising C, the aspect of interpenctration of the universal reality, for it was heavily involved in deconstructing Abhidharma's substantialist philosophy. In other words, it was concerned with the aspect of Form-is-Emptiness, and later Hua-yen philosophy explored the remaining aspect of Emptiness-is-Form.

THE HUA-YEN ONTOLOGY

HUA-YEN BUDDHISM

The Hua-yen (Flower Ornament) school of Buddhism was one of the highest achievements of Buddhist philosophy developed during the T'ang dynasty (618-907) in China,[5] then in Korea and Japan. According to Garma Chang (1971, x), "Hwa Yen [Hua-yen] is a synthesis of all major

Mahayana thoughts, a philosophy of *totalistic organism.*" Hua-yen philosophy' is a holistic philosophy of all-embracing "Totality."

Hua-yen philosophy is particularly important for our discussion of holistic education, for it refined the idea of "Interpenetration" (Ch. *hsiang-ju*; J. *sonyu*), one of the most profound concepts of relationships developed in Buddhist ontology. Suzuki (1953/1970, 87) says:

> The fundamental insight of the *Gandavyuha* [Flower Ornament] is known as Interpenetration.... This perfect network of mutual relations has received at the hand of the Mahayana philosopher the technical name of Interpenetration.

Izutsu (1981b, 358) also celebrates this idea: "The Hua Yen philosophy of the interpenetration of all things is ... a very peculiar form of Oriental ontology, standing unique and matchless in the entire history of Buddhist thought."

At first glance, the concept of Interpenetration seems to be identical with the concept of interconnection presented in contemporary holistic education, yet the Interpenetration here in question, according to Hua-yen philosophy, arises only after Enlightenment as the transformed mode of interconnection. It is the mode of relationships appearing in the universal reality, not in the cosmic reality. At this particular point, there is a unique contribution of Hua-yen philosophy to holistic thought.

The Hua-yen school emerged from studies in the *Avatamsaka* (*Gandavyuha*) *Sutra,* or *The Flower Ornament Scripture* (Cleary 1984/1993)—one of the principal texts of Mahayana Buddhism.[7] This scripture provides a comprehensive view of Mahayana Buddhism and especially describes Buddha's Enlightenment and the way of Bodhisattvas. Buddha, who appears as the central figure throughout the text, is called "Virocana," or "the all-illuminating Light," a representative "cosmic" Buddha in Mahayana Buddhism. In this sutra, according to Thomas Cleary (1984/1993, 1), the English translator of this text, "The Buddha shifts from an individual to a cosmic principle and manifestations of that cosmic principle." In general, compared to Early Buddhism, Mahayana Buddhism has laid more emphasis on the cosmic Buddha than the historical Buddha. Also, it has stressed the way of Bodhisattva, or the "enlightening being," towards the stage of Buddha. This scripture illustrates the way of Bodhisattvas in such well-known books as *The Ten Stages* and *Entry into the Realm of Reality.*

As Chang (1971, ix) emphasizes, "The Hwa Yen Sutra has one central concern: to reveal the Buddha-Realm of Infinity." The fifth book entitled *The Flower Bank World* describes Virocana's enlightened world called "the Flower Bank Array ocean of worlds." Among the dazzling descriptions of this world, addressed by a Bodhisattva called "Universally Good," appear such phrases as:

> In each atom of the Flower Bank world
>
> Is seen the universe of the elemental cosmos. (Cleary 1984/1993, 204)
>
> And into each atom of those buddha-fields
>
> Also enter all lands. (p. 206)
>
> One world system enters all,
>
> And all completely enter one;
>
> Their substances and characteristics remain as before, no different:
>
> Incomparable, immeasurable, they all pervade everywhere. (p. 215)

These phrases portray Interpenetration between one and all. The "atom"—literally "particle of dust" (*anuraja*)—is not a substantial entity but a microcosmic unit of being that contains the macrocosm. As each atom is empty of its own self-nature, the entire universe pervades it.[8]

Interpenetration of all beings is also called "the net of Indra" in the scripture: "These seas of fragrant waters, numerous as atoms in unspeakably many buddha-fields, are in the Flower Bank Array ocean of worlds, spread out like the net of Indra, king of the gods" (p. 215). The god Indra from the Indian myth has a palace where countless jewels form networks; each jewel reflects each other and in each jewel all the others are infinitely reflected. The net of Indra is a pictorial representation of Interpenetration. In his famous treatise *On the Golden Lion*[9] (Chang 1971, 224-30), Fa-tsang describes it as follows:

> [I]n each of the lion's eyes, in its ears, limbs, and so forth, down to each and every single hair, there is a golden lion. All the lions embraced by each and every hair simultaneously and instantaneously enter into a single hair. Thus in each and every hair there are an infinite number of lions. Furthermore, each and every hair containing infinite lions returns again to a single hair. The progression is infinite, like the jewels

of Celestial Lord Indra's net; a realm-embracing-realm ad infinitum is
thus established, and it is called the realm of Indra's net. (p. 229)

Interpenetration described in the scripture should not be confused
with a description of empirical reality. It describes Buddha's "Flower
Bank World" illuminated in Virocana's contemplative awareness called
"Ocean Seal Samadhi." "What Hua Yen is interested in is," as Izutsu
(1981b, 380) says, "the depth-structure of the empirical things to be disclosed only to the depth-consciousness as it is realized in the state of *samadhi.*"

THE FOUR DHARMADHATUS

Hua-yen philosophy was informed by Madhayamika's
deconstructive concept of Emptiness; however, it was more concerned
with the reconstructive aspect of Emptiness (Dependent co-arising C),
on which the concept of Interpenetration flourished. Differently put, it
concerned the universal reality as the phenomenal manifestation of the
absolute Emptiness. As Chang remarks, Hua-yen philosophers explored
the all-embracing "Totalistic" aspect:

> The Totalistic Voidness presented in Hwa Yen literature reveals many
> hidden facets of Sunyata which are not immediately clear in the
> Madhyamika theses. Only in Hwa Yen do the far-reaching implica-
> tions of the Sunyata doctrine ... become transparently clear. (1971, x)

Hua-yen philosophers developed an ontology of the "Four
Dharmadhatus" (Ch. *fa-chieh*; J. *hokkai*), namely, "the four dimensions of
reality" (in this context, "dharma" means reality, and "dhatu" means
realm or dimension). This conception was set forth by Tu Shun and further developed by Chih-yen and Fa-tsang, then finally established by
Cheng-kuan. It is a multidimensional ontology that has the following
four dimensions (see Chang 1971, 141; Cleary 1983, 24; Izutsu 1981b, 381-
84):

- *The Dharmadhatu of shih* (Ch. *shih fa-chieh*; J. *ji hokkai*): the
  dimension of phenomenal beings; Dependent co-arising A; the
  relative Emptiness; the objective reality and the social reality.
- *The Dharmadhatu of li* (Ch. *li fa-chieh*; J. *ri-hokkai*): the dimension of
  the deepest reality; Form-is-Emptiness; Dependent co-arising B;

the absolute, unmanifest Emptiness; the infinite reality. (The literal meaning of *li* includes "noumenon" or "principle.")

- *The Dharmadhatu of li-shih* (Ch. *li-shih wu-ai fa-chieh*; J. *ri-ji muge hokkai*): the dimension of unobstructed Interpenetration of *li* and *shih*; the dimension of noninterference between the deepest reality and the phenomenal reality; Dependent co-arising C; Emptiness-is-Form; the returning path from the infinite reality to the universal reality.

- *The Dharmadhatu of shih-shih* (Ch. *shih-shih wu-ai fa-chieh*; J. *ji-ji muge hokkai*): the dimension of unobstructed Interpenetration of *shih* and *shih*; the dimension of noninterference among phenomenal beings; the physical manifest Emptiness; the universal reality.

In this scheme, the Chinese philosophers of the Hua-yen school preferred to use the two Chinese words *shih* and *li* for Form (*rupa*) and Emptiness (*sunyata*), because they found them more appropriate to convey the true meanings of Form and Emptiness than their Chinese equivalents, *se* and *k'ung*.

The four dimensions of reality do not imply that four different realms exist, but that they represent the four different views of reality seen from different states of consciousness. While the first dimension is the world seen in the ordinary state of consciousness, the other three dimensions are the views of reality seen in the three different modes of Enlightenment.

- *The Dharmadhatu of shih:* This dimension represents the phenomenal, empirical, and objective world with a multitude of beings, in which all beings are perceived by our ordinary discriminating minds as distinct objects with their particularity and individuality. On this level, everything is separated by boundary (obstruction and interference).

- *The Dharmadhatu of li: Li* means the absolute Emptiness. This dimension, in Izutsu's words, refers to "the absolute metaphysical Reality," or the "metaphysical non-articulation" that is "absolutely nothing" and dissolves any kinds of obstruction and interference caused by selfhood of individual

beings. The attainment of *li* in the seeking path is called
Mahaprajna, or the Great Wisdom.

- *The Dharmadhatu of li-shih:* The third dimension asserts that *li*
does not exist apart from *shih,* that *li* and *shih* are identical in
unobstructed Interpenetration. Suzuki (1948) comments on this
"perfect mutual unimpeded solution" between *li* (*ri*) and *shih* (*ji*)
as follows:

*[R]i is ji, ji is ri, ri and ji are identical (J. soku); ri and ji are mutually
merged, immersed in each other. Ji has its existence by virtue of ri,
ji is unable to subsist by itself, ji is subject to a constant change. Ri
on the other hand has no separate existence; if it has, it will be
another ji and no more ri; ri supplies to ji a field of operation, as it
were, whereby the latter may extend in space and function in
time; ri is a kind of supporter for ji but there is no real supporter
for ji as such on the plane of distinction. (p. 50)*

The "noninterference" or "non-obstruction" between *li* and *shih*
means the aspect of Emptiness-is-Form. It reveals the returning movement from the infinite reality to the universal reality. In this third phase, *li*
serves as the ontological ground for the creation of all beings. In
Mahayana concept, this creative arising is called *Mahakaruna,* or the
"Great Compassion." According to Suzuki, "The Great Compassion is
creator while the Great Wisdom contemplates" (1948, 65).

- *The Dharmadhatu of shih-shih: The fourth and final dimension is the
dimension of noninterference among phenomenal beings, of the
unobstructed Interpenetration of all beings. On this level, everything
mutually interpenetrates into everything else in infinite freedom. For
Hua-yen philosophers, as Chang insists, this is "the ultimate and the
only Dharmadhatu that truly exists" (1971, 153, original in italics):
"The only Dharmadhatu that actually exists is Shih-shih Wu-ai, and in
its dimension each and every individual Shih enters into and merges
with all other Shih in perfect freedom, without the aid of Li" (p. 153).
This ultimate dimension corresponds to the universal reality.*

Chih-yen and Fa-tsang explored characteristics of the Dharmadhatu
of *shih-shih* in the doctrine of the "Ten Mysterious Gates." Fa-tsang's
view includes the following gates (Cleary 1983, 33-39; see also Fa-tsang
1989, 109-22):

- *The gate of simultaneous complete correspondence:* As all beings come from dependent co-arising, they form simultaneously "one whole." This is "the total aspect of universe of the mutual noninterference among phenomena." (p. 34)
- *The gate of freedom and noninterference of extension and restriction:* As one being conditions the existence of all other beings, the power of one being is unbounded. This is the aspect of extension. On the other hand, it retains its bounds, and this is the aspect of restriction. (p. 34)
- *The gate of one and many containing each other without being the same:* As all beings are interrelating, the power of one being enters all other beings, while the power of all others enters into one. Yet the very relationships among all beings keep them as they are. (p. 34)
- *The gate of mutual identification of all things:* When one being enters all beings, that one is a part of all beings. At the same time, when all beings enter one being, they lose their identity to the one. One equals all, and all equals one. (p. 35)
- *The gate of the existence of both concealment and revelation:* When one being is identical with all beings, then the all is manifest, and that one is concealed. When all beings are identical with one, then that one is manifest, and the all is concealed. (p. 37)
- *The gate of the establishment of mutual containment even in the minute:* The most minute particle contains the whole, and the whole is an integral part of each particle. (p. 37)
- *The gate of the realm of Indra's net:* In this net of Indra, "not only does each jewel reflect all the other jewels but the reflections of all the jewels in each jewel also contain the reflections of all the other jewels, ad infinitum. This 'infinity of infinities' represents the interidentification and interpenetration of all things" (p. 37).
- *The gate of using a phenomenon to illustrate a principle and produce understanding:* Since one contains the whole, any one being can be used to illustrate the whole. (p. 38)
- *The gate of separate phenomena of the ten time frames variously existing:* The ten time frames include the past of the past, the present of the past, the future of the past, the past of the present,

the present of the present, the future of the present, the past of the future, the present of the future, the future of the future, and the totality of all of these times. These time divisions interpenetrate each other. (p. 38)

- *The gate of the principal and satellites completely illuminated and containing all qualities:* In the Interpenetration of all beings, one being becomes the principal if it is made the focus, while everything else is a satellite of the principal. (p. 39)

According to Izutsu (1981b, 383), "The interpenetration of *shih* and *shih* represents the highest point reached by Hua Yen philosophy characterizing it in the most original and profound way." This aspect of Interpenetration reveals that "the universe in its entirety is an infinitely vast multilayer structure of manifoldly interrelated things" (p. 386). In this universe, not only does the entire universe embrace everything (one in all), but also everything embraces the whole universe (all in one). Taking a flower, for example, Izutsu explains:

Even the tiniest flower owes its existence to the originating forces of all other things in the universe.... Indeed, the whole universe directly and indirectly contributes to the coming-into-being of a single flower which thus stands in the midst of a network of intricate relations among all things. A flower blooms in spring, and the whole universe arises in full bloom. (p. 384)

He goes on to say, "reality in its metaphysical-ontological depth-structure is a continuum, vertically as well as horizontally. The individual things as discrete ontological units are nothing but appearances of that metaphysical continuum to our empirical consciousness" (p. 391). Therefore, in the universal reality such as this, "even the slightest change in the tiniest part of it cannot but affect all the other parts. A mote of dust arises, and the whole universe is by structural necessity moved thereby" (p. 385).

Hua-yen philosophy disclosed infinite Interpenetration embodied in each phenomenal existence. Kukai (774-835), who was strongly influenced by Hua-yen philosophy in his formation of Esoteric Buddhism,[10] brought this idea into his essential thought of "embodied existence" (*sokushin*)[11] and said: "Infinitely interrelated like the meshes of Indra's net are those which we call [embodied] existences" (Hakeda 1972, 227).

SOME IMPLICATIONS FOR HOLISTIC EDUCATION

From the Buddhist perspectives discussed above, it becomes possible to reconsider the basic ideas of holistic education. First of all, Buddhist philosophy can enrich the idea of interconnection with various interpretations of dependent-arising. As we have seen, Buddhist ideas of dependent-arising embrace multidimensional ideas of relationships. What is more, they embrace the metaphysical dimension—*nirvana, sunyata,* and *li*—which plays a central role in realizing the ultimate dimension of relationships as grasped by Hua-yen philosophy in the concept of Interpenetration.

The Hua-yen concept of Interpenetration signifies a mode of relationships that is radically transformed in the infinite reality and emerges in the universal reality. Therefore, it differs from the "interrelation" of the social reality and from the "interconnection" of the cosmic reality. Interrelation involves the relationships of coded meanings of the social world, and interconnection is the organic ecological connections of nature and the systemic functional relations of the universe. On the other hand, Interpenetration arises when any objective, social, and cosmic relationships are negated and emptied in the absolute Emptiness. *Interpenetration means relationships in absolute infinite freedom.* This aspect is called *wu-ai* ("non-obstruction" or "noninterference"), meaning liberation from any conditions (obstructions) of relationships. "Non-Obstruction" means "the total freedom from all clinging and binding" (Chang 1971, 4).

Hua-yen philosophy finds unobstructed liberation in the midst of the objective, social, and cosmic relationships. Yet it becomes possible only by the realization of Emptiness (by Enlightenment). As Chang says, "It is because of Voidness or Emptiness (Sunyata) that the mutual penetration and Non-Obstruction of realms become possible" (p. 12). In other words, it is through the second and third Dharmadhatus that unobstructed Interpenetration on the final Dharmadhatu becomes possible.

However, it is likely that holistic thinkers refer to the Hua-yen concept of Interpenetration as a representative Eastern view of interconnection with no reference to the preceding phases. In this regard, criticizing "pop mysticism," Ken Wilber (1983/1996, 163) once said, "Now the last item [the realm of *shih* and *shih*] has been seized, isolated from its context, and made the basis of pop holistic philosophy. It's very misleading." Unless the preceding three Dharmadhatus were taken into account as necessary stages, the heart of Hua-yen philosophy would never be fully understood.

Here another aspect of Buddhist philosophy becomes apparent, the aspect of contemplation. Interpenetration reveals itself to the transformed state of consciousness through contemplation. It appears in the returning mode after Awakening. Accordingly, the practical aspect of contemplation is indispensable in the quest of Interpenetration. The three Dharmadhatus leading up to the final Dharmadhatu designate a Buddhist path of contemplation. Therefore, if holistic education helps us attain Interpenetration, it needs to involve the path of contemplation.

NOTES

1. This concept has been differently represented in English in terms such as the chain of causation, dependent origination, conditioned co-production, arising due to conditions, conditioned arising, conditioned genesis, dependent co-arising, and others. In this study, I will use "dependent-arising" or "dependent co-arising."

2. Vasubandhu, who himself belonged to another school, successfully surveyed the system of the Vaibhasikas in his *Abhidharma-kosa* and its commentary *Abhidharma-kosa-bhasya*, which became one of the classical studies of Abhidharma Buddhism. For the cosmology of Abhidharma Buddhism, see Sadakata (1997).

3. *Maha-prajna-paramita Sutra* is a comprehensive collection of *Prajna-paramita Sutras* by Hsuan-chuang (Conze 1975). However, it does not include the *Prajna-paramita-hridaya Sutra*.

4. His principal work *Middle Stanzas* (*Mulamadhyamakakarika*) is composed of 450 verses, divided into 27 chapters.

5. The founders of this school include Tu Shun (557-640), Chih-yen (600-668), Fa-tsang (643-712), Cheng-kuan (738-839 or 760-820), and Tsung-mi (780-841); however, in practice, Fa-tsang's *Treatise on the Five Teachings* (*Wu chiao chang*) established the entire system of Hua-yen Buddhism.

6. Francis Cook (1977) and Shigeo Kamata (1983/1988) provide systematic introductions to the philosophy of Hua-yen Buddhism.

7. It is said that this scripture was compiled at Khotan in Central Asia, located on the Silk Route, around the fourth century, and then it was introduced to China. Though the original Sanskrit text was lost, there remain several translations in Chinese. Buddhabhadra's version (A.D. 418-420) has 34 books and Shikshananda's more com-

plete version (a.d. 695-699) has 39 books. Cleary's English translation (1984/1993) is based on the Shikshananda's version.

8. Hua-yen thought may have a Western counterpart in Leibniz's "monadology." A "monad," a metaphysical unit without material extension, embraces the entire universe. Leibniz (1989, 220) says: "This interconnection or accommodation of all created things to each other, and each to all the others, brings it about that each simple substance has relations that express all the others, and consequently, that each simple substance is a perpetual, living mirror of the universe." A monad as a "living mirror of the universe" seems to be coincident with the atom of the Flower Bank world. In addition to this, Steve Odin (1982) has attempted to establish a dialogue between the Hua-yen Buddhist worldview and Whitehead's process philosophy. Also, the Hua-yen worldview has been compared to the holographic views of the universe in science (e.g., Talbot 1991). However, it is important to note that the Hua-yen worldview can arise only in the deep states of contemplation. Without this component, it would be pointless to compare the similar outlooks of thought.

9. *On the Golden Lion* has been said to be originally a lecture addressed by Fa-tsang to the ·Empress Wu Tse-Tien at the palace where the statue of the golden lion was guarding the hall.

10. Esoteric Buddhism is also important as a philosophical and ontological foundation of holistic education, because it has been concerned with the procreative and dynamic aspects of the Hua-yen ontology. Though this study has no space for their explication, it is to be noted that Shin'ichi Nakazawa (1992) has illuminated them in his important study in the thought of Kumagusu Minakata (1867-1941), who penetrated to both Hua-yen and Esoteric Buddhist worldviews. In his attempt, Nakazawa also has drawn upon the rDzogs-chen ontology laid out by Herbert Guenther (1984), a holistic ontology developed in the tradition of Tibetan Buddhism.

11. Seigo Matsuoka (1984) highlights Kukai's central idea regarding the identification of "embodied existence" with the Indra's net as a summit of the entire philosophy of the body (pp. 223, 320).

Eastern Views of Pedagogy

This chapter will examine some pedagogical concepts from Eastern points of view in order to arrive at constructive contributions of Eastern philosophy to our understandings of education. The first half will focus on the aim of education in terms of Hinduism and the idea of nature in Taoism, and the second half will deal with issues regarding language, learning, and development from the perspectives of Taoism, Early Buddhism, and Zen Buddhism. These considerations intend to illuminate the pedagogical aspects of Eastern philosophy that have been less explored.

HINDUISM AND THE AIM OF EDUCATION

THE INTEGRAL EDUCATION OF SRI AUROBINDO AND THE MOTHER

The aims of education have been diversely defined; generally speaking, they have been formulated, on the one hand, in terms of the development of the physical, emotional, and intellectual faculties from an individualistic viewpoint, and, on the other hand, in terms of the social and moral formation from a collectivist viewpoint. These aims are mainly concerned with the individual and social worlds. By contrast, holistic education has attempted to incorporate deeper dimensions into education; it has formulated the aim of education in terms of the cosmic reality and the infinite reality. In this regard, Hindu philosophy is of paramount importance because of its recognition of the supreme aim of education.

Modern Hinduism has given rise to a considerable number of important thinkers for education such as Rabindranath Tagore (1861-1941), Mohandas K. Gandhi (1869-1948), and Sri Aurobindo Ghose (1872-1950) as well as distinguished spiritual teachers such as Paramahamsa Ramakrishna (1836-1886), Swami Vivekananda (1863-1902), Ramana Maharshi (1879-1950), Nisargadatta Maharaj (1897-1981), and many others.[1] Their thoughts on education and their pedagogical practices including the foundation of educational institutes represent not only the Hindu approach but also the entire Eastern approach to holistic education.[2]

The Hindu view of holistic education captures the multiple dimensions of the human being with a special emphasis on the spiritual dimension. For example, Gandhi (1938/1947) referred to a holistic concept of the human being and education like this: "By education I mean an all-round drawing out of the best in child and man—body, mind and spirit" (p. 2); "True education is that which draws out and stimulates the spiritual, intellectual and physical faculties of the children" (p. 23). Tagore stressed the spiritual aspect of education when he said: "Our ideal should be to make ample provision in our homes and in our schools for that development of our spiritual relationship with the Supreme Being, which may best give us a sense of freedom in all departments of life" (Tagore and Elmhirst 1961, 93-94).

The holistic view of education in Hinduism may find a systematic expression in the philosophy of "integral education" inspired by Sri Aurobindo and developed by his former disciple and collaborator The Mother (Mirra Alfassa, originally French, 1878-1973) (e.g., Aurobindo and The Mother 1956, 1992/1995). "The single most important contribution made by The Mother to contemporary philosophy of education," according to Ranjit Sharma's (1992, 209) account, "is the clarification of the integral approach to education." On the basis of Aurobindo's Integral Philosophy and Integral Yoga, The Mother (1984) describes the five dimensions of the human being and education: "Education to be complete must have five principal aspects corresponding to the five principal activities of the human being: the physical, the vital, the mental, the psychic and the spiritual" (p. 7). Integral education embraces multiple "beings" of the human being in their inseparable integrity. With regard to this, David Marshak[3] (1997, 91) comments:

> The term integral education also speaks to the purpose of education: helping the various beings and their faculties unfold according to their potential and learn to work together for a common purpose, a purpose that is conveyed from the spirit through the psychic being.

The first three dimensions—the physical, the vital, the mental—involve the formation of the individual personality, and the last two—the psychic and the spiritual—imply transpersonal development. As for the latter, The Mother discerns "psychic education" and "spiritual education." Psychic education concerns the cosmic reality, for its goal is "a higher realization upon earth" (1984, 33). She says, "the psychic life is immortal life, endless time, limitless space, ever-progressive change, unbroken continuity in the universe of forms" (p. 33). On the other hand, spiritual education concerns the infinite reality, for its goal is "an escape from all earthy manifestation, even from the whole universe, a return to the unmanifest" (p. 33). "The spiritual consciousness ... means to live the infinite and the eternal, to be projected beyond all creation, beyond time and space" (p. 33). Marshak (1997, 111) rephrases this:

> Psychic education, the education of the soul or psychic being, involves the person's knowing of the divine immanent within herself. Spiritual education, the education of the spirit, involves the person's complete surrender to the transcendent divinity.

In this way, The Mother describes a framework of holistic integral education. However, her ideas actually come from traditional Indian philosophy; as Sharma observes, "This integral approach is characteristic of Indian philosophy right from the beginning" (1992, 209). The idea of "spiritual education" is nothing but a classical idea of Indian spirituality. Therefore, we will see the essential teachings of Hindu philosophy in the following.[4]

THE UPANISADS AND THE BHAGAVAD GITA

The roots of Indian philosophy go back to the period of the *Vedas* (1000 B.C.), especially the *Upanisads*, or *Vedanta*, the secret doctrines of the

Vedas. Jogeswar Sarmah (1978) describes the aim of education in the *Upanisads* as follows:

> The highest aim of *Upanisadic* education was man making, character building and the realization of the *Supreme Spirit*. The ancient seers laid great emphasis on the spiritual enlightenment of the individual which consists in gaining a vision of the *self*. (p. 274)

The supreme aim of life in ancient India was a perfect liberation (*moksa*) in the Spirit. The "Supreme Spirit" has been called *Brahman*, and the inmost "Self" that realizes *Brahman* has been called *Atman*. *Brahman* is the absolute reality in Hinduism. As Radhakrishnan (1953/1994) says, "the Absolute is all-inclusive and nothing exists outside it" (p. 68); "While it [*Brahman*] is non-empirical, it is also inclusive of the whole empirical world" (pp. 68-69). *Atman* is the ultimate depth of the Self that is unified with *Brahman*. So the search for *Atman* leads to *Brahman*. The Upanisad philosophy called this identity *tat tvam asi,* or "That art thou" (*Chandogya Upanisad* VI. 8. 7. in Radhakrishnan 1953/1994, 458). Based on the idea of *Atman-Brahman* identity, theories and methods of Self-realization have developed in India.

Traditionally, Hinduism has celebrated the "four stages of life" as an ideal human life course: (a) *brahmacharya,* the stage of the student, or the period of discipline in formal education, (b) *garhasthya,* the stage of the householder, or the period of working in the market-place, (c) *vanaprasthya,* the stage of the forest dweller, or the period of retreat from the world, and finally (d) *pravrajya,* the stage of the wandering monk (*sannyasin*), or the period of spiritual quest. These four stages describe a course of life starting from the physical and mental stages, through the social and moral and then the religious and contemplative stages, ending with the spiritual stage. In this view, each developmental stage is organized to contribute to the final goal, namely, the spiritual realization of *Atman-Brahman*.[5] Tagore (1931, 199) appreciated this idea: "From individual body to community, from community to universe, from universe to Infinity—this is the soul's normal progress."

In this life journey, the most important stage comes last—the stage of the *sannyasin,* who renounces everything in order to devote all her or his life to the final liberation. *Sannyasins* no longer belong to any place in society so that their spirits can attain unification with the Absolute.

Radhakrishnan (1939/1989, 381) says, "Hinduism has given us in the form of the *sannyasin* its picture of the ideal man." Indian society thus created a unique system of transcending itself in the form of *sannyasin*.

The *Bhagavad Gita* (Radhakrishnan 1948/1973), originally a part of the great epic *Mahabharata*, and composed of the teachings of Krishna (The Lord Bhagavad) to Arjuna, became the most beloved text of Hinduism. According to Aldous Huxley (1944/1972, 22), "The Bhagavad-Gita is perhaps the most systematic scriptural statement of the Perennial Philosophy." The "Divine Ground" or *Brahman* is symbolized as the mythic figure of Krishna. As for his (or her) transcendental and all-encompassing nature, Krishna relates: "By Me all this universe is pervaded through My unmanifested form. All beings abide in Me but I do not abide in them" (Radhakrishnan 1948/1973, 238); "I am the origin of all; from Me all (the whole creation) proceeds" (p. 258). The ultimate purpose of life is to attain "unitive knowledge of the Divine Ground" (Huxley 1944/1972, 13) by realizing *Atman* through contemplation (yoga). The *Gita* reads: "He whose self is harmonized by yoga seeth the Self abiding in all beings and all beings in the Self" (Radhakrishnan 1948/1973, 204).

Hinduism has developed three major paths of yoga—*Jnana yoga, Bhakti yoga,* and *Karma yoga*. As a whole, they form a holistic way, for *Jnana yoga* is the path of knowledge (the mind), *Bhakti yoga* is the path of love and devotion (the heart), and *Karma yoga* is the path of action and work (the body).[6]

SANKARA'S ADVAITA VEDANTA PHILOSOPHY

Among the six major schools in Hindu philosophy, the most famous was the Vedanta school, a school that explored the philosophical dimension of the *Upanisads*. This school is important for the philosophy of education as well, because it has been a source of philosophical and spiritual inspiration for Tagore, Aurobindo, Ramana Maharshi, and many other Hindu teachers. Throughout the entire history of Vedanta philosophy or even in all of Indian philosophy, Sankara (700-750) stands out as the greatest philosopher. His position is called "Advaita Vedanta," or the non-dualistic view of Vedanta philosophy.

Sankara held that *Brahman* is identical with *Atman*. In his *Upadesasahasri* [A Thousand Teachings] (Mayeda 1979/1992, 126), he said, "I am *Atman, i.e.,* the highest *Brahman;* I am Pure Consciousness only and always non-dual." Also, the *Viveka Chudamani* (Swami Prabhavananda and Isherwood 1947/1978, 69), ascribed to Sankara, reads: "The Atman is one with Brahman: this is the highest truth. Brahman alone is real." Identity of *Atman-Brahman* is the deepest reality, yet, on the surface phenomenal level, there are "differences" or "diversity" between the individual beings. Faced with this problem, Sankara explored how "false" perception on the surface dimension takes place and alienates us from *Atman-Brahman* identity.

At this point, Sankara went beyond the preceding mythic thought, penetrating to the structure of human consciousness, and found that the core difficulty consists in "nescience" (*avidya*), whose principal function is "superimposition" (*adhyasa*). "Nescience is [defined as] the superimposition of the qualities of one [thing] upon another" (Mayeda 1979/1992, 235). A "non-Atman" component is superimposed upon *Atman-Brahman.* Superimposition is not a special function of the mind (*manas*) but rather a primary function of the mind to discriminate the One into the many. Indeed, the phenomenal world is the fabrication of superimposition: "Everything comes from nescience" (p. 162). For this reason, Advaita philosophy regards the phenomenal world as an illusional existence (*maya*). Sankara said, "This whole [universe] is qualification ... which is superimposed [upon Atman] through nescience. Therefore, when *Atman* has been known, the whole [universe] becomes non-existent" (p. 116).

Advaita philosophy focuses on how to eradicate "nescience" in order to realize *Atman-Brahman.* One of the most persistent examples of nescience is the sense of the self, or "the notion of 'I.'" The notion of "I" is an element of non-Atman superimposed upon *Atman.* Sankara said, "Whoever looks upon the *Atman* as the bearer of the 'I'-notion ... is not a knower of the *Atman*" (p. 138). Sengaku Mayeda (1979/1992, 78) comments on this: "Ordinary people think of the bearer of 'I'-notion as *Atman.* But this is not right since the bearer of 'I'-notion is merely the bearer of the notion that 'I am Atman.'"

Ramana Maharshi (1972/1988), in the same vein, sees that the very formation of self-identity veils the "Self," or "I-I" (*Atman*), and causes the false notion of the "ego" or I-am-this. He says:

"I-I" is the Self. "I am this" is the ego. When the "I" is kept up as the "I" only, it is the Self. When it flies off at a tangent and says "I am this or that, I am such and such,"—it is the ego. (p. 64)

Nisargadatta Maharaj also insists: "There is no such a thing as a person. There are only restrictions and limitations. The sum total of these defines the person" (Powell 1992, 80). However, the human being tends to confuse such "restrictions and limitations" with the true self. In particular, the erroneous notion of "I" is associated with the bodily existence; in this respect, this notion precisely corresponds to what Alan Watts (1966/1989, ix) calls "a separate ego enclosed in a bag of skin." (In fact, Watts conceived this popularized idea, inspired by Vedanta philosophy.)

Sankara asserted that *vidya*, or the true knowledge of *Brahman-Atman*, can remove nescience (*avidya*) and superimposition: "Only knowledge [of *Brahman*] can destroy ignorance" (Mayeda 1979/1992, 103). He highlights the path of knowledge (*Jnana-marga*); however, "knowledge" in this sense is quite different from our common-sense understandings of knowledge. It is an immediate intuition of *Atman-Brahman*. Sankara used to ask his disciple: "Who are you, my dear?" (p. 214). If his disciple answered the question with reference to some qualifications such as social position, family class, bodily existence, and so on, he immediately pointed out that they were not the true Self. Any identification must be negated in recognition that "I am not this. I am not this" (p. 108).

Ramana Maharshi followed this method, which he called "self-inquiry" (*vichara*), and recommended his disciples to ask, "Who am I?" to see where absolute negation would take them. He says:

> The gross body ... I am not; the five cognitive sense organs ... I am not; the five conative sense organs ... I am not; the five vital airs ... I am not; even the mind which thinks, I am not.... (1972/1988, 3)

What remains after the negation of all identifications is *Atman*, or "that I am." *Atman* is not gained or reached, because it is already always there: "When the not-Self disappears, the Self alone remains" (p. 61). Ramana Maharshi says:

> The fact is, you are ignorant of your blissful state. Ignorance supervenes and draws a veil over the pure Self, which is Bliss. Attempts are directed only to remove this veil of ignorance, which is merely wrong knowledge. The wrong knowledge is the false identification of the self

with the body, mind, etc. This false identification must go, and then the Self alone remains. (p. 62)

In this way, self-inquiry for Self-realization is none other than *Atman-Brahman* Realization.

The realization of *Atman-Brahman* marks the turning point of the way of contemplation. The world has to be abnegated in *Brahman* (the infinite reality), and then it reemerges as the manifestation of *Brahman* (the universal reality). "This universe is an effect of Brahman. It can never be anything else but Brahman" (Swami Prabhavananda and Isherwood 1947/1978, 70). The world and *Brahman* are now seen in a non-dualistic identification. As Toshihiko Izutsu (1977a, 396) says, "The world is nothing but Brahman seen or experienced *as* the world." He explains this:

> In the view of Vedanta, Brahman is the ultimate Reality which is eternally one and immutable. Brahman only *appears* to our finite consciousness as diversified into many different things. Under the infinite diversity of appearances Brahman always remains changeless, unmoved and unaffected. (p. 397)

In this returning phase, the world diversifies itself through the same function of superimposition of the mind. "The universe, therefore, is nothing but Brahman. It is superimposed upon Him" (Swami Prabhavananda and Isherwood 1947/1978, 70). As mentioned before, to realize *Atman-Brahman*, superimposition must be completely removed; however, the same function now takes part in the creation of the phenomenal world. Nisargadatta Maharaj correctly states:

> Before the mind—I am. "I am" is not a thought in the mind; *the mind happens to me, I do not happen to the mind.* And since time and space are in the mind, I am beyond time and space, eternal and omnipresent. (Powell 1992, 70)

"I am" refers to the fundamental state of *Atman-Brahman*, and the mind articulates it into phenomenal diversity. Maharaj says, "In reality all is here and now, all is one. Multiplicity and diversity are in the mind only" (p. 81).

Advaita Vedanta discerns the twofold aspect of *Brahman*: *nirguna* and *saguna*. On the one hand, *Brahman* as the unmanifest Absolute transcends any kinds of definition, qualification, and form, and can be described only in a negative term such as "not-this, not-this" (*neti neti*). This negative aspect of *Brahman* is called *nirguna Brahman* (the infinite reality). According to Eliot Deutsch (1969/1973, 12), "*Nirguna* Brahman—Brahman without qualities—is just that transcendent indeterminate state of being about which ultimately nothing can be affirmed." On the other hand, *saguna Brahman* means the aspect of *Brahman* that has appeared through the human consciousness. In Deutsch's definition: "*Saguna* Brahman—Brahman with qualities—is Brahman as interpreted and affirmed by the mind from its necessarily limited standpoint" (p. 12). In other words, *saguna Brahman* is the phenomenal appearance of *nirguna Brahman*. *Brahman* is now known in the fullness of Being as *saguna Brahman* (the universal reality). Radhakrishnan (1953/1994, 64) maintains:

> *Brahman* is not merely a featureless Absolute. It is all this world....
> *Brahman* sustains the cosmos and is the self of each individual. Supracosmic transcendence and cosmic universality are both real phases of the one Supreme. In the former aspect the Spirit is in no way dependent on the cosmic manifold; in the latter the Spirit functions as the principle of the cosmic manifold. The supra-cosmic silence and the cosmic integration are both real.

In this way, *Brahman* as such is multidimensional. As Haridas Chaudhuri (1974, 66) says, "The Absolute is multidimensional Being." In this ontology, *nirguna Brahman* is "the boundless and inexhaustible energy in endless varieties of determinate modes of existence, and yet remain full and infinite (purnam)" and "the creative source of endless determinations" (pp. 66-67). To use Phiroz Mehta's (1989) concepts, from *nirguna Brahman* arises "the creative activity of Transcendence" (p. 5); out of Transcendence, or what he calls "the Primordial Undifferentiated Creative Energy," evolves the whole universe. "The Primordial Creative Energy holds everything within itself in potentiality; the creative process brings forth all that is potential into existence; and thus the Universe manifests" (p. 84). Mehta also describes this creative process as follows:

> Origin is Absolute Transcendence—Primordial Undifferentiated Creative Energy.... It is infinite, self-subsisting, self-replenishing, inexhaustible, indestructible, eternal, potentially holding within itself all that will emerge out of it. Through its ceaseless creativeness, it emanates itself as inter-related and interactive spheres within spheres of

transcendent grades of being, unknowable by us, endowed with the
nature of Origin, till it reaches a limited state of emanation which for
us is. (p. 16)

This creative activity of Transcendence transforms the world into a sacred reality: "All existence is sacred, for it was created by Transcendence
and procreated through Nature, which is one with Transcendence" (p.
4). Mehta's accounts refer to *saguna Brahman*.

As we have seen, Advaita Vedanta clearly grasps a model of multidimensional ontology and the twofold movement of contemplation; the
world of appearance is abnegated to realize *Atman-Brahman*, and then
the world will be redeemed as *saguna Brahman*. Therefore, we need to understand Hindu views of holistic education and their emphasis on the
spiritual education in this context, in which education is a path to the
fullness of the world by realizing *Atman-Brahman*.

NATURE IN TAOISM

The idea of "nature" has always played a significant role in the formation of educational thought. Naturalism has been one of the most influential currents in the philosophy of education. This makes sense, for the
practice of education has inevitably to do with what is "naturally" given
to the human being, which we call intrinsic tendency, disposition, tem-
perament, talent, ability, and so on. Education cannot succeed in attaining its objectives if it ignores the aspect of human nature. Therefore,
pedagogical thinking has reflected on what human nature is, giving rise
to a strong current that may be called *pedagogical naturalism*. Thinkers
such as Rousseau, Pestalozzi, Froebel, Emerson, Montessori, Steiner,
and Dewey have provided a variety of ideas of pedagogical naturalism.
The central idea of pedagogical naturalism is that education must follow
the natural path of human growth, but annoying questions arise concerning human nature, because it is not something that can be defined in
an objective and empirical way. What follows will discuss the idea of nature unfolded in Taoist philosophy, for Taoism[7] can best illuminate Eastern ideas on nature and their implications for education.[8]

NATURE AND TAO

The Taoist philosophy of nature is understood in the ontology of *Tao*, for the concept of nature in Taoism not only means a physical and biological nature, within or without, but also involves the metaphysical dimension of *Tao*. In other words, Taoist nature is a multidimensional concept.

Chuang Tzu describes a multidimensional reality as follows:

> The understanding of the men of ancient times went a long way. How far did it go? To the point where some of them believed that things have never existed—so far, to the end, where nothing can be added. Those at the next stage thought that things exist but recognized no boundaries among them. Those at the next stage thought there were boundaries but recognized no right and wrong. (Watson 1968, 41)

Chuang Tzu's multidimensional reality starts from the fundamental dimension of Non-Being ("things have never existed") through the deep dimension of interconnection ("things exist but recognized no boundaries among them") to the phenomenal dimension of discrete beings ("there were boundaries"). Taoist ontology regards *wu* (Nothingness or Non-Being) as the deepest ground, out of which all other dimensions emerge. Lao Tzu[9] says, "Ten thousand things in the universe are created from being. Being is created from non-being" (Chang 1975, 112). The Taoist Non-Being is the foundation for Being.

The cosmic reality has been referred in Chinese philosophy to as "Heaven and Earth," and *Tao* is the ontological source of Heaven-and-Earth. Unlike our common-sense understanding of nature as "Heaven and Earth," the Taoist concept of nature involves Non-Being, a deeper dimension than that of Heaven-and-Earth. In Chuang Tzu's words: "Before Heaven and earth existed it [*Tao*] was there.... [I]t gave birth to Heaven and to earth" (Watson 1968, 81).

The ontology of *Tao* is delineated in terms of symbolic numbers that clearly show the multiple dimensions of reality. In Lao Tzu's words: "From the *Tao*, one is created, / From one, two, / From two, three, / From three, ten thousand things" (p. 118). *Tao* as Non-Being is the metaphysical Zero Point. As Izutsu (1983/1984) states, the "Non-Being" signifies "the Absolute in its absoluteness, or Existence at its ultimate state ... transcending all qualifications, determinations, and relations" (p. 486). *Tao* as

Non-Being is Absolute Nothingness without determinations. (This aspect of the indeterminate *Tao* is called the "unnameable" or the "nameless.") Since *Tao* is Absolute Nothingness, the universe is fundamentally empty. "The entire universe is basically void" (Chang 1975, 18).

Then, Non-Being transforms itself into the "One," or the primordial Being, from which the entire cosmos evolves. As Izutsu states, "the 'One' in the Taoist system is conceptually to be placed between the stage of Non-Being and that of Being" (1983/1984, 487). It denotes the primordial Unity: "The One is ... the metaphysical Unity of all things, the primordial Unity in which all things lie hidden in a state of 'chaos' without being as yet actualized as the ten thousand things" (p. 400). In this respect, the One symbolizes the immanent aspect of *Tao*. Although *Tao* as Non-Being implies the transcendental aspect of *Tao*, *Tao* is not absolutely detached from the dimensions of Being but dwells in everything. It is immanent in all beings. "The magnificent *Tao* is all-pervading" (Chang 1975, 97).

Tao enters the creation of the cosmos by articulating the primordial One into the multiplicity of beings ("ten thousand things"). Out of the primordial One arises the primary division of the "Two," or *yang* and *yin*. Like other schools of Chinese philosophy, Taoist philosophy conceives the creation of beings in interactions between the primary forces of *yin* and *yang*.

Tao not only gives rise to all beings but also nourishes and sustains them. "*Tao* furnishes all things and fulfills them" (Chang 1975, 116). This aspect is called *Te* (Virtue). "*Tao* creates all things, *Te* cultivates them" (p. 140).

NATURE AS NON-ACTION

Tao is deep within the human being. The Taoist way of life arises in accordance with *Tao*, and this is what Taoists mean by nature or naturalness. The "natural" way of human life is possible only if *Tao* is fully realized in human existence. At this point, Taoist education becomes important, for we are so alienated from *Tao*. Taoist education takes an opposite direction to conventional education; it has a strong tendency to return to *Tao*. Historically speaking, it was in opposition to Confucian education, which celebrated the artificial (cultural and moral) refinement of the human being over the natural state. As David Kinsley (1995,

80) remarks, "Human nature, for the Confucians, needs refinement, training, education, and civilization before it can fully mature and express itself. For the Taoist, this is nonsense. Human nature is just fine the way it is."

Taoist education seeks to transform one's consciousness to attain *Tao*. "To speak about the Tao is," as Livia Kohn (1993, 11) says, "in fact, to 'tao' it." "Crucial to the religious experience of Taoism, the Tao is always there yet has always to be attained, realized, perfected" (p. 11). It can be attained by spiritual intuition. As Chang Chung-Yuan (1975, xv) remarks, "In the traditional Chinese interpretation, *Tao* is the highest attainment of primordial intuition." Here, contemplation comes to the fore. Lao Tzu himself celebrates the value of contemplation as follows:

> Contemplate the ultimate void.
>
> Remain truly in quiescence.
>
> All beings are together in action,
>
> But I look into their non-action.
>
> Things are unceasingly moving and restless,
>
> Yet each one is proceeding back to the origin.
>
> Proceeding back to the origin is quiescence.
>
> To be in quiescence is to return to the destiny of being.
>
> The destiny of being is reality.
>
> To understand reality is to be enlightened. (Chang 1975, 47)

When the human being is in accordance with *Tao*, the mode of action would be transformed from the bottom; the action becomes "non-action" (*wu-wei*), because every action directly comes from Non-Being (*Tao*) without any intervention of the mind. The *Tao Te Ching* has a famous phrase: "Thirty spokes are joined at the hub. / From their non-being arises the function of the wheel. / … Constructed together in their non-being, they give rise to function" (Chang 1975, 35). The "function" on the surface action is fundamentally non-action. "*Tao* is real and free from action, yet nothing is not acted upon" (p. 104). Therefore, Taoist ethics sees *action as non-action* as the highest action: "The highest attainment never acts and is purposeless. / The lowest attainment acts and is purposeful" (p. 106).

Taoist "naturalness" emerges in *action as non-action* that immediately flows from Non-Being. To use Shunryu Suzuki's (1970, 105) expressions,

"Without nothingness, there is no naturalness—no true being. True being comes out of nothingness, moment after moment"; "when all you do comes out of nothingness, then you have everything.... This is what we mean by naturalness" (p. 106). The Taoist naturalness becomes manifest in spontaneous *action as non-action* flowing from *Tao*. This spontaneity of action is called "nature" (*tzu-jan*) in Taoism. Alan Watts (1975, 42) says, "the Chinese, and Taoist, term which we translate as 'nature' is *tzu-jan*, meaning the spontaneous, that which is so of itself." (This "nature" is an aspect of the universal reality.)

Taoist education may be called *radical naturalism*, for it exercises relentless criticism against the artificial way of education as a main cause of alienation from *Tao*, and instead it provides a fundamentally "natural" way of education in accordance with *Tao*. However, the same radicalism entails disadvantages in terms of a fully developed social theory, for unlike Confucian involvement with the social system, Taoism strongly facilitates liberation from the social system yet seldom provides alternative visions of the social system.

LANGUAGE AND SILENCE

If we see Eastern ideas of holistic education from Western perspectives, they may look "absurd" or very opposite to Western ideas. To be sure, this "absurdity" of Eastern ideas has prevented them from being accepted by pedagogical thinking. But the "absurd" ideas make sense if we recognize the multidimensional structures of Eastern philosophy. What is more, it becomes apparent that they can be indispensable components of educational thought, serving to complement Western theories. To recognize this, in the remainder of this chapter I will focus on three topics: language and silence, learning and unlearning, and human development.

Language is undoubtedly one of the most important faculties of the human being, and education has been virtually centered around this faculty throughout its history. Language makes it possible for us to express our feelings and ideas and to communicate with each other. It is the basis of all human knowledge and culture. Beyond that, the recent development of the philosophy of language, semantics, semiotics and other related disciplines has revealed that language constructs our life-world in accordance with its articulation of meanings. Without language, it would be impossible for us to exist as humans.

Throughout the long history of Western education, the education of language has occupied a central part of education. In the Western tradition of education, aspects regarding language—not only speaking, reading, and writing, but also logical, dialectical, discursive ways of thinking—have always been considered to be the highest abilities in human nature. Language has been thought of being endowed to humans as *logos.*

On the other hand, that has never been the case in Eastern philosophy, in which language has never won the highest status; rather, an "abnormal" degree of disrespect for language has stood out. Eastern ideas have traveled along the opposite direction to the furthest point; that is, words, concepts, logic, and knowledge—all these meant something "negative," something to be abandoned, and, instead, "silence" has achieved the highest importance. Based on penetrating insights into the nature of language, Eastern philosophy has favored silence. Eastern philosophers have regarded language as the basic hindrance to realizing a deeper reality and identified silence as an avenue to it and furthermore as the infinite reality itself.

The Buddhist tradition has ample examples in this regard. In the first place, whenever the Buddha himself was asked by his disciples to answer philosophical and metaphysical questions or was challenged by his opponents to have philosophical discussions, he is said to have always kept silent without giving any definite answer. "The Buddha himself" as Yoshinori Takeuchi (1983, 4) comments, "often warned his disciples against confusing the religious search, the 'noble quest,' with philosophical and metaphysical questions." Otherwise, they would have gone astray in the labyrinth of speculation caused by the questions, having lost sight of their noble quest for *nirvana.* Philosophy and metaphysics, that is, abstract thinking by means of language, cannot cure disciples of questions, but they can give them more. For this "pragmatic" reason, he kept silent.

In addition, according to Takeuchi (1983), the silence of the Buddha can be seen as "a sign of contemplation" (p. 12). A Zen classic, the *Wumenguan* (J. *Mumonkan,* Cleary 1993, 150), has a story: "An outsider questioned Buddha in these terms: 'I do not ask about the spoken, I do not ask about the unspoken.' / The Buddha just sat there." The silence of the Buddha does not mean that he could not find a proper answer, but, as Thomas Cleary (1993, 153) comments, that "Buddha's silence ... is an indirect teaching." Silence transmits something more than what can be spoken. It is an immediate teaching from Existence through the *presence* of the Buddha. In the story the outsider praised the Buddha for his compassionate teaching.

The *Vimalakirti Sutra* (Watson 1997), one of the essential scriptures in early Mahayana Buddhism, has a famous story in which bodhisattvas have shown their own opinions about "entering into the gate of nondualism" one by one. At last, a representative bodhisattva Manjusri gave his answer and asked Vimalakirti, an ideal figure of Mahayana Buddhism, to answer the question: However, "At that time Vimalakirti remained silent and did not speak a word" (p. 110). Faced with this, "Manjusri sighed and said, 'Excellent, excellent! Not a word, not a syllable—this truly is to enter the gate of nondualism!'" (p. 111).

Ch'an/Zen Buddhism has placed a special emphasis on silence. The *Wumenguan* has a famous story.

> In ancient times, at the assembly on Spiritual Mountain, Buddha picked up a flower and showed it to the crowd.
> Everyone was silent, except for the saint Kashyapa, who broke out in smile.
> Buddha said, "I have the treasury of the eye of truth, the ineffable mind of nirvana, the most subtle of teachings on the formlessness of the form of reality. It is not defined in words, but is specially transmitted outside of doctrine. I entrust it to Kashyapa the Elder." (Cleary 1993, 33)

Silent communion between the Buddha and Kashyapa refers to one of the four tenets of Zen: "A special transmission outside the Scriptures." The three other tenets include: "No dependence upon words and letters; / Direct pointing to the soul of man; / Seeing into one's nature and the attainment of Buddhahood" (Suzuki 1956/1996, 9). These "four Great Statements" mean that Zen is concerned with the direct realization of true Buddhahood without depending on language. The teaching devices developed in Zen such as *zazen, sanzen, koan,* and *mondo* are all based on these principles.

Mondo is the best example to show the attitude towards language in Zen. *Mondo*—literally, question and answer—is a form of verbal dialogue (or sometimes non-verbal interaction including gestures, utterances, and even hitting) that takes place between a master and a disciple when they try to test the essence of Zen with each other. Compared to other forms of discursive dialogue, *mondo* seems to be absurd, contradictory, paradoxical, and illogical. Here is an example from the *Blue Cliff Record,* another classic of Zen tradition: "A monk asked Tung Shan, 'What is Buddha?' / Tung Shan said, 'Three pounds of hemp'" (Cleary and Cleary 1977/1992, 81). From a logical point of view, this dialogue is nonsense. Yet this answer would make sense if we understand it as an immediate, spontaneous, natural response coming from the depth of Enlightenment. "Three pounds of hemp" is not merely words describing objects out there but a verbal expression of Tung Shan's Enlightenment. What happens here is a direct pointing to the universal reality through "words." In this way, Zen makes use of "words" to immediately go beyond them.

"Words" coming from a living master whose consciousness keeps in touch with the infinite reality can create situations for disciples to awaken the same deep reality. Here is another example from the *Wumenguan*:

> When Dongshan came to study with Yunmen, the teacher asked him,
> "Where have you come from?"
> Dongshan said, "Chadu."
> Yunmen asked, "Where did you spend the summer?"
> Dongshan said, "At Baoci monastery in Hunan."
> Yunmen asked, "When did you leave there?"
> Dongshan said, " August twenty-fifth."
> Yunmen said, "I forgive you threescore blows."
> The next day Dongshan went to Yunmen and asked, "Yesterday you forgave me threescore blows; I do not know where my error was.
> Yunmen said, "You rice bag! Jiangxi, Hunan, and you still go on this way!"
> At this Dongshan was greatly enlightened. (Cleary 1993, 71)

What Yunmen really asked was neither about concrete place nor about time, but he asked Dongshan (Tung Shan) to reveal his understanding of Zen. But Dongshan was captured by the logic of words. However, as he was ready to be enlightened, the last word from Yunmen served as a trigger to Dongshan's great enlightenment.

In this way, by appealing to "words," *mondo* breaks through restrictions of "words." It pushes disciples into a corner in which they cannot cope by means of their acquired knowledge. They have to renounce their clinging to it to respond from an immediate realization of a deeper reality. Masao Abe (1997, 77) points out:

> [A] Zen master tries to make his disciple face himself, to get him to return to the root-source of his being, by showing him a kind of 'aporia' in which his analytic reason and intelligence come to a deadlock that can be overcome only by the awakening of his original nature.

The unique ways of Zen teaching are "devices" for students to become aware of a deeper reality than language. However, this is far from an easy task, for we have a strong tendency to identify with language so that we hypostatize concepts language creates as if they were real objects. To use a well-known phrase of Korzybski's (1933/1958) General Semantics, although the map is not the territory (e.g., Hayakawa 1939/1978, chap. 2), we tend to confuse them. The real problem here lies in our exclusive identification with the world of language, which veils and represses the deeper dimensions of reality. In our ordinary life, language has become the only all-inclusive matrix from which all meanings of life are produced. Roberto Assagioli's (1965/1971) maxim holds true to this: "We are dominated by everything with which our self becomes identified. We can dominate and control everything from which we disidentify ourselves" (p. 22, original in italics). In this sense, Zen is a semantic therapy that enables us to disidentify with language. Indeed, it has been a radical approach to this problem more than any other.

Eastern philosophy does not see language as the all-embracing matrix or as the highest organ to grasp the universal laws (*logos*). In Taoist philosophy, the relation between language and silence is one of the central concerns. Lao Tzu loved silence, for it meant something fundamental: "One who is aware does not talk. One who talks is not aware" (Chang 1975, 154). Taoist philosophy holds that the infinite reality is absolutely ineffable, and that words serve to veil the unknown by the known. Lao Tzu was aware of the ontological function of language to create the "human" world. The opening phrase of the *Tao Te Ching* reads: "The *Tao* that can be spoken of is not the *Tao* itself. / ... / The unnameable is the source of the universe. / The namable is the originator of all things" (Chang 1975, 3). Also, "*Tao* is real, yet unnameable. / It is original non-differentiation and invisible. / ... / When discrimination begins, names arise" (p. 93). In this context, "names" are not labels on things but the originator of all things by differentiation and discrimination.

Seng-t'san, the Third Patriarch of Ch'an/Zen Buddhism, captured the same point in his *On Believing in Mind* (Suzuki 1960, 76-82), one of the essential Zen texts, as follows:

> Wordiness and intellection—
>
> The more with them the further astray we go;
>
> Away therefore with wordiness and intellection,
>
> And there is no place where we cannot pass freely. (pp. 77-78)

"Wordiness and intellection" differentiate things. Even a tiny differentiation leads to a serious dualism. "A tenth of an inch's difference, / And heaven and earth are set apart" (p. 77). Reality is "not two" but "one Emptiness": "In one Emptiness the two are not distinguished" (p. 78). Therefore, Seng-t'san requires us to go away from the dualistic function of language in order to attain the "Perfect Way." "The Perfect Way knows no difficulties / Except that it refuses to make preferences" (p. 76). Here "preference" means to differentiate a particular aspect of reality from the other aspects.

Eastern philosophy sees words and language, and the intellectual thinking based on them, as fundamental obstacles to an exploration into the deeper dimensions of reality. The Eastern way of contemplation, therefore, has focused on disidentification with them in order for "silence" to reveal itself. Krishnamurti (1970, 120-21) says:

> Meditation is the ending of the word. Silence is not induced by a word, the word being thought. The action out of silence is entirely different from the action born of the word; meditation is the freeing of the mind from all symbols, images and remembrances.

A meditative state is silent; "it is the silence when thought—with all its images, its words and perceptions—has entirely ceased" (pp. 114-15). Silence is not an intra-psychic experience, but it *is* an immediate revelation of ineffable reality. Krishnamurti described this as follows:

> That night ... the silence was as real as the wall you touched.... It was not a self-generated silence; it was not that the earth was quiet and the villagers were asleep, but it came from everywhere—from the distant stars, from those dark hills and from your own mind and heart. This silence seemed to cover everything from the tiniest grain of sand in the river-bed ... to the tall, spreading banyan tree and a slight breeze.... (p. 32)

He says: "Meditation is absolute silence of the mind.... Only in that total, complete, unadulterated silence is that which is truth, which is from everlasting to everlasting" (1999, 35).

The above does not argue that words and language are not important or useful. On the contrary, we need to develop as far as possible those linguistic abilities which are absolutely necessary in our everyday life. Eastern philosophy does not oppose this aspect. Rather, it simply warns us that language is not the ultimate ground and that it tends to conceal the deeper dimensions of reality, dimensions that are disclosed in silence. In this sense, Eastern philosophy attempts not to destroy language abilities nor to regress to the preverbal level of development but to transcend the dimension of language. To use Wilber's formulation, "there is *preverbal* (primary process), and there is *verbal* (secondary process)—and above and beyond both, as a magic synthesis, there is *transverbal*" (1980/1996, 65). What Eastern philosophy is concerned with is this "transverbal" dimension.

What is needed in education is to extend its framework so as to include transverbal silence. We already have pioneering attempts by Krishnamurti, Aldous Huxley, and Parker Palmer in this regard. Huxley's ideas of "the education of an amphibian" focus on the non-verbal aspect of education (see Chapter 6). Palmer (1983/1993), following the Quaker tradition, highlights silence in education.

> In silence more than in argument our mind-made world falls away and we are opened to the truth that seeks us. If our speech is to become more truthful it must emerge from and be corrected by the silence that is its source. (p. 80)

LEARNING AND UNLEARNING

In the history of not only Western education but also modern education around the world, learning has been one of the most central concerns. It is not an exaggeration to say that the whole effort of education has been to explicate how learning takes place and to enhance its quality. On the contrary, Eastern philosophy again seems to go in the opposite direction; it regards learning as something negative and instead celebrates "unlearning." Lao Tzu makes this point:

> To learn,
> One accumulates day by day.
> To study *Tao,*
> One reduces day by day.
> Through reduction and further reduction
> One reaches non-action,
> And everything is acted upon.
> Therefore, one often wins over the world
> Through non-action. (Chang 1975, 131)

These lines highlight the Eastern way of learning, namely, unlearning. Unlike our conventional belief that learning makes us efficient agents in a human society, Taoist philosophers hold that knowledge and skills acquired through learning build a barrier that prevents us from returning to *Tao.* Rather, we need to release anything learned and to become an "innocent" being. A Taoist story by Chuang Tzu relates this:

> Knowledge wandered north to the banks of the Black Waters, climbed the Knoll of Hidden Heights, and there by chance came upon Do-Nothing-Say-Nothing. Knowledge said to Do-Nothing-Say-Nothing, "There are some things I'd like to ask you. What sort of pondering, what sort of cognition does it take to know the Way? What sort of surroundings, what sort of practices does it take to find rest in the Way? What sort of path, what sort of procedure will get me to the Way?" Three questions he asked, but Do-Nothing-Say-Nothing didn't answer. It wasn't that he just didn't answer—he didn't know *how* to answer! (Watson 1968, 234)

This story conveys a lesson that "knowledge" is important to "get to the Way" but innocence—"Do-Nothing-Say-Nothing"—is essential.

The Eastern way of learning is to realize the deeper dimensions of reality through unlearning the learned. Therefore, the way of contemplation (at least in its initial phases) concentrates on unlearning. However, unlearning is not meant to destroy or annihilate acquired knowledge. This cannot happen simply because, after contemplation or even after Awakening, knowledge remains the same and the mind *does* function. What really happens in unlearning is that an exclusive identification with knowledge or the known is gradually reduced and eventually ceases to be. What is unlearned is this part of identification.

Dogen gives a well-known formulation of the Eastern way of learning: "To study the buddha way is to study the self. To study the self is to forget the self. To forget the self is to be actualized by myriad things" (Tanahashi 1985, 70). The "buddha way" is a quest for the true Self, yet Dogen says that it is possible only if one forgets the "self." The "self" means the surface ego that erroneously dominates the whole being of the individual. The ego has to be forgotten, or unlearned, in the pursuit of the true Self. However, "to forget the self" does not necessarily mean to destroy and eliminate the ego altogether, but rather to reduce and end the domination of the ego over the whole being. The Jungian Buddhist Mokunen Miyuki emphasizes that what really happens in this process is not "ego-dissolution," "ego-depotentiation," or "ego-negation" but "the transformation of the ego": "What is overcome is not the ego itself but the function of the ego which is to be characterized as 'ego-centric'" (Spiegelman and Miyuki 1985, 37). In this sense, "the word 'forgotten' indicates the psychological condition of 'being emptified' (*kung, sunyata*) wherein the ego is opened to the service of the activity of the Self, the matrix of life" (p. 38). "Forgetting" or "unlearning" the self refers to a transformative shift from the "ego-centric" to the "Self-centric" mode of being.

However, a problem remains in the character of the "Self" thus realized. From the Eastern point of view, the true Self (the Eastern Self) is an infinitely open existence. Shin'ichi Hisamatsu was concerned about this in his dialogue with Carl Jung. Hisamatsu insisted: "The True Self [of Zen] has no substance. The True Self has no form or substance, whatsoever" (Hisamatsu and Jung 1992, 112). And he concluded: "Ultimately, to become 'The Formless Self' [*muso no jiko*] is the essence of Zen" (p. 113).

This statement is important because only if the "True Self" is the "Formless Self" is it "actualized by myriad things."

Finally, the Eastern way of unlearning has its counterpart in Western approaches; for example, D. H. Lawrence (1921/1922/1971, 76) remarks: "The supreme lesson of human consciousness is to learn how *not to know*. That is, how not to *interfere*. That is, how to live dynamically, from the great Source." In his unique essays on education, Lawrence was extremely critical of the mind. Huxley's idea of "the art of dissociation" (1937/1966, 217-19), Assagioli's idea of "dis-identification," and Krishnamurti's key concept of "freedom from the known" share the same direction with the Eastern way of unlearning. Furthermore, some of the body-mind approaches such as the Alexander Technique, Sensory Awareness, and the Feldenkrais method are intended to unlearn the acquired inappropriate body-mind patterns. Because of this similarity, it becomes possible to integrate them with the Eastern way of unlearning (see Chapter 6).

HUMAN DEVELOPMENT AND THE TEN OXHERDING PICTURES

Since the modern age started (after Rousseau's *Emile*), the concept of "human development" has played a central role in the Western system of education. Nowadays, a common belief is that education should be applied in accordance with the developmental stages of children. Developmental psychology has provided a variety of models of human development regarding cognitive, affective, moral, psychosexual, psychosocial, and other development. One of the common features of developmental models is that most of them have adopted linear and progressive models. In addition, developmental stages usually begin with a sensory, physical, and material stage and go through intermediate stages (emotional, affective stages) to finally arrive at a rational and cognitive stage. The rational mode of being is in most cases regarded as the highest stage of development. No matter how much these models seem to articulate observable facts, it is also obvious that they reflect a Western belief system that highlights "progress" and "rationality."[10]

On the contrary, in the East, the idea has not evolved that human life goes through linear, progressive phases of development. Also, unlike

Western philosophy that takes rationality for the supreme organ to know the objective world, Eastern philosophy has never accepted rationality as the highest human ability.

THE "CHILD" AS AN IDEAL

An ideal person in the East has been sometimes described with the image of "child." Lao Tzu says, "When man is enriched with *Te* [virtue], / He may be identified with innocent child" (Chang 1975, 151). The idea of "innocent child" was basically opposed to the Confucian ideal of moral perfection in adulthood, which celebrated cultural sophistication over the natural state of a child. This "innocent child" should not literally be understood as the state of a person who has regressed to the premature level, but rather it stands for the state of a person who has gone beyond the rational and cultural modes and thereby regained higher "innocence." This is what Abraham Maslow (1971/1993) called the "second innocence." Maslow, who was strongly influenced by Taoist philosophy in his later years, coined this concept, which means that

> [innocence] of the wise, self-actualizing, old adult who knows the whole of the D-realm [the realm of deficiency], the whole of the world, all its vices, its contentions, poverties, quarrels, and tears, and yet is able to rise above them, and to have the unitive consciousness in which he is able to see the B-realm [the realm of Being], to see the beauty of the whole cosmos, in the midst of all the vices, contentions, tears, and quarrels. (p. 245)

The "second innocence" is different from the first innocence of early childhood, simply because "the adult cannot become a child in the strict sense" (p. 246). Accordingly, "The only possible alternative for the human being is to understand the possibility of going on ahead, growing older, going on ahead to the second naiveté, to the sophisticated innocence, to the unitive consciousness" (p. 247). The "innocent child" of Lao Tzu surely represents this "second innocence."

In relation to this, Nietzsche's idea of "three metamorphoses of the spirit" gives a philosophical account for the "child" as a higher state of being. In his *Thus Spoke Zarathustra*, Nietzsche (1961/1969) mentioned the "three metamorphoses of the spirit" as a transformative process in which the spirit travels from a "camel" to a "lion," and to a "child" (pp.

54-56). Using three metaphors, this process describes the maturation of the spirit; a camel, a lion, and a child represent three different modes of being. Even a small child is a "camel," or an adult with an ordinary mind, if he or she has internalized the established belief system of a given society. The "camel" is the "weight-bearing spirit" that wants to take upon itself the burden of traditional values. If education only imposes traditional values on children, it reproduces "the beast of burden."

But in the second metamorphosis a camel becomes a lion. To capture freedom, the lion is willing to fight against "the great dragon" called "Thou shalt," namely, the traditional values. The lion represents the rebellious spirit of youth:

> To create new values—even the lion is incapable of that: but to create itself freedom for new creation—that the might of the lion can do.
>
> To create freedom for itself and a sacred No even to duty: the lion is needed for that, my brothers. (p. 55)

The metamorphosis from a camel to a lion is a process of unlearning. A "sacred No" against a camel is necessary for "new creation" to take place. It is only after a "sacred No" that a "sacred Yes" can arise. At this point, a lion must turn to a child:

> The child is innocence and forgetfulness, a new beginning, a sport, a self-propelling wheel, a first motion, a sacred Yes.
>
> Yes, a sacred Yes is needed, my brothers, for the sport of creation: the spirit now wills *its own* will; the spirit sundered from the world now wins *its own* world. (p. 55)

In Nietzschean philosophy, this "child" represents the supreme mode of being, identical with the primordial power (*Macht*), the dynamic state to which "innocence" really refers. Through the innocence of the "child" a new creation takes place.

For Nietzsche the "child" is the true greatness and creativity of the human being, which overcomes the nihilistic, negative mode of the human being symbolized in "camel." Here it is necessary to discern two different levels of affirmation, or "yes," in the camel and the child. The camel, or the ordinary mind, affirms traditional values without saying "no" and thereby preserves the nihilistic mode of existence, because they negate the greatness or depth of the human being. Referring to the camel's yes, Gilles Deleuze (1983, 185) remarks, "the yes which does not know how to say no ... is a caricature of affirmation. This is precisely because it says yes to everything which is no." To overcome the negative and to restore the affirmative, it is necessary to say "no" against the "false affirmation" of the camel—the "sacred No" of the rebellious lion.

This great negation is itself the preliminary stage of the great affirmation of the child, for the great affirmation is possible only if the negative in the camel is negated in the lion. The child emerging through the negation of the negative is a "sacred Yes," or the great affirmation. In the sacred Yes, the primordial power can be released. The three metamorphoses of the spirit with the dialectic path between negation and affirmation are not only at the core of Nietzschean philosophy but can also disclose the secret of the Eastern view of human development. The following will examine the *Ten Oxherding Pictures* in the Zen tradition to take a look at a typical Eastern view of development.

THE TEN OXHERDING PICTURES

Zen has a well-known teaching material called the *Ten Oxherding Pictures* (Suzuki 1960, 129-34), ascribed to the Ch'an/Zen master Kaku-an of the Sung Dynasty in China, which describes the gradual process of attaining Enlightenment in a series of ten pictures with short introductions in prose and commentary verses. Although the basic position of Zen is the "instant, sudden enlightenment" on the practical and psychological plane, as Suzuki (1949/1961, 364) stresses, "Zen fully recognizes degrees of spiritual development." The *Ten Oxherding Pictures* represent an Eastern view of Self-actualization.[11]

The *Ten Oxherding Pictures* have ten pictures with the following headings:

1. Searching for the Ox
2. Seeing the Traces
3. Seeing the Ox
4. Catching the Ox
5. Herding the Ox
6. Coming Home on the Ox's Back
7. The Ox Forgotten, Leaving the Man Alone
8. The Ox and the Man Both Gone Out of Sight
9. Returning to the Origin, Back to the Source

10. Entering the City with Bliss-Bestowing Hands.

These ten stages describe a young person's search for the true Self. They clearly delineate the Eastern way of contemplation, that is, the two-fold movement of seeking and returning. The seeking path starts from No. 1 and goes through No. 2 to No. 7 and arrives at No. 8, which is the infinite reality. No. 9 and No. 10 show the returning path. Zen has called this twofold path *kojo* and *koge* (in Japanese), or "upward" and "down-ward."

The first seven stages describe a young man's (or woman's) existential and spiritual quest for the true Self. To use Jungian terms, the young person symbolizes the ego, and the ox described in the pictures means the Self. At the initial stage, the youth has a feeling of loss, of existential vacuum, or of meaninglessness. His present state becomes a great question, and he is driven to begin a search for the true Self. At the second stage, he learns to know spiritual teachings as guidelines for his search. Through the next three stages, he strives to see, catch, and herd the ox, which means that the ego gradually comes to terms with the Self. At the sixth, which describes the ox coming home with him on its back, his struggle is over. As Hayao Kawai (1996, 42) comments, "the sixth may well be said to represent the pinnacle. Here the ego completely relinquishes its initiative to the Self, by which it is being led." The ego comes to function in the service of the Self. Psychologically or existentially, this is the attainment of individuation or self-actualization.

However, the sixth stage is not the goal. The text says, "Riding on the animal, he leisurely wends his way home" (Suzuki 1960, 132). The ox brings him back to his "home." The existential search for the Self turns into a spiritual search for a deeper reality ("home"). Then, in the "home" (No. 7) "the ox is no more; the man alone sits serenely" (p. 132). The ego and the Self are so completely unified that a genuine person ("the man alone") arises who is the sheer manifestation of the Self. This genuine person rests in the "home" that is nature. As Kawai says, "the Self now is manifested not as an ox but as the external environment surrounding the person, taken as a whole" (1996, 42). Therefore, this stage means that the genuine person is in deep connection with the cosmic reality.

The cosmic reality of the seventh stage is not the final station of the whole journey. As Shizuteru Ueda (1982a, 11) says, "With the attainment of the seventh stage, however, the true self as Zen understands it has not yet been realized." In other words, the last three pictures from the eighth to the tenth represent the true Self in Zen that has to do with the deeper dimensions of the infinite and universal realities. With this respect, Ueda (1982a, 1982b, 1983a; Ueda and Yanagida 1982) gives us an in-depth interpretation of these three pictures as follows.

After the seventh comes the eighth, namely, "The Ox and the Man Both Gone out of Sight," where nothing is described but an empty circle. The eighth is the dimension of Absolute Nothingness (the infinite reality). The empty circle denotes the all-negating activity of Absolute Nothingness (a sacred No). "Absolute nothingness signifies in the first place … an absolute negation" (1982a, 11). It functions as endless negation or radical deconstruction. Therefore, "the transition from the seventh to the eighth is the true Greatest Death, and herein is a critical, discontinuous leap" (1982, 34, trans. Nakagawa).

> In order to achive a breakthrough to the true self that corresponds to its unconditioned selflessness, one must leap once and for all into pure nothingness. As the Zen saying has it, one must "die the Great Death." (1983a, 58-59)

The Self (the genuine person of the seventh) must be emptied in Absolute Nothingness. The Self attained through the process up to the seventh stage still retains a form of selfhood (the genuine person). If one is contented with it, there arises a false identification with the Self. Therefore, any identification with the Self must disappear in Absolute Nothingness. Only when the selfhood of the Self completely drops off, the Self becomes the "Selfless Self."

Here is a real turning point of the whole process. "Absolute Nothingness turns into Absolute Beginning. Everything begins from 'Nothingness' … anew" (1982, 45, trans. Nakagawa). This is the moment of rebirth and of a sacred Yes. "In this absolute nothingness with its desubstantializing dynamic, the fundamental turnabout occurs as a 'dying and becoming' or as a 'death and resurrection' wherein the formless takes on concrete form" (1983a, 59). Absolute Nothingness turns into Absolute Being; or, the infinite reality becomes the universal reality. The "nature" (No. 9) and the "human world" (No. 10) are the two phases of Absolute Beginning, of rebirth and resurrection, of Absolute Being, and of the universal reality. Ueda finds in this dynamic complex "the coincidence of ceaseless negation and straightforward affirmation" (1982b, 160).

> Absolute nothingness, which first of all functions as radical negation, is maintained as this dynamic coincidence of infinite negation and straightforward affirmation. In this coincidence, and because of it, a fundamental transformation and a complete return—a sort of "death and resurrection"—are achieved in *ex-sistence*. (p. 161)

The ninth picture has a tree and flower alongside a stream. The text says, "The stream flowing ... the flowers vividly red" (Suzuki 1960, 134). It is "nature" or the cosmic reality that has been totally transformed by Absolute Nothingness into the universal reality. The text reads:

> From the very beginning, pure and immaculate, the man has never been affected by defilement. He watches the growth of things, while himself abiding in the immovable serenity of non-assertion.... The waters are blue, the mountains are green; sitting alone, he observes things undergoing changes. (p. 133)

The person as the Selfless Self "watches" nature that is nothing but the Selfless Self. "Nature" is no longer an external object but a resurrected embodiment of the Selfless Self in a non-objective form: "It is a picture of reality seen as an actual appearance of the selfless self" (Ueda 1982b, 162). In other words, the person as the Selfless-Self staying in Absolute Nothingness ("abiding in the immovable serenity") "observes" nature that is also Absolute Nothingness. Through Absolute Nothingness both the person and nature are one and identical.

The tenth, on the other hand, describes the "human world" that is the social reality that has been totally transformed in Absolute Nothingness into the universal reality. "Here the true self resurrected from nothingness is at work between individuals, or comes into play there, as a selfless dynamic of the 'between'" (1982a, 19).

In the picture, an old man is encountering a young man on the road. The person (an old man) as the Selfless Self comes back to the marketplace to meet people. The text reads: "Bare-chested and bare-footed, he comes out into the market-place; / Daubed with mud and ashes, how broadly he smiles!" (Suzuki 1960, 134). He never looks like a detached, holy saint but rather like a very ordinary person or even a fool. "Carrying a gourd, he goes out into the market.... He is found in company with wine-bibbers and butchers, he and they are all converted into Buddhas" (p. 134). People he meets are no longer separate others, for he is identical with others who are in their depth equally Absolute Nothingness. Hence, his presence makes it possible that "he and they are all converted into Buddha."

Of the two figures in this picture, Ueda (1982b, 162-63) remarks:

"An old man and a youth" means the selfless self-unfolding of the old man. For the self in its selflessness, whatever happens to the other happens to itself. This communion of common life is the second resurrected body of the selfless self. The self, cut open and disclosed through absolute nothingness, unfolds itself as the "between." I am "I and Thou" and "I and Thou" are I. What we have here is the self seen as a double self grounded on selflessness in nothingness.

Here the self and the other form a "double self." The self of the other and the self of the self are the resurrected double self of the Selfless Self. The double self has a double aspect of being old and young, which again suggests the ideal image of the Eastern Self as a union of the old and the young.

According to Ueda, the last three pictures form an "invisible circle of nothingness-nature-communication" and a "threefold manifestation" of the Selfless Self. They are not distinct stages in progress but three phases of Absolute Nothingness or the Selfless Self. Furthermore, these three aspects are in a constant process of dynamic "movement" in which the Selfless Self cannot be located at any particular place, for it is a formless, dynamic movement of Emptiness itself. According to Ueda,

the self is never "there" but always in the process of transformation, always fitted to its circumstances and likewise always proceeding from out of itself, at one moment passing away into nothingness unhindered and without a trace, at another, blooming in the flowers as the selfless self, and at a third, in the encounter with the other, converting that very encounter into its own self. (1982a, 22)

In this way, the last three pictures represent three modes of the Selfless Self that realizes the infinite reality and manifests itself as the universal reality.

The *Ten Oxherding Pictures* clearly exemplifies the Eastern way of Self-realization. As we have seen, they have a certain developmental stage, yet at the same time they go beyond the idea of development as such. The introductory comment of the first picture begins with a phrase like this: "The beast has never gone astray, and what is the use of searching for him?" (Suzuki 1960, 129). In the final analysis, from the beginning, nothing is lost. This aspect is symbolized by the circles of all pictures enclosing the contents. The circle (Absolute Nothingness) is always already there from the beginning to the end.

In this regard, Kawai (1996), an experienced psychotherapist, draws an important lesson beyond the stage-centered ideas of human development, saying, "Working with clients, we need to be able to look at them both with and without stages. Buddhism offers an effective way of observing without stages" (p. 60); "as the pictures are shown in a sequence from first to tenth, they appear to be indicating real stages, but this is only for convenience" (pp. 60-61). Then he comments on the idea of "progress":

> Modern man likes the word *progress*. I think contemporary people are still dragging that idea around. It is easy to accept that logic which proposes a diagram of "progress," progress with stages rising in a line. On this point, Jungian ideas are pretty flexible, while Buddhism is utterly open. There is no first and last, no beginning or end. Buddhism shows us the world of everything as it is, as a whole. No real change is going on. (p. 61)

From the viewpoint of Absolute Nothingness, there is no stage of development. Therefore, what is important is to have views of both development and non-development. The following comments on clinical practice by Kawai are of special importance for education as well:

> [T]he greater part of my effort is spent in contact with the realm which is unrelated to the developmental changes. This attitude of mine was acquired and cultivated during my long clinical experience, as I repeated many mistakes as a result of dwelling too heavily on the scheme of developmental changes. (pp. 62-63)

The discussions in this chapter have explored some of the characteristics of Eastern holistic education that seem to be very different from or opposite to the Western ideas of education. In these expositions, how-

ever, I have never intended to raise an either-or question. My point has
been to show that from the Eastern perspectives there can be a different
view of education that can complement the Western ideas of education.
The pedagogical implications of Eastern philosophy are significant because they can contribute to a comprehensive view of education.

NOTES

1. Jidu Krishnamurti is also an important Indian thinker like them, but he is not included
   in this list because he rejected belonging to any kind of religious tradition including
   Hinduism. Hazrat Inayat Khan (1960) is also an important Indian thinker on education.
   Yet he is not included here because he was a Sufi mystic.

2. Besides their own writings, see also Cenkner (1976); Patel (1953); Pavitra (1961/1991);
   Sharma (1992); and Marshak (1997).

3. Marshak provides a comparative study between Aurobindo, Hazrat Inayat Khan, and
   Rudolf Steiner.

4. For systematic introductions to Hinduism, see Klostermaier (1994), Radhakrishnan
   (1923/1996a, 1923/1996b), and others.

5. The "bridge" model of "conscious education" presented by Philip Gang, Nina Lynn,
   and Dorothy Maver (1992) has a similar framework to the Hindu view of life. This
   "bridge" model has four stages of life: self, others, the world, and the universal; we start
   our lives as self-centered beings and come to terms with others and then the world, and
   finally become involved with the universal and spiritual realm.

6. Jal Jehangir Nanavaty (1973) provides an in-depth exploration into educational thought
   in ancient India, including the *Veda*, the *Upanisads*, and the *Bhagavad Gita*.

7. "Taoist philosophy" or "Taoism" in this study fundamentally refers to the philosophies
   of Lao Tzu and Chuang Tzu, and this "philosophical Taoism" is distinct from Taoism as
   religious movements that became popular in the period of the Six Dynasties (420-581)
   in China. It is important to note that the philosophies of Lao Tzu and Chuang Tzu
   strongly influenced the development of both Ch'an and Pure Land Buddhist thoughts.
   To use the *pinyin* system, Taoism is represented as Daoism, Lao Tzu as Laozi, Chuang
   Tzu as Zhuangzi.

8. Callicott and Ames (1989) provide an overview of various ideas of nature developed in
   Asian thought.

9. Among many other English translations of Lao Tzu's *Tao Te Ching*, throughout this
   study I have used Chang Chung-yuan's *Tao: A New Way of Thinking* (1975), for it was
   made with special attention to the philosophical and ontological aspect of Lao Tzu's
   ideas. For a recent study, see Csikszentmihalyi and Ivanhoe (1999).

10. In addition to this, some of the prominent trends in the perennial philosophy (Theoso-
    phy, Anthroposophy) and transpersonal psychology (Wilber) have heavily drawn on

linear progressive models of development, even if they go beyond the rational stage and acknowledge the trans-rational stages. In this respect, it is important to note the work of Thomas Armstrong (1985), who provided an alternative view of development that includes both "strands" of the "body up" and the "spirit down" development. The "body up" strand encompasses the whole aspects of the material development throughout childhood. On the other hand, "[the] 'spirit down' strand of growth defines the journey from a higher/broader/deeper/more comprehensive level of nonmaterial existence to a narrower/more confining/more separate/material or bodily existence" (p. 7). Armstrong demonstrated that both lines of development are necessary to comprehend the whole dynamics of development. Interestingly, he mentioned Eastern views of development in this regard.

11. For psychological interpretations, see Kawai (1996), Spiegelman and Miyuki (1985); and for philosophical interpretations, see Ueda (1982a, 1982b, 1983a), Ueda and Yanagida (1982).

SEARCHING FOR THE OX

SEEING THE TRACES

SEEING THE OX

CATCHING THE OX

HERDING THE OX

COMING HOME ON THE OX'S BACK

THE OX FORGOTTEN, LEAVING THE MAN ALONE

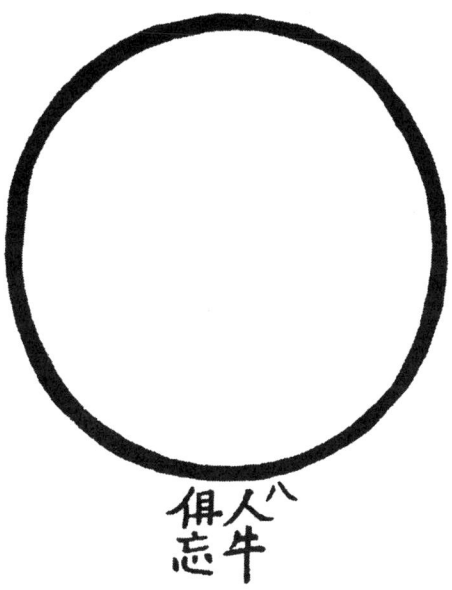

THE OX AND THE MAN BOTH GONE OUT OF SIGHT

RETURNING TO THE ORIGIN, BACK TO THE SOURCE

ENTERING THE CITY WITH BLISS-BESTOWING HANDS

Eastern Ways of Holistic Education

This chapter and the next will explore Eastern ways of holistic education, or some practical aspects of Eastern philosophy that are relevant to holistic education. The Eastern ways of practice for self-cultivation and spiritual transformation have been not of secondary but of primary importance; they have not been subordinate to theories as mere means, but both have stood in reciprocal relationships in such ways that theories have developed in reflecting on the experiences attained in practices and in turn have provided useful instructions for practices. Eastern philosophy has involved practices as its integral parts; in this sense, it has never been an idealistic speculation or a religious doctrine or a mere belief system but a practical, operational, and transformative discipline.

Izutsu (1983/1984) discerns two types of philosophy—the "normal" or "ordinary" philosophy and the "abnormal" or "extraordinary" philosophy. The "normal" or "ordinary" type is based on "the ordinary experience of Existence shared by all men on the level of common sense" (p. 474). "A philosopher of this type is a man standing on the level of the 'worldly mode of being'" (p. 474). In spite of its penetrating thinking, the most part of Western philosophy may belong to this type, for it lacks systematic practice to transform "the worldly mode of being." On the other hand, Eastern philosophy belongs to the "abnormal" or "extraordinary" type, exploring "the real metaphysical depth of Existence" (p. 474)

through "spiritual transformation." Referring to the worldviews of Ibn
Arabi, Lao Tzu, and Chuang Tzu, Izutsu asserts that Eastern philosophy
is "an extraordinary world-view because it is a product of an extraordinary vision of Existence as experienced by an extraordinary man" (p.
474). To penetrate into "the mystery of Existence," "the spiritual eyesight"[1] is necessary, and to obtain it "man must experience a spiritual rebirth and be transferred from the 'worldly mode of being' to the
'otherworldly mode of being'" (p. 474).

The truth of Eastern philosophy is revealed in an awareness cultivated by practice. According to Yasuo Yuasa (1987), "cultivation" (J.
shugyo) is a methodological foundation for metaphysical and philosophical quests. On the uniqueness of Eastern philosophy, he remarks:

> One revealing characteristic is that personal "cultivation" (*shugyo*) is
> presupposed in the philosophical foundation of the Eastern theories.
> To put it simply, true knowledge cannot be obtained simply by means
> of theoretical thinking, but only through "bodily recognition or real-
> ization" (*tainin* or *taitoku*), that is, through the utilization of one's total
> mind and body.... Cultivation is a practice that attempts, so to speak,
> to achieve true knowledge by means of one's total mind and body. (pp.
> 25-26)

In terms of multidimensional reality, "cultivation is a process in which
one's soul progresses gradually from the physical to the metaphysical
dimension" (p. 217). For example, in the Buddhist context, "Cultivation's ultimate goal is wisdom (*prajna*).... Buddhism contends that this
goal can be attained only through cultivation" (p. 98). Cultivation has
been "a *method* to reach the wisdom of *satori* [Enlightenment], a passage
to it" (p. 27). This holds true to other traditions of Eastern philosophy,
each of which has developed a variety of systems of cultivation.[2]

Eastern methodologies of cultivation attempt to transform a total being in pursuit of the Eastern Self, the Self who has embodied full
dimensionality in her or his transformed existence. Cultivation includes
two major fields of practice—contemplation (meditation) and arts. The
following discussion will expound a basic structure of contemplation
and art.

THE WAY OF CONTEMPLATION

It is no exaggeration to say that the way of contemplation has been the royal road to Awakening in the traditions of Eastern philosophy for thousands of years. For example, Dogen valued *zazen* (sitting meditation) over anything else as "the true gate to buddha-dharma" (Okumura & Leighton 1997, 29). According to Dogen,

> All buddha-tathagatas together have been simply transmitting wondrous dharma and actualizing anuttara samyak sambodhi [the supreme enlightenment of Buddha] for which there is an unsurpassable, unfabricated, wondrous method....
>
> For disporting oneself freely in this samadhi, practicing zazen in an upright posture is the true gate. Although this dharma is abundantly inherent in each person, it is not manifested without practice, it is not attained without realization. (p. 19)

By the same token, each tradition and each school of Eastern philosophy has refined numbers of methods and techniques of contemplation (yoga, meditation).

Today many of them have been introduced to the West. In the field of education, various attempts were made from the 1960s to the 1970s by pioneers in humanistic and transpersonal psychology including Michael Murphy, George Leonard, Deborah Rozman, Gay Hendricks, Thomas Roberts and others, to incorporate the methods of contemplation as significant tools of self-inquiry and learning.

Contemporary holistic education has enlarged this approach; for example, pioneers such as John Miller (1988/1996, 1993a, 1994) and Richard Brown (1991, 1998/1999) have highlighted roles of contemplation in educational settings and have put it into practice in their fields.[3] In particular, they have demonstrated that contemplation can play a significant role in teachers' personal development in both pre-service and in-service programs. Miller (1994) points out four aspects of contemplation applied to higher education; that is, contemplation allows the teacher to develop Self-learning, to cope with daily stress, to overcome the sense of separateness, and to teach from the Self (pp. 120-122).

Brown (1991) designed a comprehensive teacher training program in which the Buddhist contemplation occupies a central place. As he remarks:

> Previously neglected in teacher training was the Asian notion of "training of the heart." When the heart is opened and nurtured in teacher training, there is the possibility of connecting with the best in our children, with the disciplines of study, and with the student-teacher's own resourceful nature. Effectiveness in teaching is derived in large part from this directness, openness, passion, and sensitivity. The meditative approach deepens our training to inspire that kind of wholeheartedness. (p. 16)

What is needed in teachers' development is not only theories and skills they can make use of, but also "the inner preparation of the teacher" (p. 16), because a real effectiveness in education comes ultimately from the inner qualities of the teacher that can be cultivated by contemplative practice. Brown states: "Before we can teach others holistically, we must begin to familiarize ourselves with, and then unlearn, the habits that inhibit us from being truly whole as teachers" (p. 17). Contemplation, or what Brown calls "contemplative observation," can help us realize who we really are. "Once we have made peace with our own style of being, then awareness and compassion extend beyond our own agendas and our teaching can take on an effective fluidity" (p. 17). The way of contemplative education can deeply affect the quality of educational practice through cultivating the inner qualities of the teacher.

THE ART OF AWARENESS

Generally speaking, contemplation or meditation[4] is *an art of awareness* in its basic forms; it is the art of being aware of that which is taking place in the present moment without intervention of the mind. Awareness in this sense is alternately called "attention," "mindfulness," "witness," and "observation." The Buddhist tradition calls it "mindfulness." According to Thich Nhat Hanh (1998/1999, 64), "Right mindfulness (*samyak smriti*) is at the heart of the Buddha's teachings."[5] Here "mindfulness" means "remembering to come back to the present moment" (p. 64). In addition, Buddhist meditative practice has been called *dhyana*,[6] which, as Chögyam Trungpa (1973) says, "literally means 'awareness,' being in a state of 'awake'" (p. 177). The principles of mindfulness and *dhyana* are extremely simple for they are just *to see what is* here and now within and without. After Trungpa (1969/1985, 73), "Meditation is just trying to see what *is*, and there is nothing mysterious about it." He also mentions a "panoramic awareness":

> [O]ne has to develop a panoramic awareness, an all-pervading aware-
> ness, knowing the situation *at that very moment*. It is a question of
> knowing the situation and opening one's eyes to that very moment of
> nowness, and this is not particularly a mystical experience or anything
> mysterious at all, but just direct, open and clear perception of what *is
> now*. (p. 47)

However, on the other hand, the practice of awareness is far from an easy work because "the whole idea of meditation is to develop an entirely different way of dealing with things" (Trungpa 1969/1985, 60). The whole effort of meditation is dedicated to cultivating and enhancing awareness so as to disidentify with the predominant power of the mind. In the ordinary state of consciousness, only the mind is predominant; it is always actively functioning—interpreting, categorizing, evaluating, criticizing, and judging—and thereby producing "ordinary" experiences in accordance with the habitual patterns of thinking, feeling, and moving. Our exclusive identification with the mind results in preventing us from knowing a deeper reality. As opposed to this, meditation attempts to disidentify with the mind through enhancing awareness; it observes how the mind works with no attachment, so that the mind learns to wither and become less dominant. That is why the great T'ien-t'ai master Chih-i (538-579) identified the essence of Buddhist meditation with "stopping and seeing," that is, stopping the mind and seeing the true reality (Chih-i 1997).

Awareness is distinct from the ordinary function of consciousness (the mind); it is a consciousness *of* consciousness, or a meta-consciousness. According to "the radical view of the mind" by Charles Tart (1975/1983), awareness is not "a function of the brain" (p. 29) but "something that comes from outside the structure of the physical brain, as well as something influenced by the structure of the brain (thus giving consciousness) and the cultural programming" (p. 30). Likewise, Arthur Deikman (1982) calls awareness "the observing self" as distinct from "the thinking self," "the emotional self," and "the functional self." "The observing self is the transparent center, that which is aware. This fourth self is most personal of all, prior to thought, feeling, and action, for it experiences these functions" (p. 94). It is a deeper self than other selves. "We *are* awareness, and that is why we cannot observe it; we cannot detach ourselves from it because it is the core experience of self" (p. 103). Contemplation or meditation cultivates this observing self and thereby enters the deeper dimensions of the Self and reality. Miller (1994, 121) describes this as follows:

> Meditation lets us witness the striving of the ego. During meditation practice, we compassionately witness all our thoughts and ego trips, and very gradually we begin to see that our fundamental identity is not the thoughts that form our ego structure, but the clear awareness that is witnessing the arising and falling of all of this. This basic insight is the beginning of liberation and compassion.

The discovery of awareness, or the observing self, is surely one of the greatest contributions of contemplative traditions to education, because it has disclosed a different aspect of the human being other than the mind, the body, and the emotion. The history of education has paid little attention to this aspect; therefore, it would be a primary task of holistic education to develop a system of education that includes the art of awareness as an integral part. The following is an attempt of this kind.[7]

AN INTEGRAL VIEW OF CONTEMPLATION

A basic framework of contemplation in holistic education may include not only meditation in the traditional sense but also "somatic education" (Murphy 1992, 386) (so-called bodywork) and a part of psychotherapy developed in the West. The somatic and psychotherapeutic approaches can be associated with meditation under the umbrella of contemplation. There are several rationales for this integration.

First of all, a holistic understanding of the human being as an integral being—a being with body, emotion, mind, soul, and spirit—requires various approaches hitherto developed separately to form an integral methodology. Claudio Naranjo (1994), who advances the idea of "an integral education: an education of body, feelings, mind and spirit" (p. 67), calls for an integration such as this; "only artificially can we divorce the provinces of education, psychotherapy, and the spiritual disciplines, for in truth there is a single process of growth-healing-enlightenment" (p. 56). The fields of bodywork, psychotherapy, and meditation can be combined in holistic education.

Next, some of the body-mind works such as the Alexander Technique, the Feldenkrais Method, and Sensory Awareness contain to a great extent meditative aspects in their emphasis on bodily awareness, and, at this point, they can serve as meditative practices. On the other hand, we can use a large part of meditation for therapeutic purposes as suggested by Watts (1961/1975) and Wilber (1979/1985), demonstrated in transpersonal psychotherapy (e.g., Wilber, Engler, and Brown 1986; Boorstein 1996, 1997). These factors also encourage us to develop an integral model of holistic education practice.

Most importantly, the multidimensional theory requires such an integration in its own right. The social system imposes itself on the body-mind and, in order to explore the deeper dimensions, it is necessary to release social conditionings by working on the body-mind. At this point, the body-mind system is not only a physical organism but rather a "social body." Mary Douglas (1970/1973) refers to "the social body" that is predominant over the physical body: "The social body constrains the way the physical body is perceived. The physical experience of the body, always modified by the social categories through which it is known, sustains a particular view of society" (p. 93). Michel Foucault (1977/1979) also contends that "in every society, the body was in the grip of very strict powers, which imposed on it constraints, prohibitions or obligations" (p. 136). And Don Johnson (1983), a leading somatic philosopher, observes: "Each of our bodies is an artifice, a community project visibly manifesting the values of those implicated in the task" (p. 66).

The body is strongly conditioned by the social system. It is an embodiment of the social system in a human being. Psychosomatically, this takes place in such a way that the mind (the ego or the self-image), which is itself conditioned by the social system, tries to dominate the body as a material object. Somatic thinkers have been fully aware of this. For example, according to Alexander Lowen (1967/1969, 7), "As it [the ego] develops ... it becomes antithetical to the body—that is, it sets up values in seeming opposition to those of the body." The domination of the mind has to do with the function of language. Moshe Feldenkrais (1972/1977) refers to the "tyranny" of abstraction and verbalization: "As verbal abstraction becomes more successful and more efficient, man's thinking and imagination become further estranged from his feelings, senses, and even movements" (pp. 51-52).

Aldous Huxley (1956/1975, 13) concludes: "Language, it is evident, has its Gresham's Law. Bad words tend to drive out good words, and words in general . . . tend to drive out immediate experience and our memories of immediate experience." In his notion, a human being is an "amphibian" that exists in the two worlds of language and the "first-order experiences," but the world of language tends to suppress the first-order experiences. In this way, the body (the organismic system in the cosmic world) becomes subordinate to the social dimension through the dominant power of the mind (language). The body-mind system involves such a repressive structure within itself.

Therefore, the transformative work of holistic education must start with the body-mind to release the organismic body from the domination of the social mind (the ego, the social world). This is what Norman Brown (1959/1985) once called "the resurrection of the body," and what Herbert Marcuse (1969, 1972) called the "emancipation of the body." As society creates the "second" nature in the body, the social change must involve "the biology of the individual." Marcuse (1969, 16-17) claimed that "the radical change which is to transform the existing society into a free society must reach into a dimension of the human existence ... the "biological" dimension.... [L]iberation presupposes changes in this biological dimension, that is to say, different instinctual needs, different reactions of the body as well as the mind." He also called for the "emancipation of the senses." As "the existing society is *reproduced* not only in the mind ... but *also in their senses*" (1972, 71), the senses become the basis for the transformation in the interest of liberation: "'*Emancipation of the senses*' implies that the senses become 'practical' in the reconstruction of society" (p. 64).

The transformation of the body-mind has been explored and *practiced* in somatic approaches including the Alexander Technique, Bioenergetics, the Feldenkrais Method, and Sensory Awareness (e.g.,

Johnson 1995). They all attempt to recollect the primordial bodily processes in which the division of the mind and the body dissolves away. In other words, somatic education brings about liberation from the social dimension to explore a deeper reality. In this sense, it is a way of *social criticism* after the definition given by Alan Watts (1961/1975). He says that

> the therapist who is really interested in helping the individual is forced into social criticism. This does not mean that he has to engage directly in political revolution; it means that he has to help the individual in liberating himself from various forms of social conditioning....
> (p. 8)

Somatic education can transform the body-mind from *the communicative body to the communal body*. In the communal body is revealed the interconnectedness of the cosmic reality. Lowen (1967/1969) calls this reality "the ego-body-nature continuum": "Reality as seen from the inside, that is, from the point of view of the body, is a continuum in which ego, body, and nature are linked by similar processes" (p. 255). Lowen (1972/1973) also observes that the grounding in the body through Bioenergetics brings about an eco-spiritual experience. He says, "true spirituality has a physical or biological basis" (p. 12) and remarks that "faith is rooted in the deep biological processes of the body" (p. 12).

> Faith is a quality of being: of being in touch with oneself, with life, and with the universe. It is a sense of belonging to one's community, to one's country, and to the earth. Above all it is the feeling of being grounded in one's body, in one's humanity, and in one's animal nature. It can be all these things because it is a manifestation of life, an expression of the living force that unites all beings. It is a biological phenomenon and not a psychic creation. (p. 219)

A person with faith in this sense is one who is connected with her or his body and thereby "with all life and with the universe" (p. 318).

Johnson (1983) regards the transformation of the body as a shift from "alienation" to "authenticity" and calls the somatic methods "the technology of authenticity." This shift "requires diverting our awareness from the opinions of those outside us toward our own perceptions and feelings" (p. 154). In the authentic mode of the body, no part is predominant over other parts, but every part interconnects with each other

(p. 167), and, moreover, an openness to others becomes remarkable (p. 177). Johnson also regards these refined experiences of the body as " consensual spirituality" rooted in communal sensual experience (pp. 205-206).

Furthermore, the communal body is what David Michael Levin (1988) calls the "transpersonal body" and the "ontological body" as distinct from the "ego-logical body" that is the communicative body. While the "ego-logical body" is "the civic body, socially constituted in the economy of a body politic" (p. 47), the "transpersonal body" is "that dimension of our bodily being through which we experience our connectedness with all sentient beings, our participation in nature's organic processes" (p. 47). As Levin recognizes, the stages of the transpersonal and ontological bodies "go beyond what society requires. We might call them 'spiritual' stages" (p. 48).

Somatic education can be succeeded by meditation to explore the deeper dimensions of reality. However, in reality, their boundary is not so clear, for somatic education can enhance awareness and meditation necessarily involves approaches to the body-mind.[8]

ALDOUS HUXLEY'S IDEAS
ON THE NONVERBAL HUMANITIES

An attempt to integrate somatic education with meditation has already been made by Aldous Huxley (1937/1966, 1956/1975, 1962/1972, 1965, 1969, 1977; see also Nakagawa 1992a) especially in his conception of the "nonverbal humanities."

Huxley developed a multidimensional concept of the human being called "multiple amphibians" that involves not only the conscious self, or the verbal level (language), but also the unconscious deeper layers of "not-self" including the vegetative soul, the worlds of insights and inspiration, of archetypes, of visionary experience, and the "universal Not-Self" (1956/1975, 17-18). The deeper not-selves constitute the foundations of the human being, yet the conscious ego and the subconscious layers of "the personal not-self" (inappropriate habits, neurosis caused by repressed emotions, and other conditioned behaviors of the body) tend to obstruct the deeper not-selves. He says:

> Man ... is a self associated with not-selves. By developing bad habits, the conscious ego and the personal sub-conscious interfere with the normal functioning of the deeper not-selves, from which we receive the animal grace of physical health and the spiritual grace of insight. (p. 23)

The "nonverbal humanities" try to dissolve barriers the ego and the personal subconscious have created. They include "Training of the kinesthetic sense. Training of the special senses. Training of memory. Training in control of the autonomic nervous system. Training for spiritual insight" (p. 19). They have psychosomatic and contemplative trainings from East and West—the Alexander Technique, the training of perception such as Gestalt Therapy, the art of wise passiveness, the art of meditation in the East such as yoga, Tantric training, and others. To use his favored phrase, this is an attempt to "make the best of both worlds." These methods serve as "the art of combining relaxation with activity" in which the ego and the personal subconscious are relaxed and at the same time the vegetative soul and the deeper not-selves are activated.

These methods are called "nonverbal," because Huxley regards their essence as the nonverbal aspect:

> In most societies ... very little effort has been made to educate children and adults systematically on the nonverbal level of first-order psychophysical experience.... What is needed, if more of the potentialities of more people are to be actualized, is a training on the nonverbal levels of our whole being as systematic as the training now given to children and adults on the verbal level. (1965, 37)

The system of the nonverbal humanities is a holistic model of education. In his last novel *Island*, Huxley (1962/1972) refers to the education of the whole person as follows:

> What we give the children is simultaneously a training in perceiving and imagining, a training in applied physiology and psychology, a training in practical ethics and practical religion, a training in the proper use of language, and a training in self-knowledge. In a word, a training of the whole mind-body in all its aspects. (p. 208)

Huxley himself had been involved in the Alexander Technique, a body-mind approach developed by F. M. Alexander (1923/1985, 1932/1984) in the early twentieth century as a method of conscious control of "the use of the self," or of the psycho-physical organism. Huxley found that John Dewey had also practiced it under Alexander and celebrated it as an essential contribution to education. Just as Alexander himself regarded his technique as a way of "re-education" of "the use of the self," so Dewey viewed it as a "constructive education." In his introduction to the work of Alexander, Dewey (1923/1985, xxxiii) recognized that "the method is not one of remedy; it is one of constructive education." Dewey later went so far as to say that: "It [the technique of Mr. Alexander] provides ... the conditions for the central direction of all special educational processes. It bears the same relation to education that education itself bears to all other human activities" (1932/1984, xix). However, his voice had been ignored even among progressive educators. Huxley commented on his statements as follows:

> These are strong words; for Dewey was convinced that man's only hope lies in education. But just as education is absolutely necessary to the world at large, so Alexander's methods of training the psycho-physical instrument are absolutely necessary to education. (1956/1975, 21)

These statements by Dewey and Huxley must be recalled as historic voices in the development of somatic education.[9]

The nonverbal humanities are the art of awareness. Huxley focuses on this aspect and associates the somatic approaches with meditation, providing a comprehensive view of *the education of awareness* that starts with the elemental level and reaches to the deeper level. Most of the somatic approaches can contribute to the training of "elementary awareness": "Education in elementary awareness will have to include techniques for improving awareness of internal events and techniques for improving awareness of external events as these are revealed by our organs of sense" (1969, 155). In his view, the Alexander Technique is a way to enhance the elementary awareness of the kinesthetic sense, which reveals the first-order experience of the psycho-physical organism. This is important because "[t]he kinesthetic sense is the main line of communication between the conscious self and the personal subconscious on the one hand and the vegetative soul on the other" (1956/1975, 19).

Elementary awareness can provide a basis for the further evolution of awareness in meditation. "A good physical education should teach awareness on the physical plane" (1937/1966, 221). Similar ideas are found in the somatic work of Sensory Awareness and the Feldenkrais Method. Sensory Awareness, developed by Elsa Gindler and Charlotte Selver, may be called a meditation in action, a way of enhancing awareness through paying attention to immediate experiences of the senses. (see Brooks 1974/1982).

Feldenkrais (1972/1977) developed a method of movement that can remarkably enhance awareness. He discerns ordinary consciousness and awareness.

> There is an essential difference between consciousness and awareness, although the borders are not clear in our use of language.... Awareness is consciousness together with a realization of what is happening within it or of what is going on within ourselves while we are conscious. (p. 50)

Awareness is the meta-consciousness of consciousness and something that has to be cultivated. Awareness of this sort may lead to a spiritual unfolding.

> In those moments when awareness succeeds in being at one with feeling, senses, movement, and thought, then man can make discoveries, invent, create, innovate, and "know." He grasps that his small world and the great world around are but one and that in this unity he is no longer alone. (p. 54)

The Feldenkrais Method is not a mere training for physical functioning but is designed to bring about a spiritual awakening.

In *Island*, Huxley (1962/1972) celebrates not only the somatic work but also every human activity that can be the art of awareness, which he calls "the yoga of everyday living": "Be fully aware of what you're doing, and work becomes the yoga of work, play becomes the yoga of play, everyday living becomes the yoga of everyday living" (p. 149). For him, awareness is the key to Enlightenment. "This is the only genuine yoga, the only spiritual exercise worth practicing" (p. 40). He concludes: "Everybody's job—enlightenment. Which means, here and now, the preliminary job of practicing all the yogas of increased awareness" (p. 236). In other words, Enlightenment is the realization of "the ultimate Not-Self" (1956/1975, 33).

From Awareness to Awakening

Meditation (contemplation) is designed to bring about *a transformation of consciousness* through a cultivation of awareness. According to Robert Ornstein (1972/1975, 124), it is "an attempt to inhibit the usual mode of consciousness, and to cultivate a second mode that is available to man." The ordinary, normal state of consciousness is marked by its "verbal," "rational," "analytic," "linear," and therefore fragmentary modes. On the contrary, the transformed state of consciousness is "intuitive," "receptive," and "holistic": "The techniques of meditation ... are in their totality designed to cause a shift from the ordinary analytic consciousness to the holistic" (p. 246). Meditation is able to temporarily undo the superficial function of the mind so as to allow the deeper levels of holistic consciousness to emerge.

The total transformation of consciousness has been called "awakening" in the literature of meditation. Ralph Metzner (1986, 17) states that "the transformation of consciousness is like the change from dreaming to waking." "Awakening" is a common metaphor to describe the transformation of consciousness among spiritual traditions. For example, in Buddhism, the word "Buddha" means "the awakened one," and the whole effort of Buddhist meditation is dedicated to attain awakening, or *bodhi*. In terms of Zen, D. T. Suzuki (1964/1991, 95) says, "*Satori* is the sudden flashing into consciousness of a new truth hitherto undreamed of." Likewise, Masao Abe (1997, 76) remarks:

> What the Zen master tries to lead his disciple to and the disciple wants to attain, is not the intellectual knowledge of the natural world nor the understanding of cultural conditions and values, but the disciple's awakening to his original nature.

In Sufism, the Sufi masters have highlighted "awakening" in their teachings. For example, Rumi (1994) discerns two different modes of consciousness: "heedlessness" and "heedfulness." The mode of "heedlessness" means the ordinary mode of consciousness that constructs the ordinary reality; he says, "the world subsists through heedlessness. If there were no heedlessness, this world would cease to be" (p. 114). When a transformation of consciousness occurs, we enter the awakened mode of "heedfulness." Rumi describes it as follows:

From infancy, when he begins to grow, man exists in heedlessness; otherwise he would never grow at all. Then, when he has reached full maturity in heedlessness, God imposes pain and strife upon him by means of determination and free will in order to wipe clean that heedlessness and make him pure. After that he can become acquainted with the other world. (p. 209)

"Awakening" refers to the sudden realization of the infinite reality. Compared to the awakened state, the ordinary state is seen as a "dreaming" process in "sleep." Chuang Tzu wrote: "Only after he wakes does he know it was a dream. And someday there will be a great awakening when we know that this is all a great dream" (Watson 1968, 47). However, it is rare for a great awakening to take place, because the ordinary mode of consciousness, or "sleep," is so dominant that it excludes other modes of consciousness.

A modern esoteric philosopher, G. I. Gurdjieff, who was greatly influenced by Sufism, discerns the "four states of consciousness" available to the human being: (a) ordinary sleeping and dreaming, (b) ordinary waking state, (c) self-consciousness, and (d) objective consciousness (Ouspensky 1950/1965/1987, 141; Tart 1986/1987, 212). Gurdjieffian psychology holds that only a "fully developed man" can possess all the states of consciousness, and ordinary states are occupied with the first two modes.

In this psychology, the second mode, ordinary waking state, does not mean "awakening" but being spiritually "asleep": "*He lives in sleep.* He is asleep" (cited in Ouspensky 1950/1965/1987, 143). In other words, without "self-consciousness," the human being is unconsciously subject to the forces of predominant subpersonalities—mind, body, and emotions at the moment. In this respect, Gurdjieff used to regard the human being as a "machine." E. F. Schumacher (1977), inspired by Gurdjieffian thought, remarks: "Without self-awareness ... man acts, speaks, studies, reacts mechanically, like a machine" (p. 75). Gurdjieff gives an account of how "sleep" takes place in the human consciousness:

[H]e [a man] is born among sleeping people, and, of course, he falls asleep among them just at the very time when he should have begun to be conscious of himself. Everything has a hand in this: the involuntary imitation of older people on the part of the child, voluntary and involuntary suggestion, and what is called "education." Every attempt to awaken on the child's part is instantly stopped. This is inevitable. And a great many efforts and a great deal of help are necessary in order to awaken later when thousands of sleep-compelling habits have been accumulated. And this very seldom happens. In most cases, a man when still a child already loses the possibility of awakening; he lives in sleep all his life and he dies in sleep. (cited in Ouspensky, 1950/1965/1987, 144)

To awaken from sleep to self-consciousness and then to objective consciousness, the practice of awareness or attention is necessary, which Gurdjieff calls "self-observation" and "self-remembrance." He says, "in observing himself a man notices that self-observation itself brings about certain changes in his inner processes. He begins to understand that self-observation is an instrument of self-change, a means of awakening" (pp. 145-146). According to Tart (1986/1987, 193), "In its most general form self-observation means paying more attention to everything in your world and everything in yourself." The state of "sleep" is caused by exclusive identification with the ordinary mode of consciousness filled with physical, emotional, and mental contents. Gurdjieff says, "Man is always in a state of identification, only the object of identification changes" (p. 150). Accordingly, the practice of self-observation is an exercise of "disidentification" by "seeing" identification of any kind to its very root. For instance, Schumacher (1977) refers to "bare attention" in terms of thinking: "Bare Attention is attainable only by stopping or, if it cannot be stopped, calmly observing all 'inner chatter.' It stands *above* thinking, reasoning, arguing, forming opinions" (p. 70).

"Self-remembering" is another exercise of attention that requires us to remember all the aspects of the self at the present moment. After Tart (1986/1987, 197), "It involves a deliberate expansion of consciousness such that the whole (ideally) of your being, or at least aspects of that whole, are kept in mind simultaneously with the particulars of consciousness." To this end, Gurdjieff himself created various methods including bodily movements that require the fullest attention. The self-consciousness can emerge through efforts of self-remembering. The transformation of consciousness leading to "objective consciousness" is possible by becoming fully awake of everything. As Deikman (1982, 176) says, "The observing self can be a bridge between the object world and the transcendent realm. Without the enhancement and development of the observing self, the further step to the Self cannot be taken."

Awareness is to observe what is taking place within and without, but this does not mean to create another dualistic division between subject and object. Rather, it is a way to disidentify with the very dimension where the mind creates dualism. Awareness is a deeper dimension than the mind and can witness how the mind creates divisions within the world. Therefore, it can bring us to the primordial non-dual state of consciousness. The great awakening may happen in the process of enhancing awareness and fostering disidentification. Roger Walsh and Frances Vaughn (1980, 58-59) point this out:

> Finally, awareness no longer identifies exclusively with anything. This represents a radical and enduring shift in consciousness known by various names, such as enlightenment or liberation. Since there is no longer any exclusive identification with anything, the me/not me dichotomy is transcended and such persons experience themselves as being both nothing and everything. They are both pure awareness (no thing) and the entire universe (every thing). Being identified with both no location and all location, nowhere and everywhere, they experience having transcended space and positionality.

To use Ken Wilber's (1979/1985) terms, this is a shift from "transpersonal witness" (or the "transpersonal self") to "unity consciousness." The transpersonal self is "a center and expanse of awareness which is creatively detached from one's personal mind, body, emotions, thoughts, and feelings" (p. 128). However, the transpersonal self is not synonymous with "unity consciousness."

> Although the transpersonal experiences are somewhat similar to unity consciousness, the two should not be confused. In unity consciousness the person's identity is with the All, with absolutely everything. In transpersonal experiences, the person's identity doesn't quite expand to the Whole, but it does expand or at least extend beyond the skin-boundary of the organism. (p. 8)

Before the unity consciousness (awakening) takes place, "one must first discover that transpersonal witness, which then acts as an easier 'jumping-off point' for unity consciousness" (p. 130). In his recent work,

Wilber (1996) uses the term "the observing Self" for the transpersonal self and finds that "this observing Self eventually discloses its own source, which is Spirit itself, Emptiness itself" (p. 199).

> When, as a specific type of meditation, you pursue the observing Self, the Witness, to its very *source* in pure Emptiness, then no objects arise in consciousness at all. This is a discrete, identifiable state of awareness—namely, *unmanifest absorption* or *cessation*, variously known as nirvikalpa, samadhi, jnana samadhi, ayin, vergezzen, nirodh, classical nirvana. (1996, 220)

The "pure Emptiness" is, in his words, the state of "the causal" which means "pure formless awareness, pure consciousness as such, the pure Self as pure Spirit (Atman = Brahman)" (1995, 301).

However, this attainment of the causal is not the final stage of the whole way of contemplation but marks the turning point from the seeking to the returning mode. Here opens the gate of "the nondual," or the universal reality. Wilber (1997) describes what happens in contemplation at this moment as follows:

> When I rest in the pure and simple Witness, I will even begin to notice that the Witness itself is not a separate thing or entity, set apart from what is witnesses. All thing arise within the Witness, so much so that the Witness itself disappears into all things. (p. 292)

In this way, all things, the world, arise again as they are in the Witness. The nondual means the nondual identity between the Witness and the world.

> When one breaks through the causal absorption in pure unmanifest and unborn Spirit, the entire manifest world (or worlds) arises once again, but this time as a perfect expression of Spirit and as Spirit. The Formless and the entire world of manifest Form—pure Emptiness and the whole Kosmos—are seen to be not-two (or nondual). (1995, 308)

Wilber follows the Mahayana tradition of the non-dualism: Emptiness-is-Form. "The pure *Emptiness* of the Witness turns out to be one with every *Form* that is witnessed, and that is one of the basic meanings of 'nonduality'" (1996, 228). Now Emptiness is "not a *discrete* state, but the reality of *all* states, the Suchness of all states" (p. 227). Enlightenment no longer abides in the causal but manifests itself in the nondual, in the midst of the world. "Enlightenment is an ongoing process of new Forms arising, and you relate to them as Forms of Emptiness. You are one with all these Forms as they arise" (p. 239). And this is the final phase of contemplation.

EDUCATION FOR AWAKENING:
KRISHNAMURTI AND SOCRATES

The ideas of awareness and awakening are important for education if it tries to involve the transformation of consciousness by way of contemplation. In practice, however, these ideas have never captured serious attention from modern mainstream education and pedagogy.[10] As Ornstein (1972/1975, 180) remarks, "Western educational systems largely concentrate on the verbal and intellectual. We do not possess a large-scale training system for the other side." But it seems to be appropriate to enlarge the concept of education to embrace not only the reflective but also the contemplative approach, as exemplified in holistic education. Education can be an attempt for awakening through the practice of awareness. In this regard, it is worthwhile recalling the work of Krishnamurti and Socrates.

Krishnamurti regards the heart of both education and meditation as the art of awareness, and, importantly, he has stressed this in his educational practices. He calls the art of awareness "choiceless awareness" (1954/1975, 94-98): "Awareness implies an observation in which there is no choice whatsoever, just observing without interpretation, translation, distortion" (1999, 73). And this is meditation; meditation is awareness (or attention) through which the dimension beyond "thought" or "the known" will be revealed. "Meditation is the seeing of what is and going beyond it" (1979, 18). Attention makes it possible for us to be aware of thought and thereby to disidentify with it. "Meditation is the freedom from thought, and a movement in the ecstasy of truth" (1970, 107). This "freedom" allows "the immeasurable" to manifest itself. Krishnamurti says:

> Thought has always a horizon. The meditative mind has no horizon.
> The mind cannot go from the limited to the immense, nor can it transform the limited into the limitless. The one has to cease for the other to be. Meditation is opening the door into spaciousness which cannot be imagined or speculated upon. (1970, 40)

Krishnamurti has put forth different views of education. He maintains that it is in choiceless awareness that "intelligence" can function and "learning" takes place. Therefore, the functions of intelligence and learning have nothing to do with accumulating knowledge, but rather intelligence is an alert attention to the present moment. "Intelligence is the seeing of what is" (1970, 155). On learning, he says: "There is a difference between learning and acquiring knowledge. Learning ceases when there is only accumulation of knowledge. There is learning only when there is no acquisition at all" (1974, 101-102). Learning is to directly know what is moment to moment with no projection of acquired knowledge. He says, "learning is pure observation—not only of the things outside you but also of that which is happening inwardly" (1981, 29).

For Krishnamurti, "self-knowledge" means to be aware of what I am, and he sees it as having a grave importance in the entire work of education. "Understanding comes only through self-knowledge, which is awareness of one's total psychological process. Thus education, in the true sense, is the understanding of oneself, for it is within each one of us that the whole of existence is gathered" (1953, 17). Self-knowledge in this sense can reveal the deeper dimensions of the Self and life, or what he calls "the wholeness of life": "To understand life is to understand ourselves, and that is both the beginning and the end of education" (p. 14).

It is also important for educators to enhance their own self-awareness and self-knowledge. As Krishnamurti observes, "The right kind of education begins with the educator, who must understand himself and be free from established patterns of thought; for what he is, that he imparts" (1953, 98).[11]

His idea is the same as that which Brown (1998/1999) and Miller (1994) try to fulfill in their teacher training programs. Both are influenced by Buddhist perspectives; Miller's program intends to cultivate the teacher as "the contemplative practitioner," and Brown provides a program of "contemplative education for teachers." According to Brown, "Contemplative teaching begins by knowing and experiencing ourselves directly" (p. 70). For this purpose, he has developed a practice called "contemplative observation." "In contemplative observation, we observe not only what is happening in the environment, but also what is simultaneously occurring within ourselves" (1998/1999, 70). What is observed includes senses, thoughts, and emotions taking place during teaching and other occasions. In his view, it is through contemplative observation that "the sacredness of ordinary teaching and learning" (p. 73) will appear. Contemplation or meditation is a way to transform the reality of teaching and learning from its radical ground.

Finally, we need to turn to the work of Socrates, because, at the very beginning of Western education, he had laid a foundation of contemplative education. In the *Apology*, Socrates declared the purpose of his activities to people as follows:

> [A]ll day long I never cease to settle here, there, and everywhere, rousing, persuading, reproving every one of you.... I suspect, however, that before long you will awake from your drowsing, and in your annoyance you will take Anytus' advice and finish me off with a single slap, and then you will go on sleeping till the end of your days....
> (Hamilton and Cairns 1961, 17)

The primary concern for Socrates was to awaken people from their wretched sleep. Featuring "the transformative tradition" in education as opposed to "the mimetic tradition," Philip Jackson remarks: "In the person of Socrates we witness perhaps the most famous of all transformative teachers in action" (126). Jacob Needleman (1982, 39) also highlights the transformative aspect of Socrates as follows:

> Socrates is far more than an interrogator who exposes illusions; he is also a presence, a personal force, who through his interaction with the other awakens in him the taste of conscience and inner divinity.... The being of Socrates transmits the taste of the higher; the interrogation of Socrates brings awareness of one's corruption and illusions.

The Socratic method of *interrogation* in dialogues is a device for awakening like Zen *mondo*, not necessarily aimed at the intellectual investigation of concepts. According to Needleman, "*the interrogation is itself a material, chemical process* by which the transformation begins to take place within oneself. This fact, and only this fact, can explain the greatness and mystery of Socrates" (p. 25).

Socratic "self-knowing" or "self-inquiry" may mean to enhance the level of self-awareness. This is also referred to as "the care of the soul" which, as Needleman says, requires a cultivation of attention to the *soul*, or the deeper level of the Self (pp. 55-56).[12]

The Socratic way of the teacher known as the Socratic art of "mid-wifery" gives us a classical metaphor of an education for awakening, for awakening is not to produce something but to rediscover what is always already, and "midwifery" is to help such an awakening to take place. Abe (1997) recognizes an affinity of the Socratic way with the way of a Zen master. A Zen master cannot give a *satori* to a disciple, simply because "*satori* is the self-awakening of one's original nature" (p. 77). In the ultimate sense, "a master is necessary only as a midwife, i.e., not as a *satori*-giver but as a *satori*-helper" (p. 77).

In other words, the education for awakening has nothing to teach in the usual sense. From the beginning nothing is lost, and everything is ever present. As Suzuki (1964/1991, 92) says, "there is in Zen nothing to explain, nothing to teach, that will add to your knowledge." The whole-ness of reality *is* all the time, and what is necessary is to become aware of it. As Trungpa (1973, 4) says, "Enlightenment is permanent because we have not produced it; we have merely discovered it."

THE WAY OF ART

ART AS CONTEMPLATION

The Eastern way of art has been a form of contemplation. Art as contemplation involves the twofold path of seeking and returning; the practice of art follows the seeking path, and the artistic expressions occur in the returning path. Therefore, in the East artistic expressions have been respected as expressing something ultimate. The present discussion[13] will focus on the way of art (J. *geido*) especially developed in Japan under the strong influence of Zen.[14]

The way of art is a way of spiritual cultivation. Yuasa (1987) recognizes this in his comment on the art of poetry as follows:

> Just as the practicing monk leaves behind his own egoism and deep-ens his *satori* by experiencing cultivation with body-mind, so too, the poet enhances his or her state of mind as a poet by training in composi-tion. Therefore, training in artistry is a kind of personal cultivation: one not only studies a certain technique but also, in so doing, enhances one's own personality. (p. 103)

The training and mastery of an art (*keiko*) and the cultivation of the self (*shugyo*) are united in the way in which art becomes a path of the heart. Yukihiro Kurasawa (1983/1993) remarks: "The way of art (*geido*) is a 'path' from 'art (*gei*) and form (*sugata*) to the heart (*kokoro*)' and then 'from the heart to art and form'" (p. 45, trans. Nakagawa). Here, the "heart" means the "true heart," or the deeper dimensions of the self. "'The path to the heart' in the way of art is the path of deepening and enhancing the heart through the training of the art and its form" (p. 46, trans. Nakagawa).

The way of art as a path to the heart attempts to explore the deeper dimensions of reality. As Toshimitsu Hasumi (1962, viii) says, "The way of art helps us to penetrate deep into the inner structure of the cosmos." In this sense, it is called the "spiritual way" (*do*). With Hasumi, "art is the way to the Absolute and to the essence of human life. This he [the Japanese] designates as 'DO'" (p. 79).

Once the way of art attains the Absolute, the returning mode of the art can occur, in which artistic expressions come into being. This represents "the path from the heart to art and form." According to Hasumi, "The way to the NOTHING is the innermost art of Japan, and out of it all formative art unfolds" (p. xi). Here, the artistic creation (form) embodies formless Nothingness and expresses the infinite reality in its finite form by the artist who is fundamentally transformed in Absolute Nothingness. In other words, the art becomes an expression of the universal reality as such.

THREE STAGES IN TIIC WAY OF ART: THE HERRIGELS' STORIES

Some fascinating stories that exemplify a transformative process in the way of art relate the experiences of Eugen Herrigel (1953/1999) and his wife Gustie (1958/1974), who stayed in Japan for six years from 1924 to 1929 and intensively learned Zen art. Eugen learned the art of archery (*kyu-do*) and Gustie the art of flower arrangement (*kado*) under the great masters of the day.

Eugen Herrigel (1953/1999) correctly grasps the essence of the way of archery as "spiritual exercise." He says, "by the 'art' of archery he [the Japanese] does not mean the ability of the sportsman ... but an ability whose origin is to be sought in spiritual exercises and whose aim consists in hitting a spiritual goal" (p. 4). In terms of spiritual exercise,

> archery can in no circumstances mean accomplishing anything outwardly with bow and arrow, but only inwardly, with oneself. Bow and arrow are only a pretext for something that could just as well happen without them, only the way to a goal, not the goal itself, only helps for the last decisive leap. (p. 7)

From the reports by the Herrigels, we can trace three distinctive phases of the practice of art.

First, the way of art requires the student to transcend the ego and to realize the egoless state of consciousness called in Zen "no-mind" (*mushin*) or "no-ego" (*muga*). To use the words of Karlfried Graf Dürckheim (1987/1991), this is the process of "dismantling the ego": "Zen is not in the business of destroying the ego, but of transforming the merely world-centered ego and changing the person determined solely by that ego into a person determined by his true nature" (p. 89).[15]

In pursuit of dismantling the ego, the way of art usually does not allow the student to express her or his egocentric uniqueness; art should not be an expression of personal feelings, skills, ideas, and beliefs. Gustie Herrigel (1958/1974, 12) says, "personal idiosyncrasies and originality in making new experiments met with little recognition." The student must admit that "any sort of ambition is a hindrance, and that any desire for personal uniqueness stands in the way of development" (p. 22).

The story of Eugen provides an outstanding illustration of transcending the ego, which was the most difficult task for him as a philosopher trained in logical thinking. (Eugen came to Japan from Germany to teach philosophy at Tohoku Imperial University). He struggled with "letting go of himself" in his practice. The following conversation with his master Kenzo Awa reveals this:

> I said, "I draw the bow and loose the shot in order to hit the target. The drawing is thus a means to an end, and I cannot lose sight of this connection...."
>
> "The right art," cried the Master, "is purposeless, aimless! The more obstinately you try to learn how to shoot the arrow for the sake of hitting the goal, the less you will succeed.... What stands in your way is

that you have a much too willful will. You think that what you do not
do yourself does not happen." (E. Herrigel 1953/1999, 31)

The primary task of the master is to help the student disidentify with the
egocentric "doer" and learn that "all right doing is accomplished only in
a state of true selflessness, in which the doer cannot be present any longer as 'himself.' Only the spirit is present, a kind of awareness which
shows no trace of egohood" (p. 44)

To this end, the way of art requires the student to practice "patterns"
(*kata*) and "forms" (*katachi*) demonstrated by the master. The teaching
and learning process consists of the demonstration of patterns by the
master and the imitation and mastery of them by the student through re-
peated practices, in which the egocentric desires of the student come to
wither. As Gustie says,

> To begin with the European finds it difficult to understand why he
> should fit himself into a pattern and only then work free of it. But bit by
> bit he begins to realize, and perhaps also to experience, that this "fit-
> ting in" is actually a springboard for true creativity. (1958/1974, 23)

Patterns and forms are not arbitrarily imposed on the student but are
designed for the student to fit in the essence of what is being learned; that
is, "the pattern, which at first appears merely as an outward form, becomes the inner form of flower arrangement as soon as the rules enter
into life itself" (G. Herrigel 1958/1974, 24). At this point, the master is
not an instructor of patterns but one who invites the student into the
heart of the art.

The practice such as this may include at least two essential aspects in
terms of transcending the dualistic division between subject and object.
The first aspect concerns the process of learning in which the student becomes one with the thing to be learned. Keiji Nishitani (1982) regards
"learning" as follows: "The Japanese word for 'learn' (*narau*) carries the
sense of 'taking after' something, of making an effort to stand essentially
in the same mode of being as the thing one wishes to learn about" (p.
128). For example, the art of ink-painting teaches that "spend ten years
observing bamboo, become a bamboo yourself, then forget everything
and—paint" (E. Herrigel 1953/1999, 77).

According to Izutsu (1977/1982), this is a crucial factor in the practice
of the art: "This positive aspect of the Zen discipline is known ... as 'one's

becoming the thing'" (p. 79). In an actual situation, "the painter should *become* the thing which he wants to paint. The painter who is going to paint a bamboo must, before taking up his brush, sit in contemplation until he feels himself completely identified with the bamboo" (p. 79). In one's becoming the thing, the true reality of the thing comes to manifest itself in the no-mind state of the artist. From the state of complete unification in which there remains no trace of distinction between the painter and the bamboo, "the bamboo draws its own picture on the paper. The movement of the brush is the movement of the inner life of the bamboo" (p. 80).

Another aspect of the practice is concerned with the art of awareness. Like somatic education and meditation, the practice of art can enhance the level of awareness. Eugen Herrigel calls it the "right presence of mind":

> This means that the mind or spirit is present everywhere, because it is
> nowhere attached to any particular place. And it can remain present
> because, even when related to this or that object, it does not cling to it
> by reflection and thus lose its original mobility. (1953/1999, 37)

This is also what Takuan (1986) called the "no-mind" state of consciousness in his teachings on the way of swordmanship and what Zeami called the "observing with a detached seeing" (*riken no ken*) in his teachings on the way of *No* play. Yuasa refers to the latter as follows: "'Observing with a detached seeing' is the state in which the self's consciousness of itself ... disappears and the actor sees even his own dancing figure from the outside" (1987, 108). This "seeing" is none other than the awareness we have discussed before.

The second phase of practice is to attain the ultimate depth of the art. The practice can attain the infinite reality in the egoless state of one's becoming with what is learned. Gustie Herrigel describes this as "the Principle of Three" in which the Three—the heart of the flower, the heart of the human being, and the universal heart—are unified.

> Sunk deep in herself, she sought to attain that state of mind in which it
> is possible to become one with the heart of flower.... For only when
> this union of her own heart with the flower's heart—and indeed with
> the "universal heart" ... is truly established, does she rest in that un-

moved stillness from which creation proceeds as if of itself, entirely unpurposingly. (1958/1974, 28)

It is in one's becoming the thing that the infinite reality is disclosed. Here, "flower-heart, man's heart and universal heart are one. Man lives in essential communion with the plant as with the whole universe.... [E]verything forms the unbroken Three-in-One" (p. 37). At this stage, three poles (poleless-poles) are completely unified: the person (one's deepest consciousness), the particular art work (flower), and the universe (the infinite reality). As Hasumi admits, "The essence of Japanese spiritual creations is rooted in this unfathomable source, deep in the ground of the transcendent cosmic law and of the immanent consciousness of the inward man" (1962, 80).

This stage marks a culmination in the whole process of the way of art. Eugen had to spend four years until this took place.

> Then, one day, after a shot, the Master made a deep bow and broke off the lesson. "Just then 'It' shot!" he cried....
>
> "What I have said," the Master told me severely, "was not praise, only a statement that ought not to touch you. Nor was my bow meant for you, for you are entirely innocent of this shot. You remained this time absolutely self-oblivious and without purpose in the highest tension, so that the shot fell from you like a ripe fruit." (1953/1999, 52-53)

The shot happened in his egolessness, in which "It" appeared. "'It' takes aim and hits, so here 'It' takes the place of the ego" (p. 76). In his last stage of practice, he remarks as follows:

> "Do you now understand," the Master asked me one day after a particularly good shot, "what I mean by 'It shoots,' 'It hit'?"
>
> "I'm afraid I don't understand anything more at all," I answered, "even the simplest things have got in a muddle. Is it 'I' who draw the bow, or is it the bow that draws me into the state of highest tension? Do 'I' hit the goal, or does the goal hit me...? Bow, arrow, goal and ego, all melt into one another, so that I can no longer separate them. And even the need to separate has gone. For as soon as I take the bow and shoot, everything becomes so clear and straightforward and so ridiculously simple...."
>
> "Now at last," the Master broke in, "the bowstring has cut right through you." (p. 61)

Two comments can be made about these statements. Suzuki (1959/1993) applies the term "Cosmic Unconscious" to the ultimate experience happening in the way of art. In his definition,

> underneath all the practical technique or the methodological details necessary for the mastery of an art, there are certain intuitions directly reaching what I call the Cosmic Unconscious…. [T]he fundamental experience is acknowledged to be an insight into the Unconscious itself as source of all creative possibilities, all artistic impulses…. [T]he Unconscious then permits its privileged disciples, masters of arts, to have glimpses of its infinite possibilities" (pp. 192-193).

Suzuki discerns "several layers of consciousness," relying on the Mind-Only theory in the Yogacara school of Mahayana Buddhism, which include the following(pp. 242-243):

- The ordinary consciousness—dualistic perception
- The semiconscious plane—the realm of accessible memories
- The Unconscious—the realm of lost memories
- The Collective Unconscious—the bedrock of our personality, the basis of our mental life (*alaya-vijnana*, or the Storehouse-Consciousness)
- The Cosmic Unconscious—the principle of creativity, the moving force of the universe (*sunyata*).

Herrigel's "It" corresponds to the Cosmic Unconscious (or the infinite reality).

Furthermore, to use Muneyoshi (Soetsu) Yanagi's (1972/1989) account, "It" means the realm of the "Non-dual Entirety," as is shown in Eugen's phrases such as "Bow, arrow, goal and ego, all melt into one another, so that I can no longer separate them. And even the need to separate has gone." According to Yanagi, this is but a state of Enlightenment: "Enlightenment becomes synonymous with the realization of Non-dual Entirety, with abiding in undifferentiated integrity" (p. 128).

Then, out of "It" (the Cosmic Conscious or the Non-dual Entirety) the third phase of the way of art emerges—the stage of creation. The creation (artistic work and performance) flows directly from the infinite depth; in other words, the infinite reality manifests itself in the visible forms of art. With Suzuki (1959/1993, 242-243), "The Cosmic Unconscious is the principle of creativity.... All creative works of art ... come from the fountain-head of the Cosmic Unconscious." In terms of "Oriental [Eastern] Nothingness," Izutsu (1977/1982, 82) remarks:

> The Oriental Nothingness is not a purely negative ontological state of there being nothing. On the contrary, it is a plenitude of Being. It is ... so full that it can manifest itself as anything in the empirical dimension of our experience, as a crystallization of the whole spiritual energy contained therein.

Gustie Herrigel makes the same point: "He [the artist] himself lives and fashions his work from the 'formless Form.' The artist combines in himself the creative impulse with its realization, emptiness with full-ness" (1958/1974, 90). Eugen describes a master as follows:

> Every Master who practices an art molded by Zen is like a flash of lightening from the cloud of all-encompassing Truth. This Truth is present in the free movement of his spirit, and he meets it again, in "It," as his own original and nameless essence. He meets this essence over and over again as his own being's utmost possibilities, so that the Truth assumes for him—and for others through him—a thousand shapes and forms.

Centered in "It" (Emptiness or Nothingness), the artist creates an art work in spontaneity. At this stage, he or she no longer depends on the es-tablished patterns; instead, the art becomes a spontaneous expression of sheer freedom. Suzuki says, "The artist's world is one of free creation, and this can come only from intuitions directly and immediately rising from the isness of things" (1959/1993, 17). This is called the state of the "Master" (*meijin*).

However, what really matters in creation is not the artwork itself but the liberation of the artist from dualistic judgment, attachment, inten-tion, calculation, and purpose. This is called in Zen *muge.* According to Yanagi, "It means the state of liberation from all duality, a state where there is nothing to restrict or be restricted" (1972/1989, 130). *Muge,* or freedom, comes from the recognition of the non-dual reality. On the na-ture of "beauty" Yanagi makes a significant comment: "Beauty, then, ought to be understood as the beauty of liberation or freedom from im-pediment" (p. 130). In other words, "true beauty" has nothing to do with any relative standards or categories regarding the beauty and the ugly:

[F]rom the Buddhists' point of view, the "beauty" that simply stands
opposed to ugliness is not true beauty. It is no more than a relativistic,
dualistic idea. True beauty exists in the realm where there is no distinction between the beautiful and the ugly, a realm that is described as
"prior to beauty and ugliness" or as a state where "beauty and ugliness are as yet unseparated." (p. 130)

Thus, "true beauty"—real work or performance—comes into being in a
spontaneous way from the artist who abides in the non-dual deepest dimension "prior to beauty and ugliness"; "only the beauty of Non-dual
Entirety can be true" (p. 151). In this sense, Yanagi (1995) calls "true
beauty" alternately "the beauty of the non-dual" (*funibi*), "the beauty of
spontaneity" (*jizaibi*), or "the beauty of freedom" (*jiyubi*).[16]

Finally, it is also important to add that the art of the Master is no longer
separated from her or his everyday living. "The man, the art, the
work—it is all one" (E. Herrigel, 1953/1999, 45). In other words, living itself becomes an art. The art fundamentally transforms her or his life so
that the way of art can become the art of living. Everything in everyday
living is now opened up to the infinite depth and appears in the phase of
the universal reality. Everyday living becomes Enlightenment in action.
This is the ultimate goal of the way of art, for it is fundamentally the way
of self-cultivation.

QUESTIONS ABOUT CREATIVITY

The preceding discussion on the way of art will make clear important
aspects of the questions about creativity.[17] First, the way of art has nothing to do with creativity in problem-solving. It pays little attention to
each problem. On the contrary, it solves the problem of the "self." In the
Eastern perspective, the self is the fundamental difficulty which brings
about every other kind of problem. In this sense, the way of art is a way to
resolve the problem of the self. For example, as Eugen Herrigel says, in
the art of archery "fundamentally the marksman aims at himself and
may even succeed in hitting himself" (1953/1999, 4). Differently put, creativity in the way of art means a re-creation of the self.

Second, creativity in the way of art can to some extent be taught, but
this happens in the mode not of transmission or transaction but of transformation. In general, the way of art stresses the crucial importance of

the relationship between the master and the student. The master must be not only a skillful teacher but also an embodiment of the spirit of the art. The point in teaching is that the master helps the student realize the same spirit through spiritual communion, or "communication from heart to heart" (*ishin-denshin*) (G. Herrigel 1958/1974, 15). Spiritual communion between them plays the central part in the lessons. However, in the final stage, creativity can never be taught, because it becomes a direct and spontaneous manifestation of one's Enlightenment. When Eugen asked his master, "And who or what is this 'It'?" the master replied, "Once you have understood that, you will have no further need of me" (1953/1999, 52).

Third, creativity in the way of art is not necessarily age-related. Most ways allow anyone to start practice whenever he or she wants to learn it. But ideally, one should start learning from an early age. A famous instruction on age-related learning is found in Zeami's *Kadensho* (1408?) [Transmission of the Flower], which had long been a secret doctrine of the *No* play. Zeami, a remarkable master and a philosopher of the *No* play, used the metaphor of "flower" (*hana*) to describe the "seven ages of training" starting from the seven-year-old beginner through to the fifty-year-old mature artist (true flower) (Ze-ami 1968, 17-24). These stages illustrate a path to spiritual perfection of a person as well as perfect mastery of the art.

Fourth, creativity in the way of art is fundamentally spontaneous. Indeed, it appeals to patterns, but they basically serve to transform the egocentric attitude of the student so that he or she can eventually attain absolute freedom. The way of art is designed to tap a creative force hidden in the deepest layer of consciousness. If one masters an art, the art becomes an "artless art." Eugen says, "art becomes 'artless,' shooting becomes not-shooting, a shooting without bow and arrow" (1953/1999, pp. 5-6).

The ways of contemplation and art have long been practical forms of Eastern philosophy. In terms of holistic education, they can become integral parts of the practice of holistic education, essential contributions from Eastern philosophy to holistic education.[18]

More importantly, the Eastern way of art will require education itself
to be a "way" (*do*) in the same sense of the "way" of art. The way of art is
not only a section of holistic education practice but also a model for education as a whole.

NOTES

1. In Ken Wilber's (1983/1996, chap. 1) terms, "the spiritual eyesight" corresponds to "the
   eye of contemplation," and the normal or ordinary eyesight to the other two modes of
   seeing; "the eye of flesh" (perception of the external world of time and space) and "the
   eye of reason" (knowledge of the mind).

2. In this regard, to use Kathleen Kesson's (1994, 1997) terms, Eastern philosophy can be
   marked by "contemplative spirituality" or "process spirituality" rather than "religion."
   She says: "The important distinction here is that between spirituality as a dynamic, ex-
   ploratory *process* and religion as the structured *form* that emerges to contain, and to
   some extent control the process" (1997, 11); "Process spiritualities tend towards the
   mystical and the personal, while religion tends towards the social and the institutional.
   Process spirituality, with its emphasis on exploration, maintains the capacity to under-
   mine dogma and rigid faith systems" (p. 14).

3. Miller has provided an in-service program for teachers and professionals that includes
   courses entitled "The Teacher as a Contemplative Practitioner" and "Spirituality in Education" at the Ontario Institute for Studies in Education of the University of Toronto.
   Brown has created a Buddhist-inspired teacher training program in the department of
   Early Childhood Education at The Naropa University (Boulder, Colorado) that was
   founded in 1974 by Chögyam Trungpa.

4. Given the numerous techniques of meditation evolved in the East and the multitude of
   recent studies of them appearing in the West, it is neither possible nor necessary in this
   small study to detail the issues concerning the types of meditation, concrete techniques,
   physio-psychological effects, and other related matters. Some of the essential studies
   are found in the work of Naranjo and Ornstein (1971), Naranjo (1989/1990), Ornstein
   (1972/1975), LeShan (1974/1975), Goleman (1977/1988), Ram Dass (1978), Deikman
   (1982), Shapiro and Walsh (1984), Murphy and Donovan (1988), Murphy (1992), Tart
   (1975/1983), Wilber (1979/1985), and Wilber, Engler and Brown (1986).

5. Right mindfulness constitutes a part of the Eightfold Path, the Early Buddhist way of
   practice, which includes right view, right thinking, right mindfulness, right speech,
   right action, right diligence, right concentration, and right livelihood (see Thich Nhat
   Hanh 1998/1999, 49-118).

6. *Dhyana* is one of the Six Paramitas, the six basic Mahayana Buddhist practices, which include *dana* (giving), *shila* (precepts), *kshanti* (inclusiveness), *virya* (diligence), *dhyana*
   (meditation), and *prajina* (wisdom) (see Thich Nhat Hanh 1998/1999, 192-213).
   Nathaniel Needle (1999) has explored educational implications of these Six Paramitas.

7. The importance of contemplative education has been explored in both East and West. Though my studies focus on the Eastern traditions, Jacques Maritain (1962/1967), for instance, emphasizes the role of contemplation in the Christian tradition as follows. "[I]f the word 'contemplation' is taken in its original and simplest sense (to contemplate is simply to see and to enjoy seeing), leaving aside its highest—metaphysical or religious—connotations, it must be said that knowledge is contemplative in nature, and that education, in its final and highest achivements, tends to develop the contemplative capacity of the human mind. It does so ... in order that once man has reached a stage where the harmony of his inner energies has been brought to full completion, his action on the world and on the human community, and his creative power at the service of his fellow-men, may overflow from his contemplative contact with reality—both with the visible and invisible realities in the midst of which he lives and moves" (p. 54).

8. A main difference is that the framework of somatic education reaches the dimension of the cosmic reality yet mostly does not involve the deeper dimensions of the infinite reality and the universal reality, but, on the other hand, meditation works on the body-mind in order to explore those deeper dimensions.

9. As for the relationship between Alexander and Dewey, see Jones (1976/1979).

10. It is worth noting that Otto Friedrich Bollnow (1959/1977) revealed pedagogical implications of "discontinuous" existential moments occurring in life, including awakening. Yet his discussion did not include the contemplative aspect of awakening.

11. When I visited Brockwood Park School in England, one of the schools founded by Krishnamurti, I realized that this school has tried to implement what Krishnamurti taught in terms of awareness. Their curriculum includes courses called Self-Observation and Inward Journey.

12. Although Plato's own philosophy has differed from Socrates' teachings, I think that his definition of education as "an art of turning around" given in the *Republic* may resonate with the work of Socrates. Plato states, "the instrument with which each learns ... must be turned around from that which is *coming into being* together with the whole soul until it is able to endure looking at that which *is* and the brightest part of that which *is*" (Bloom 1968 197). Education is an art that induces a "turning around" in the easiest and most effective way.

13. A large portion of the following discussion appeared in my article "Holistic Education in Japan: Three Approaches" published in *Encounter* 11(3), 1998. It is reprinted here by permission of Holistic Education Press with considerable modifications.

14. The way of art includes tea ceremony (*sado*), flower arrangement (*kado*), black-and-white ink-painting (*suibokuga*), gardening, architecture, calligraphy (*shodo*), poetry (*kado*), *Haiku*, No play (*nogaku*), and some of the martial arts (*budo*) such as archery (*kyudo*) and swordmanship (*kendo*). Most of them have a history of over several hundred years and developed their own systems of practice. According to Shin'ichi Hisamatsu (1971), Zen aesthetics has "the Seven Characteristics," which includes asymmetry (*fukinsei*), simplicity (*kanso*), austere sublimity or lofty dryness (*kokou*), natural-

ness (*shizen*), subtle profundity or deep reserve (*yugen*), freedom from attachment (*datsu-zoku*), tranquillity (*seijaku*) (pp. 28-38).

15. Dürckheim (1960/1974, 1962) gives us excellent accounts of the Eastern way of self-cultivation.

16. Importantly enough, in his attempt to develop "Buddhist aesthetics," Yanagi found that not only the great works of the talented artists but also the ordinary goods made by the ordinary anonymous crafts workers often show the true beauty of spontaneity and freedom. Yanagi maintained that the crafts workers had advantages in attaining the nondual state; unlike the artists with ample knowledge and the strong ego, the crafts workers were at their time usually ignorant, naive-minded people, not obsessed by the values of the beautiful and the ugly. In addition to this, the very nature of craft did not demand that they express individualistic components in the work, for the goods made by them were used in folks' daily lives. Given these conditions, the crafts workers did not develop egocentric attitudes towards the work and so entered a nondual state. With this finding and his involvement in Pure Land Buddhism, Yanagi identified the way of the artist with "the Way of Self-Power" or "the Way of Hardship," and the way of the craft worker with "the Way of Other Power" or "the Easy Way." The Herrigels described the former way, yet Yanagi's emphasis was on the latter. Yanagi's ultimate concern was with "the Pure Land of Beauty" in which ordinary people like crafts workers can be saved. We need to embrace both ways of Self-Power and Other Power if we have a comprehensive look at the way of art.

17. Originally, these questions were put forth by Professor Emeritus John A. Eisenberg in his course entitled "Creativity and Education" held at OISE/UT, which I attended in the summer of 1997.

18. In particular, Shuji Wada (1995, chap. 11) recognizes the importance of the art of tea ceremony as an Eastern model of holistic education, which was originally refined by Shin'ichi Hisamatsu as "the tea of the heart" (*shincha*).

Society and Eastern Philosophy

FROM PERSONAL TO SOCIAL TRANSFORMATION

The Eastern way of action seems to be quite different from the Western way of action. The Eastern way is mostly concerned with the "inner" transformation of individuals through contemplative practices, yet it has paid little attention to the "outer" transformation of social systems. On the other hand, the Western way of action is much more oriented towards the outer visible transformation of social systems through social criticism, activism, and engagement. It attempts to create a society where social injustice is solved by our conscious efforts. Seen from this perspective, the Eastern way of action must appear to have nothing to do with a meaningful social transformation. Indeed, Eastern philosophy and its practices have rarely been action-oriented, but rather they have celebrated the way of *inaction* (*non-action*). And this apparent passivity in social activism seems to have contributed to the preservation of the existing social order.[1]

Contemporary holistic education (and the holistic movement in general) finds itself in a similar situation to the Eastern way of action. As a general characteristic, it tends to stress the inner aspect of personal transformation more than the transformation of social systems. Therefore, even its proponents have been critical of this tendency. Ron Miller

(1993b), for example, regards the "popular" holistic movement as a "subjectivist" position:

> A primary flaw in popular holistic thinking is its idealist, subjectivist, solipsistic epistemology; rather than linking mind and world, subject and object in a larger ecology of meaning (the aim of a genuine holism), this subjectivist holism reduces concrete historical and cultural issues to phenomena of personal consciousness. (p. 14)

Kathleen Kesson (1991, 1993, 1996) has also criticized holistic education (holism) as an idealist, subjectivist, and visionary position devoid of critical, historical, political, and socio-economical perspectives. For example, she says:

> Holism ... is a somewhat amorphous activist movement that tends to be nontheoretical and relatively acritical, but which has an almost magical faith in the cultural transformation that will result when sufficient numbers of people experience a "shift" in consciousness. (1993, 96)

"Holistic thinkers," in her view, "have a powerful transformative vision, but generally fail to turn their critical attention upon themselves" (1991, 48). Therefore, Kesson strongly requires that holistic education be informed by critical theory. "I strongly believe that holism, both as a social movement and a theoretical perspective, would be enriched by the inclusion of new ideas from the sociology of knowledge, feminist thought, and critical theory" (1993, 95).

In the same vein, Jeffrey Kane and Dale Snauwaert (1998) have raised awareness that "holistic education must be 'socially engaged'" to counter "the debilitating effect of social injustice in all of its various dimensions" (p. 3). David Purpel (1996) has called for "a *truly* holistic education—one that seeks to integrate the inner self with the outer self and thereby connect the personal with our social, cultural, moral, political, and economic contexts" (p. 26). These claims not only encourage holistic education to be more socially concerned but also require it to become an effective agent of social transformation.

From the Western point of view, the inner transformation of the self should be linked with the outer transformation of social systems. Here is a place where the Eastern and the Western ways of action can meet. In reality, we are witnessing the emergence of new branches such as "deep ecology" and "Engaged Buddhism" that contain both components.[2] To use Leonard Angel's (1994) terms, these phenomena exemplify meetings of "Enlightenment East" and "Enlightenment West." While "Enlightenment East" is centered around "mystical awakening," "Enlightenment West" is a thought in which "the central value is the humanistic pursuit of social and individual well-being, justice, and scientific rationalism" (p. 3). Angel calls for an integration of both ways as follows:

> The Enlightenment West project of making scientific and social prog-
> ress must be informed by Enlightenment East mysticism. And devel-
> oping Enlightenment East mystical doctrines, practices and
> institutions must be informed by Enlightenment West values of clarity
> in thought, scientific knowledge, and awareness of social justice. (p. 4)

To use Donald Evans' (1993) terminology (he uses it within a discussion of Christianity), the Eastern way may be called "contemplative spirituality," and the Western way, "social-activist spirituality." He maintains that "contemplative spirituality needs to be balanced and corrected by social activist spirituality" (p. 226). The movements of deep ecology and Engaged Buddhism may be forms of Enlightenment East and West, and of contemplative and social-activist spirituality.

One of the basic assumptions of these movements is that the inner transformation of the self leads to a social transformation. For example, as discussed before (Chapter 3), relying on the Buddhist ideas, Joanna Macy (1991b) refers to the transformation of the self from "the ego-self" to "the ecological self or the eco-self"—the self that arises through a deep realization of interconnectedness with all beings. Then she claims:

> Now the sense of an encompassing self, that deep identity with the
> wider reaches of life, is a motivation for action. It is a source of courage
> that helps us stand up to the powers that are still, through force of iner-
> tia, working for the destruction of our world. This expanded sense of
> self serves to empower effective action. (pp. 184-185)

A deep sense of interconnectedness through an inner transformation will lead to action on the social plane. Likewise, of Engaged Buddhism Kenneth Kraft (1985/1988, xiii) says: "The touchstone for engaged Buddhists is a vision of interdependence, in which the universe is experienced as an organic whole, every 'part' affecting every other 'part.'"

Then he remarks that "awareness of interconnectedness fosters a sense of universal responsibility" (p. xiv).

In the field of contemporary holistic education, a similar idea has been put forth by John Miller (1988/1996, 26): "The realization of the fundamental unity of existence leads to social action to counter injustice and human suffering." In the same way, *Education 2000* says:

> By fostering a deep sense of connection to others and to the Earth in all its dimensions, holistic education encourages a sense of responsibility to self, to others, and to the planet. We believe that this responsibility is not a burden, but rather arises out of a sense of connection and empowerment. (Flake 1993, 246)

This means that an inner transformation for interconnectedness will bring about a social transformation.

Henry Weerasinghe's (1992) notion of the Buddhist "peace education" agrees with the position of contemporary holistic education in this respect. In his notion, the Buddhist peace education begins with cultivating "inner peace": "The teachings of the Buddha may be regarded as peace pedagogies. Education in its true sense is rooted in inner peace" (p. 77). The "inner peace" can be cultivated by "meditation": "The peace pedagogies of the Buddha are based on a practical educational principle commonly known as meditation" (p. 74). Then he refers to the social implication of inner peace:

> Buddhist theory of education takes its shape from the key Buddhist concept of peace (*santi*). It is stressed that peace must originate from the individual himself and from there it should radiate into man's social milieu. In more precise terms, peace in society becomes a reality only when man has learnt how to experience it himself. (p. xvi)

Deep ecology, Engaged Buddhism, and contemporary holistic education are based on the fundamental assumption that out of the inner transformation of the self, which realizes the interconnectedness of all beings, may arise a meaningful social action or engagement to transform the social systems. This assumption would make sense if we recognize that the realization of interconnectedness presumably changes our ways of thinking and feeling to cultivate such qualities as compassion, solidarity, responsibility, and energy, which would encourage authentic activities to take place.

The association of the inner with the outer transformation is indeed an integration of the Eastern and Western ways of action, which can benefit both sides; it gives the Eastern way of action a path of self-expression in social circumstances, and it provides the Western way of action with a deeper foundation of action in which social action is grounded.

Having said all that, however, I think that there is another possibility for exploring the social implications of Eastern philosophy. In reality, the first direction mentioned above—I do not doubt its importance—has been mostly explored by Buddhist activists in the West under the Western framework of social action where "action" means a visible, active engagement in social problems. From this perspective, the Eastern way of action seem to be actionless self-indulgence. It seems that, without the strong influence of this Western perspective, those movements of deep ecology and Engaged Buddhism would have never appeared.

However, it is the same perspective that prevents us from becoming aware of the deeper, true aspect of the Eastern way of action. From the Eastern perspectives, the social implications of action are more multidimensional; that is, not only evident, social activism but also deeper invisible dimensions have relevant social implications.

Furthermore, as a crucial problem, we need to recognize that the whole discussion of inner-and-outer transformations seems to be based on a subject-object dichotomy. In spite of the effort of holistic thinking not to lapse into a dualistic idea, here most of us easily accept such a dualism. In this sense particularly, we need to explore deeper foundation of action that is liberated from dualistic thinking.

Eastern philosophy requires us to examine the concept of social action and to expand it so as to encompass the deeper aspects of action. In other words, just as the Eastern way of action needs to expand its boundary to incorporate Western social activism for its own transformation, so *the Western way of action needs to deepen its insight into the deeper dimensions of action rather than social activism for its own transformation.* In the following part, I will illuminate social implications of the Eastern way of action.

Two Concepts of Freedom

A difference between the Eastern and Western ways of action is revealed in their notions of *freedom.* Although both ways seek after freedom, their implications are quite different. To elucidate differences between them, let us compare critical theory with Zen Buddhism.

Underlying the ideas of critical theory are assumptions that the external social system has an objective reality; the states of human existence are basically determined by the objective reality of society; the causes which prevent us from enjoying freedom but instead create injustice and suffering fundamentally stem from the social structure; social reality is a human-made system, and therefore we can change it by our conscious commitment in social criticism and activism. In this regard, the call for freedom takes the form of political struggle whose effort is to reform or transform the social systems, in which education is seen as an instrument to fulfill social criticism and activism.

An example can be found in Paulo Freire's ideas of the "pedagogy of the oppressed." Freire (1970/1996) defines freedom as a liberation of both the oppressed and the oppressors from the oppressive situation of society, and as a transformation from "dehumanization" to "humanization."

> To surmount the situation of oppression, people must first critically
> recognize its causes, so that through transforming action they can cre-
> ate a new situation, one which makes possible the pursuit of a fuller
> humanity. (p. 29)

To transform the world, "praxis" is needed that is "reflection and action" (p. 33): "[T]he oppressed unveil the world of oppression and through the praxis commit themselves to its transformation" (p. 36). The struggle for freedom can eventually lead to the production of "a new man" who is liberated from the oppressor-oppressed contradiction. However, this is a difficult task for the oppressed who have internalized the value system of the oppression. In this regard, the pedagogy of the oppressed serves to help the oppressed realize their situation: "The pedagogy of the oppressed is an instrument for their critical discovery that both they and their oppressors are manifestation of dehumanization" (p. 30). Education thus becomes a "practice of freedom." In particular, Freire introduced the idea of "problem-posing education," or a "liberating education," as opposed to what he called the "banking education," or a conservative education that served to perpetuate the oppressive situation in both education and society. The problem-posing education "strives for the *emergence* of consciousness and *critical intervention* in reality" (p. 62). In this way, Freire's ideas of the pedagogy of the oppressed call for a transformation of the objective social reality by raising critical consciousness of the oppressed and involving them with social action.[3]

On the other hand, Eastern philosophy has developed a totally different view of freedom or "liberation." In the East, liberation, diversely called *moksha* in Hinduism, *nirvana* in Early Buddhism, and *satori* in Japanese Zen Buddhism, has been regarded as the highest aim of life. For example, D. T. Suzuki (1956/1996) characterizes Zen as follows: "Zen moves along with infinite possibilities; Zen enjoys unlimited freedom because Zen is freedom itself" (p. 265). In another place, Suzuki (1959/1993, 5-6) remarks:

> Zen is discipline in enlightenment. Enlightenment means emancipation. And emancipation is no less than freedom. We talk very much these days about all kinds of freedom, political, economic, and otherwise, but these freedom are not at all real. As long as they are on the plane of relativity, the freedoms or liberties we glibly talk about are far from being such. The real freedom is the outcome of enlightenment. When a man realizes this, in whatever situation he may find himself he is always free in his inner life, for that pursues its own line of action.

Suzuki's "freedom" is quite different from Freire's libertarian "freedom," for it means "absolute" freedom released from any conditions, as distinct from "relative" freedom conditioned by the social systems. We have called those who have realized absolute freedom the Eastern Self (Chapter 2). Deeply rooted in Emptiness and Nothingness, the Eastern Self is free from attachment of any sort, even from Enlightenment.

THE SOCIAL IMPLICATIONS
OF THE EASTERN WAY OF ACTION

Next, we turn to social implications of the Eastern way of action, which are explored multidimensionally in the twofold movement of seeking and returning; in other words, what are the social implications of contemplation and Enlightenment?

Contemplation as Social Criticism: At first, the way of contemplation is a radical form of social criticism. The view that separates personal transformation from social transformation and then tries to associate them is fundamentally misleading, because it unconsciously assumes that there are two domains of transformation. However, in reality, the self and society can never be separated; society is *within* ourselves; we are socially conditioned in the body-mind structure, and in this sense "we are the society." The way of contemplation is an attempt to disidentify us with social conditionings to explore the deeper dimensions of reality. It is an act of *social* transformation and also a *radical* criticism of society, for it seeks after emancipation from the social domination built in the body-mind system from within.

Alan Watts (1961/1975) captures the essential aspect of the Eastern way of "liberation" when he says, "the main function of a way of liberation is to release the individual from his 'hypnosis' by certain social institutions" (pp. 46-47). Thich Nhat Hanh (1987) refers to this point as follows:

> The kind of suffering that you carry in your heart, that is society itself. You bring that with you, you bring society with you. You bring all of us with you. When you meditate, it is not just for yourself, you do it for the whole society. You seek solutions to your problems not only for yourself, but for all of us. (p. 47)

Furthermore, Krishnamurti sees an identity of the self with society, which he has often called "you are the world." "The world is not separate from us; we are the world, and our problems are the world's problem" (1954/1975, 42). He goes on to say that "revolution in society must begin with the inner, psychological transformation of the individual" (1954/1975, 38); "[T]his society can be changed only when the individual human being really transforms himself radically" (1991b, 7). This is not to say that changes in the individual later lead to a social change at large, but that the inner transformation itself is immediately the transformation of society, for "[t]he outer *is* the inner. The inner *is* the outer. There is no difference between the outer and the inner; they are totally related to each other" (1991b, 10). If we really understand that "we are the world," we can realize the social implication of contemplation.

Action as Contemplation: From a contemplative point of view, so-called "social action" can be a contemplation, because *every action can be a contemplative path.* The way of contemplation can encompass the entire realm of everyday living other than specific fields such as meditation and art. The idea of "way" delineated in the way of art (Chapter 6) suggests this possibility. Martin Buber's (1960) notion of "the way" is also important here:

> There is no separation within the human world between the high and the low; to each the highest is open, each life has its access to reality, each nature its eternal right, from each thing a way leads to God, and each way that leads to God is *the* way. (p. 149)

As far as "social action" is concerned, it can serve as the art of awareness, or the way of self-cultivation. This has been explored by Ram Dass (Ram Dass and Gorman 1985; Ram Dass and Bush 1992), who has initiated several social actions such as the prison project and the dying project on the basis of the tradition of *karma yoga,* or the path of action. According to his definition of "the path of action," "[t]his spiritual path uses as its vehicle for transformation our actions themselves; that is, we gain internal freedom through external action" (1992, 134).

Among all the possible actions, Ram Dass highlights the action of service or helping others. The action of service becomes a form of contemplation that requires "the inner work" as well as external action—"the inner work, the work on ourselves, which is the foundation of all true service, and the only way, finally, to maintain energy and inspiration" (1985, 211). In other words, as "at the deepest level we help through who we *are*" (p. 227), the work of service and the inner work become one and the same thing. "We work on ourselves, then, in order to help others. And we help others as a vehicle for working on ourselves" (p. 227). In the reciprocal way the work and the contemplative practice make a seamless fabric.

> It [service] is a vehicle through which we reach a deeper understanding of life. Each step we take, each moment in which we grow toward a greater understanding of unity, steadily transforms us into instruments of that help which truly heals. (p. 224)

In Buber's (1958/1988, 225) impressive phrase: "You cannot really love God if you do not love men, and you cannot really love men if you do not love God."

Ram Dass finds an essential role of awareness in the work of service that enables us to become disidentified with our self-image as the "actor" or the "doer." In awareness we witness what we are doing moment to moment without attachment. "Quite remarkable, moreover, we also notice that while our identification as the doer is falling away, *much is still being accomplished*. We're still setting about our work, perhaps even more productively" (1985, 195). If the actor or the doer falls away through awareness, the primary obstacle to compassionate actions is removed. Then action becomes a spontaneous expression from the compassionate heart. In this way, Ram Dass finds stages in the transformative process in the path of action:

> In the beginning, I felt that I was doing it. Then I felt that I was observing it. And now I sometimes find myself absent and the compassionate action just occurring, rising out of the momentary conditions of the situation, having little to do with me at all. (1992, 149)

The point is that *any* action can be a contemplation. A classical example is found in the *Bhagavad Gita*, in which Krishna encourages Arjuna to fight in the war. From the viewpoint of social justice, this may be judged immoral. However, as Thomas Merton (1995, 50) says, "The *Gita* is not a justification of war," but the main point is on another dimension—the contemplative aspect of action. The text reads, "without attachment, perform always the work that has to be done, for man attains to the highest by doing work without attachment" (Radhakrishnan 1948/1973, 138). "Without attachment" means to enhance awareness while one is doing work. Merton says, "The *Gita* is saying that even in what appears to be most 'unspiritual' one can act with pure intentions and thus be guided by Krishna consciousness" (1995, 51). According to Ram Dass (1992, 142),

> In the *Bhagavad Gita* we are enjoined to "be not attached to the fruits of the action." After all, if we are performing the action appropriate for us at this moment, doing it as skillfully as we are able, and attempting to use it as a means of awakening, then we have done what we can to realize the immediate fruits of the action.

This does not, of course, do away with moral judgment of the fruits of the action, but it is equally important to recognize the contemplative dimension in every kind of action.

Human life is composed of countless actions that are related with each other, and to do them in a contemplative way is to transform society. Contemplation in everyday living is a path of social transformation. The true meaning of Engaged Buddhism is this. According to Thich Nhat Hanh (1987, 53),

> Engaged Buddhism does not only mean to use Buddhism to solve social and political problems, protesting against the bombs, and protesting against social injustice. First of all we have to bring Buddhism into our daily lives.

Nhat Hanh underlines the importance of "being peace" of the individual in the peace movement. "Peace work means, first of all, being peace" (p. 80). If we separate peace movement from other actions of everyday living, it would bring about another fragmentation and conflict.

As we have seen, the social implications of the Eastern way of action are found in contemplation itself on the one hand, and every action including "social action" can be a contemplative practice on the other hand. The point is that the contemplative action can disclose the deeper dimensions of reality through enhancing disidentification with the social reality. A society will be transformed in this multidimensional realization of the deeper dimensions of reality.

THE ACTION OF ENLIGHTENMENT

Now let us see the social implications of Enlightenment that reveal themselves in the returning path. If Enlightenment were completely isolated from the social reality, it would be nonsense to ask for its social implications. But that is not the case, for those who are enlightened never disappear in cessation but ever dwell *in* a society, albeit their existence has been totally transformed in realizing the infinite reality.

Enlightenment changes the perception of reality, which may be represented, to borrow Evans' (1993) conception, as "appreciative awareness"—an aspect of what he calls "contemplative spirituality." In his definition,

> Contemplative spirituality includes an appreciative awareness that everything is okay as it is—indeed, not merely okay but wondrous and radiant and harmonious and good—in an ultimate sense of "good" which transcends our usual dichotomy between good and evil. (p. 221)

Mahayana Buddhism has called the appreciative awareness *tathata*, or "Suchness," which is paired with *sunyata*, or Emptiness. While in

Emptiness absolute negation of all beings happens, in Suchness everything is reborn and affirmed again as it is. This affirmation is not a relative but an *absolute affirmation* through absolute negation. After Suzuki
(1956/1996, 263), "*Tathata* is the viewing of things as they are: it is an affirmation through and through."

> If *sunyata* denies or rejects everything, *tathata* accepts and upholds ev-
> erything; the two concepts may be considered as opposing each other,
> but it is the Buddhist idea that they are not contradictory.... In truth,
> *tathata* is *sunyata*, and *sunyata* is *tathata*; things are *tathata* because of
> their being *sunyata*. (p. 264)

Keiji Nishitani (1982) makes the same point: "Being is only being if it is
one with emptiness. Everything that is stands on its own home-ground
only on the field of emptiness, where it is itself in its own suchness" (p.
124). In our concept, Suchness is another name for the universal reality.

According to Toshihiko Izutsu (1981b), a being appearing in Suchness
is "physical sunyata" as the manifestation of the "metaphysical
sunyata." The physical sunyata is not the same as "the empirical world"
seen in an ordinary perception.

> There is a profound and essential difference between the original em-
> pirical world as seen through the eyes of ordinary people and the em-
> pirical world once dead and now reborn before the eyes of the sage.
> For the latter is still permeated by the *sunyata* which is now positively
> functioning as physical *sunyata* as distinguished from the metaphysi-
> cal sunyata which it has gone through at the previous stage. The em-
> pirical world as it is reflected in the consciousness of a sage is the
> metaphysical *sunyata* phenomenalized, appearing in the form of
> physical things. (pp. 365-366)

The absolute affirmation in Suchness means that everything is fundamentally liberated from relative, conventional values or judgments, for
they have disappeared in the absolute negation of Emptiness. Emanci-
pated from relative distinctions, everything rests in Suchness as it is.
Nobuhiro Hayashi (1993) calls it "ontological peace," in which "the
trans-existential consciousness totally affirms all that which is as it is" (p.
159, trans. Nakagawa). The "ontological peace" has nothing to do with a
psychological harmony or a political peace but refers to absolute accep-
tance of all that which is as it is without such dualism as good or bad,

right or wrong. It is an appreciative awareness of "is-ness" of all that which is prior to the interventions of judgment. In the "ontological peace," one is no longer bound by any duality, oppositions, or conflicts found in the conventional reality, and in this sense absolutely free even in the midst of them.

The action of Enlightenment occurs in this ontological peace, or absolute freedom, in which no action is bound by conventional restrictions. It does not always follow pre-established rules, as embodied in the unexpected actions of Ch'an/Zen masters. It is neither predictable nor predetermined, let alone ordered or controlled by others. Rather, it is a sheer spontaneous action, which has been called *tzu-jan* in Taoism or *muge* or *jizai* in Japanese Zen Buddhism. Watts (1961/1975) regards this aspect as playfulness. As opposed to a "society" controlled by social rules, "the world is play" (p. 24); "the world has no *fixed* order" (p. 27). The liberated one is "the artist" who plays in this world. "He [the 'liberative artist'] is the artist in whatever he does, not just in the sense of doing it beautifully, but in the sense of *playing* it…. Whatever he does, he *dances* it" (p. 183). Playfulness is a basic feature found in the action of Enlightenment which correctly corresponds to the Nietzschean "child" (Chapter 5).

Enlightenment may find any form of action as its manifestation, whether it is everyday ordinary action or social action. A social action in Enlightenment may be remarkably different from social actions in a conventional sense, because it comes from the absolute affirmation in Suchness that has transcended the relative, conventional judgments. Presumably, the enlightened ones enhance their intuition and insight into the heart of the issues in question, and here discernment arises which will show them possible ways of action. Liberated from conventional judgments, they can discern what is with clarity in accordance with the "natural" order of things. This impartial view does not necessarily bring about a degeneration of committed action; rather, as they are no longer captured by their own egocentric components, it is expected that their commitments may become much more intensified. However, this intensity would always be one with playfulness and freedom.

At this point, Suzuki's conception of "differentiation undifferentiated" (*mufunbetsu no funbetsu*) provides an explanation of discernment. It means that differentiation needs to be once negated in Emptiness to turn into the undifferentiated. Then the undifferentiated is to be differentiated in Suchness. Suchness is the dimension of "differentiation undifferentiated." According to Suzuki (1956/1996), in "differentiation undifferentiated,"

> the whole is intuited together with its parts; here the undifferentiated whole comes along with its infinitely differentiated, individualized parts. The whole is seen here differentiating itself in its parts, not in a pantheistic or immanentist way. The whole is not lost in its parts, nor does individuation lose sight of the whole. The One is the all without going out of itself, and each one of the infinitely varied and variable objects surrounding us embodies the One, while retaining each its individuality. (pp. 272-273)

"Differentiation undifferentiated" refers to the nature of discernment arising in Suchness. It is in this contradictory identity of undifferentiated continuum and differentiation that each action comes to take a form.

Suzuki's concept of "differentiation undifferentiated" has its precedent in the epistemology of the Yogacara school in Mahayana Buddhism, which has captured discernment arising in Suchness as "the knowledge acquired subsequently" (*tat-prsthalabdha-jnana*). The Yogacara epistemology classifies knowledge into three levels. The first is the discriminative knowledge on the preparatory stage of the seeking path (*prayogika-jnana*). The second is the non-discriminative wisdom (*nirvikalpa-jnana*) attained in Emptiness. The third level of knowledge arises in the returning phase, subsequent to the experience of the non-discriminative wisdom. According to Gadjin Nagao (1991, 223), "*[t]at-prsthalabdha-jnana*, the knowledge acquired subsequently, is obtained from and arises from non-discriminative knowledge." The subsequent knowledge is a discriminative knowledge rooted in the non-discriminative wisdom. As Nagao states, the action of Enlightenment takes place in accordance with this subsequent knowledge. "[I]t is exactly this knowledge that the Enlightened One must employ as the 'descent' from the *dharmadhatu* and that is made to work in this world for the purpose of benefiting others" (p. 224).

It is also helpful to see Wilber's (1997) discussion on what happens to the body-mind existence after Enlightenment. He says that "you will arise, from the ground of ever-present awareness, and you will embody any of the highest possibilities of that ground" (p. 297). He suggests that an embodiment may occur in relation to "the native dispositions and particular talents of your own individual bodymind" (p. 299). At the bottom of consciousness, you are totally released from any restriction; however, in the phase of embodiment, "you will manifest certain qualities, qualities inherent in intrinsic Spirit, and qualities colored by the dispositions of your own bodymind and its particular talents" (p. 300). This illustrates how differentiation of the undifferentiated can take place in accordance with the dispositions or talents of the individuals, which are no longer restrictions but rather gateways to the phenomenal plane.

History in the East has shown us that a large number of the enlightened ones have become spiritual teachers or masters to help students attain Awakening. This is undoubtedly a remarkable form of social engagement that has emerged in the East. Their styles of teaching have varied due to their dispositions and talents,[4] but, more importantly, their *presence* has helped students awaken to their Atman or Buddhahood or the selfless Self. When asked by a disciple "Does my Realization help others?" Ramana Maharshi (1972/1988) replied as follows:

> Yes, and it is the best help that you can possibly render to others. Those who have discovered great truths have done so in the still depths of the Self. But really there are no "others" to be helped. For the Realized Being sees only the Self.... The realized One does not see the world as different from himself. (pp. 63-64)

It is this Self-to-Self communion that can eventually bring about students' awakening to their own Self. In other words, through their work as teachers, they have served as "openings" through which the deepest reality has revealed itself in our society. As Phiroz Mehta (1989, 75) says, "Since the person in holistic consciousness is at home in the context of infinity and eternity, he can act as a conduit for the healing or whole-making power of the Primordial Creative Energy."

However, we need to understand that the action of Enlightenment does not always find itself in extraordinary actions but rather in ordinary actions of everyday living. There is no difference of value between any forms of action; *no action is special in Emptiness, every action is special in Suchness.* Zen has stressed this aspect in its appreciation of everyday living. Yun Men's renowned phrase in the *Blue Cliff Record,* "Every day is a good day" (Cleary and Cleary 1977/1992, 37), relates to this. In Ho Koji's words, "How wondrous this, how miraculous! / I carry fuel, I draw water" (cited in Suzuki 1959/1993, 16). The *Wumenguan* has a story as follows:

> A monk asked Zhaozhou, "I have just joined the community, and I request the teacher's instruction."
> Zhaozhou inquired, "Have you had your breakfast gruel yet?"
> The monk said, " I have had my gruel."
> Zhaozhou said, "Then go wash your bowl."
> That monk had an insight. (Cleary 1993, 39)

The heart of Zen teaching lies not in a special act but in a very ordinary activity like carrying water or washing a bowl. As Suzuki (1972/1994, 12) emphasizes, "Zen is the living, Zen is life, and the living is Zen." If we make a special attachment to something in our lives, we are bound to go astray into judgment. Lin-chi says that "the Dharma of the buddhas calls for no special undertakings. Just act ordinary, without trying to do anything particular. Move your bowels, piss, get dressed, eat your rice, and if you get tired, then lie down" (Watson 1993, 31); "The man of value is the one who has nothing to do. Don't try to do something special, just act ordinary" (p. 29).

This "ordinariness" arises in Suchness. Every "ordinary" action is equally important because it reveals the universal reality in Suchness. For example, the great Zen master Bankei (1622-1693), who has realized Enlightenment as "the Unborn," says: "The man of the Unborn abides at the *source* of all buddhas. That which is unborn is the source of all things, the starting point of all things" (Haskel 1984/1989, 5). Suzuki (1972/1994) comments on Bankei's Unborn as follows:

> The Unborn was the content of Bankei's satori which sprang up from his whole being, and enveloped it, so that he felt as if he were living in and with the Unborn all the time. Every moment of his life was the expression of the Unborn. (p. 122)

Finally, we need to recognize that the agent of action no longer exists in the action of Enlightenment, for the selfless-Self comes in the place of the ego. There is no "doer." Ramana Maharshi (1972/1988) says as follows:

> As the activities of the wise man exist only in the eyes of others and not
> in his own, although he may be accomplishing immense tasks, he re-
> ally does nothing.... [H]e knows the truth that all activities take place
> in his mere presence and that he does nothing. Hence he will remain as
> the silent witness of all the activities taking place. (p. 29)

Actions continue to arise, but the empty center of action remains still, ir-
relevant to apparent activities. In silence everything happens and nothing is done. This is what the Taoist concept of "non-action" (*wu-wei*)
means. In Lao Tzu's words: "The best action is free from marks" (Chang
1975, 79); "He [the wise] completes all things / Without action" (p. 129).
In accordance with *Tao*, the highest action naturally takes place in non-
action.

THE WAY OF COMPASSION

The Eastern way of action has culminated in the way of compassion
(*karuna*) developed in Mahayana Buddhism. Compassion is the altruistic aspect of Enlightenment, which arises in the returning phase of practice. It has been looked upon as the final goal of the Buddhist practice (of
bodhisattvas) by Mahayana thinkers.[5] Even one's Enlightenment has to
be sought for this ultimate end. Enlightenment brings about a realization
that every being is the same manifestation of the infinite reality, or the
universal reality, which transforms one's concern for others. Wilber
(1996) describes it as follows: "With the supreme identity, you are established in radical Freedom, it is true, but that Freedom *manifests* as compassionate activity, as agonizing concern. The Form of Freedom is
sorrow, unrelenting worry for those struggling to awaken" (pp. 316-
317). Together with "wisdom" (*prajna*), compassion underpins the
whole edifice of Mahayana Buddhism; that is, wisdom is the ultimate insight disclosed in Enlightenment, and compassion is the energy flowing
out from the Enlightenment.[6]

It would not be so absurd to view this Buddhist concept of compassion as a fundamental concept of education. His Holiness, the Dalai
Lama (1999), for example, highlights the importance of cultivating "an
open heart" and "a good heart" in the present situation of education and
calls for "a sense of caring or compassion, forgiveness and loving-kind-
ness" (p. 87). Also, Gisho Saiko (1988, 1995) has developed "Buddhist

counseling" based on Shin Buddhism, which, as we shall see later, gives us an example of compassionate education.

Furthermore, the way of compassion represents the Eastern view of the teacher. John Miller (1981, 1993a), for example, has identified "the holistic teacher" with "the compassionate teacher": "Holistic teachers are both authentic and compassionate. In other words, they are genuine individuals who also care deeply about other human beings" (1993a, 32). The following part will explore some aspects of compassion in relation to "caring," a key concept of contemporary holistic education, to clarify educational implications of compassion and to deepen the meaning of caring in the Buddhist perspective.

THE IDEA OF CARING

The idea of caring has attracted increasing attention from educational thinkers and educators, who think that it could break through the predicaments caused by modern education. For example, inspired by Montessori's work at *"Casa dei Bambini"* (the Children's Home), Jane Roland Martin (1992) has advocated the idea of the "Schoolhome" that emphasizes domesticity and the curriculum of "the three Cs" including care as well as concern and connection. Also, based on Daniel Goleman's idea of emotional intelligence, the projects of "Social and Emotional Learning" (SEL) are trying to foster students' social and emotional competence and life skills. SEL puts forth three major goals that include caring as well as knowledge and responsibility (e.g., Elias et al. 1997).

Nel Noddings (1984, 1992) is the foremost proponent of caring in education. She requires that schooling be based on caring, because caring as one of the "fundamental human needs" (1992, xi) has crucially been ignored in our modern life: "The need for care in our present culture is acute" (1992, xi); "Many of our schools are in what might be called a crisis of caring" (1984, 181). She describes the objective of schooling as follows:

> I will argue that the first job of the schools is to care for our children. We should educate all our children not only for competence but also for caring. Our aim should be to encourage the growth of competent, caring, loving, and lovable people. (1992, xiv)

Noddings holds that caring is not a part of education but education is included in caring, for, she thinks, it provides a broader foundation on which education can be based. She says, "when we look at 'pedagogical caring' we shall begin not with pedagogy but with caring. Then we shall see what *form* caring takes in the teaching function" (1984, 70). This suggests a radical transformation of education in which the entire activity of education is reorganized so as to foster caring in schools. In this context, the teacher becomes the "one-caring" or "caregiver" rather than the one-teaching. The relationship between teacher and student becomes an encounter between the one-caring and the "cared-for." "I am first and foremost one-caring and, second, enactor of specialized functions. As teacher, I am, first, one-caring" (1984, 176).

"Caring" was first discussed by Martin Heidegger (1996) in his *Being and Time* as a philosophical concept that characterizes the fundamental structure of human existence. Heidegger made explicit that caring (*Sorge*) is the ontological, existential structure of the human being, or, in his word, *Dasein* (Da-sein): "Dasein, *ontologically* understood, is care" (p. 53). In this context, care does not mean one of the psychological faculties or personality traits but the fundamental ontological structure of Dasein as "being-in-the-world"; that is, the very structure of caring constitutes the world in which Da-sein is: "As a primordial structural totality, care lies 'before' every factical 'attitude' and 'position' of Da-sein, that is, it is always already *in* them as an existential *a priori*" (p. 180).

Due to this characterization, Heidegger's concept of caring differs from Noddings' idea. Briefly, Heidegger's caring refers to the self-centric mode of being-in-the-world of Da-sein or the self-being. Caring makes it possible for the "world" to have a "familiarity" for the self-being by constituting "relevance" of things at hand in the world. In other words, caring constitutes the world as a relevant structure, centered around the self, in which the self can understand her or his existence in connection with the relevant, familiarized world. In caring Da-sein projects meanings to the world for the sake of its own existence. In this sense, Heidegger's caring (in *Being and Time*) is a self-centric concept. (However, this self-centered aspect of caring was later overcome by Heidegger himself.[7])

On the contrary, Noddings' idea of caring refers to an ideal mode of relationship between human beings. It has no trace of the self-centric aspect, but it is a fundamentally relational concept; "caring is a way of being in relation" (1992, 17). Referring to Heidegger, she underlines this relational aspect as follows:

> Heidegger's full range of meanings will be of interest as this exploration continues, but the meaning that will be primary here is relational. A *caring relation* is, in its most basic form, a connection or encounter between two human beings—a career and a recipient of care, or cared-for. (1992, 15)

In contrast to Heidegger, who regards human relations marked by "concern" as "falling prey" from the "authentic" mode of the selfhood, Noddings sees a caring relation as an ideal state of being, which agrees with Martin Buber's "I and You relation." Drawing on this idea, she has engaged in establishing an "ethic of caring." She insists that "relation will be taken as ontologically basic and the caring relation as ethically basic" (1984, 3).

Noddings discerns two basic conditions of the one-caring, or "engrossment" and "motivational displacement," that suggest openness to the other. "By engrossment I mean an open, nonselective receptivity to the cared-for" (1992, 15). In engrossment the one-caring receives the other's reality as it is: "I do not project; I receive the other into myself, and I see and feel with the other" (1984, 30); "When I receive the other, I am totally with the other" (p. 32). In engrossment, the other's reality becomes one's reality; "when the other's reality becomes a real possibility for me, I care" (p. 14). In this way, caring has a moment of stepping out of the self-centric structure. Then the "motivational displacement" takes place that is a responding action flowing from the one-caring towards the cared-for; "our motive energy is flowing toward others and their projects" (1992, 16). The one-caring devotes her or his energy to accomplish the other's project as if it were her or his own. In addition to these two conditions, a caring relation needs "reception," "recognition," and "response" from the cared-for to complete itself. Caring as a relation depends upon the cared-for. "The cared-for is essential to the relation. What the cared-for contributes to the relation is a responsiveness that completes the caring" (1984, 181).

In grounding the ethic of caring, Noddings appeals to a naturalistic foundation, namely, "natural caring" as experienced in a mother's relation to her child.

> Our relation to our children is not governed first by the ethical but by natural caring. We love not because we are required to love but because our natural relatedness gives natural birth to love. It is this love, this natural caring, that makes the ethical possible. (1984, 43)

She argues that the ethical caring arises out of the natural caring. This would make sense in many actual cases; however, my concern is that a natural relation between mother and child does sometimes include unconscious factors which distort their relation into a dysfunctional, neurotic one. As Alice Miller (1983/1990) has demonstrated, the natural relation between mother and child in many cases contains "poisonous" factors on its unconscious levels, which bring about destructive influences on the relation. If the one-caring who is driven by unconscious neurotic desires enters a caring relation, she or he may produce the relation that unconsciously serve to fulfill her or his desires to the detriment of the cared-for. But the projection from the one-caring is usually concealed from the conscious mind of the one-caring. Alice Miller has revealed distortions of this sort happening between parents and children, which she called "poisonous education." In other words, under the appearance of caring, poisonous education may take place. If a caring relation is "poisonous," it does not ultimately transcend the self-centric structure of the one-caring. In this regard, the naturalistic foundation needs another foundation that can be laid by the concept of compassion.

COMPASSION IN PURE LAND AND SHIN BUDDHISM

The concept of compassion was refined in the Japanese tradition of Pure Land Buddhism by Buddhists such as Honen (1133-1212), Shinran (1173-1262), and Ippen (1239-1289). Among them, Shinran founded the most influential school called Shin Buddhism. The basic teachings of the Pure Land and Shin Buddhism[8] are these: Human beings (all beings) are released from their sufferings by means of their birth in Pure Land through the help of Amida Buddha (the Buddha of Infinite Light). To save all beings is Amida's Primal Vow (honguan). Those who have the deepest faith (shinjin) in Amida's Vow will be born in the Pure Land.

To this end, a practical form of contemplation called *nembutsu* can be the way; it is to intone *namu-amida-butsu* ("I take refuge in Amida Buddha") in a wholehearted way.[9] *Nembutsu* serves to enhance trust in the work of "Other-power" (*tariki*) flowing from Amida. In this regard, it differs from the practice of Zen, which the Pure Land schools regarded as "the Path of Sages" and "difficult practice" appealing to the "self-power" (*jiriki*). In contrast, *nembutsu* is "the Path of the Pure Land" and "effortless practice." As it does not appeal to the self-power, *nembutsu* makes it easier for everyone to surrender to the Other-power, and it is in this surrender that the egocentric state dissolves and Enlightenment can take place (e.g., Yanagi 1955/1986; Unno 1998. In particular, Shin tradition calls those who have embodied the path of Other-power *myokonin* (e.g., Yanagi 1991), "a person who manifests the wonderful fragrance of spirituality" (Suzuki 1998, 69).

In agreement with Suzuki (1998),[10] we can say that Amida is not an otherworldly mythological figure but an ontological dimension hidden within: "My conclusion is that Amida *is* our inmost self, and when that inmost self is found, we are born in the Pure Land" (pp. 41-42). Amida is the deepest dimension of the Self that is opened up to the Pure Land (or the infinite reality). After Hee-Sung Keel (1995, 167), "Amida Buddha is the medium ... between the formless Buddhahood and the sentient beings living in the world of forms and discriminations." Originating from the formless Buddhahood, Amida invites us to the Pure Land. Accordingly, birth in the Pure Land is none other than Enlightenment by a total surrender of the self to the Other-power of Amida. Suzuki says, "it is only by the power of Amida that our liberation and freedom are assured. We don't add anything to Amida's working" (1998, 56). To animate the Other-power of Amida, we need to abandon egocentric "calculations" (*hakarai*) and to be empowered by the Other-power with no trace of selfhood.

The human being in the Pure Land and Shin Buddhism is a multidimensional being composed of the surface self (the level of self-power) and the inmost Amida (the Self) and the Pure Land (the infinite reality). Here we can reach a multidimensional concept of compassion. The *Tannisho* (Unno 1984), a record of Shinran's teachings, mentions two dimensions of compassion:

> There is a difference in compassion between the Path of Sages and the Path of Pure Land. The compassion in the Path of Sages is expressed through pity, sympathy, and care for all beings, but truly rare is it that one can help another as completely as one desires.
>
> The compassion in the Path of Pure Land is to quickly attain Buddhahood, saying the nembutsu, and with the true heart of compassion and love save all beings as we desire.
>
> In this life no matter how much pity and sympathy we may feel for others, it is impossible to help another as we truly wish; thus our compassion is inconsistent and limited. Only the saying of nembutsu manifests the complete and never ending compassion which is true, real, and sincere. (p. 9)

Shinran teaches us that the true compassion comes not from the personal level of the self-power, but from the Amida's Other-power. Amida's boundless compassion manifests itself through the phenomenal compassion of those who have surrendered to the Other-power. We can be compassionate, for our existence is always already embraced and cared for on the deepest level by the boundless compassion of Amida.

This multidimensional structure of compassion holds true for caring; a person who is cared for by Amida is able to care for the other on a deeper level. A caring relation has no longer one-dimensional horizontal structure but a multidimensional depth, for it includes a vertical relation within the one-caring. Saiko (1995) calls this a "twofold relationship" in his theory of Buddhist counseling: "Underneath the human dimension on which both a counselor and a client stand, there is the dimension of Buddha transcending humanness on which a Buddhist counselor stands" (pp. 45-46, trans. Nakagawa). In a counseling relation, a Buddhist counselor dwells in a personal relationship with a client, and at the same time she or he is deeply embraced by Buddha's dimension. The care for the client from the counselor involves a "twofold aspect of care"; a Buddhist counselor cares for the client not only from the humanistic perspective but also from the Buddhist perspective. Even if the counselor is a finite existence, she or she is simultaneously aware that both the counselor and the client are embraced by the infinite compassionate power of Buddha.

The action of the Buddhist counselor has no "calculation" on the part of the counselor and bears the quality of true naturalness called *jinen*. It is in this naturalness that the Other-power reveals itself. According to Keel, "*Jinen* refers to ultimate reality itself as well as the way in which this reality works for our salvation, i.e., enlightenment" (1995, 130). Also, Yoshifumi Ueda and Dennis Hirota (1989, 176-177) say: "*Jinen* or naturalness is true reality that transcends all forms, and at the same time it is always in motion, functioning as the liberating force that encompasses the lives of ignorant beings." In a twofold caring relation, *jinen* reveals the fundamental function of caring which ultimately brings about Enlightenment. Through the working of the Buddhist counselor, the Other-power works on the client to heal and transform her or his mode of existence.

The Buddhist idea of compassion can radically transform the meaning of caring. Caring learns to involve a deeper function than fulfilling basic human needs. Underlying a personal relation between the one-caring and the cared-for, another dimension of caring exists that comes from the Other-power of the infinite reality; those who care for each other are always already cared for by Amida, or Existence itself. This is an ontological foundation of caring derived from the Buddhist perspective of compassion, without which caring may not fulfill its conditions such as engrossment and motivational replacement.

TOWARDS A SOCIETY OF ENLIGHTENMENT

In closing this chapter, I will reflect again on the relationship between the Western and Eastern ways of action. In this discussion I have tried to clarify various aspects of the Eastern way of action. But this does not argue that the Western way of action (social criticism and social activism) is pointless or meaningless. Even though it is based on subject-object dualism, it is also evident that without this orientation we cannot bring about visible changes in the objective, social systems. In this respect, the thrust for social criticism and activism is obviously weak in the Eastern way of action. We need to foster an integration between the Eastern way of contemplative action and the Western way of social action, as is exemplified in such attempts as deep ecology and Engaged Buddhism.

On the other hand, as we have seen in this chapter, it is also important to acknowledge that the social implications of the Eastern way of action can provide deeper foundations for the theory of action and social transformation. In this regard, the very notion of social action should be enlarged to incorporate various aspects of contemplative action other than social activism.

This second point may require us to alter our perceptions of social reality. In the discussions regarding personal and social transformation, one remarkable tone is that personal transformation must support social transformation. It implies that the cultivation of the deeper dimensions should be subordinate to the social dimension. Here the social reality has a top priority over the other dimensions of reality. As a result, there emerges a kind of "social reductionism" that reduces all the other dimensions only to the social level. However, the multidimensional theory requires the social dimension to cease dominating the others, and to embrace them so as to support them. The social reality must be redefined in terms of the other dimensions—the cosmic reality, the infinite reality, and the universal reality.

For instance, from the viewpoint of perennial philosophy, Aldous Huxley (1946/1968) redefines the meaning of society as follows:

> [T]he important thing is that individual men and women should come to the unitive knowledge of the divine Ground, and what interests them in regard to the social environment is not its progressiveness or non-progressiveness ... but the degree to which it helps or hinders individuals in their advance towards man's final end. (p. 94)

As Huxley says, the social environment for spiritual development is crucially important; otherwise, it tends to hinder it and to produce what Buber (1958/1988) calls "the non-religious man" who is alienated from the wholeness of reality:

> [H]e can not merely be admirable in every other respect, he can even possess the wholeness in his personal life that the other lacks; but he does not have real contact with the wholeness of being, that is, his life as such is isolated over against the wholeness of being. (p. 219)

The social dimension must open itself to the deeper dimensions of reality so that they can reveal their own significance in the social reality. What is needed is a sort of Copernican revolution regarding our perceptions of the social reality, in which society will become an optimal environment for a deeper reality to arise.

In this regard, Eastern ways of action have a special importance, for they mediate the deeper reality to the social plane. A primary implication of the Eastern way consists in this activity of making connections between different dimensions. The Western way of social criticism and activism also needs to engage in creating the social systems that can nurture and cultivate contemplative spirituality as well as social justice; otherwise, it would eventually contribute to the social reductionism, repressing the deeper reality. In this effort to make vertical connections among dimensions, the Eastern way of contemplative action can cooperate with the Western way of social action.

What is needed is, therefore, to have not only the politics of democracy but also what Robert Thurman (1998) calls the "politics of enlightenment." The politics of enlightenment attempts to design and promote a social environment where everything can serve to bring about the enlightenment of individuals, for it recognizes enlightenment as "the summit of human evolution" (p. 61) and as "the most important thing for each one" (p. 38). It also understands the political and social implications of enlightenment. In his description of the Buddha's approach, Thurman says: "Once an individual attains enlightenment, society at large automatically becomes enriched. This principle was the heart of the Buddha's social revolution" (p. 33). Though it is realized in each individual, enlightenment is not only a personal matter but has a profound effect on society at large. "A society of enlightened beings is bound to be an enlightened society" (p. 87).[11]

What is more, Thurman highlights a significant role of education in the politics of enlightenment, which he calls "enlightenment education" (p. 99) or "enlightenment-oriented education system" (p. 119). In terms of the Buddha's work, he remarks: "His movement was not the founding of a religion—it was the founding of a new educational system, a cultural and social revolution" (p. 95). Also, in terms of the social and political work of Ashoka, a Buddhist emperor, Thurman refers to Askoka's "educational evolutionism": "A society geared to uncovering truth and spreading enlightened attitudes will necessarily focus intently on education, make it one of the chief preoccupations of policy" (p. 125). The following comment is important with regard to the education of enlightenment.

> Education is the major tool of truth-conquest, as well as the most important survival technique known to man. It promotes enlightenment as the flowering of the individual's own awareness, sensibility, and powers, and thereby develops a strong society. Within the context of the politics of enlightenment, it is understood that the purpose of human life is education, not that education prepares a person for some other life-purpose. Education is a requirement for accelerating the process of evolution that brings the individual to human birth and for ensuring that he or she achieves the quantum jump of awareness from the constriction of automatic self-centeredness into the freedom of selfless relativity. (p. 126)

This statement may represent not only the Buddhist but also the Eastern view of education as a whole. In a word, the Eastern way of education is the way of Enlightenment. Eastern philosophy has identified that education in its essential aspect can be the education for Awakening.

NOTES

1. We need to admit that the receptive, passive attitude of Eastern inaction (in the sense of social action) has yielded few critical oppositions to the existing social systems and little active political involvement in changing society and eventually served to maintain the status quo. However, this does not necessarily mean that Eastern philosophy is conservative, nationalistic, or totalitarian thought. But rather, I think, in its fundamental intention it is a radical attempt to transform society from a deeper reality, the aspect of which we need to become aware.

2. Although deep ecology has been evolving among Western thinkers, it has Eastern components, especially in Joanna Macy's Buddhist approach. On the other hand, Engaged Buddhism, coined by Thich Nhat Hanh, is a development of Buddhist activism, yet it has been facilitated mostly by Westerners.

3. It has to be added that the pedagogy of the oppressed *does* start with the inner transformation of the oppressed, which entails a radical transformation of their perception, thinking, and behavior, to bring about a social transformation. This inner transformation of the self can raise "critical consciousness" of social injustice, yet it does not involve contemplative awareness.

4. In this context, I do not intend to idealize the enlightened ones as the model of moral perfection, but refer to the aspect of them as the teacher of Enlightenment. In this re-

gard, I also admit Georg Feuerstein's (1990) critical examination of the Eastern guruism.

5. One of the primary figures who realized compassion is the Buddha himself, who after his great enlightenment devoted himself to guide people for forty-five years.

6. As Fujiyoshi (1989) remarks, Zen Buddhism has tended to stress the aspect of wisdom more than compassion, and, by contrast, Shin Buddhism has tended to stress the aspect of compassion.

7. After the decisive turning of his thought, Heidegger did away with the self-centric connotations of human existence found in *Being and Time*. For instance, in his "Letters on 'Humanism,'" Heidegger (1998) introduced the concept of "ek-sistence" (*Ek-sistenz*) to signify the ecstatic essence of the human being. The human being as ek-sisting is an open being who is by "being" thrown into "the openness of being" in an ecstatic way. He said: "The human being is, and is human, insofar as he is ek-sisting one. He stands out into the openness of being. Being itself, which as the throw has projected the essence of the human being into 'care,' is as this openness. Thrown in such fashion, the human being stands 'in' the openness of being" (p. 266). Thus, the human being is open in the openness of being, and "care" constitutes the ecstatic essence of the human being. "The human being is the shepherd of being" (p. 252).

8. Basic introduction to Pure Land and Shin Buddhism includes the work of Suzuki (1973a, 1998), Ueda and Hirota (1989), Unno (1998), Keel (1995), Ueda (1993), and Yanagi (1955/1986, 1991).

9. As a form of contemplation, the Pure Land way is similar to those ways such as the way of love and heart in Sufism (Harvey 1994; Helminski 1999), the way of devotional love in the *Bhakti* tradition of Hinduism, and the Christian way of prayer (Savin 1991).

10. It is less known that D. T. Suzuki was strongly impressed by Shin Buddhism and the way of *myokonin* as much as Zen Buddhism. He translated Shinran's principal work *Kyogyoshinsho* (Suzuki 1973b) into English and wrote articles on Shin Buddhism (1973a).

11. The "politics of meaning" put forward by Michael Lerner (1996) may resonate with Thurman's idea of the "politics of enlightenment." After Lerner, "The politics of meaning is a modest attempt to apply some of the ancient wisdom of the human race to our contemporary reality" (p. 18). And it is "an attempt to reconstruct the world in a way that really takes seriously the uniqueness and preciousness of every human being and our connection to a higher ethical and spiritual purpose that gives meaning to our lives" (p. 4).

Conclusion

This study has explored a philosophical foundation for holistic education from various perspectives of Eastern philosophy. Needless to say, this issue is so broad that this small study cannot go into detail; it can, however, provide an account of the major views taken on holistic education.

To integrate holistic education with Eastern philosophy has been one of my chief concerns since I encountered holistic education in the early 1990s. The encounter with holistic education has brought me a broad perspective in which various studies I had done on education became integrated. However, as I learned more about holistic education, it came upon me that something is missing in the ideas of holistic education, because it seemed to me that most notions of contemporary holistic education are based on connectionist worldviews and lack the aspect of depth; in particular, superficial understandings of connections are in danger of lapsing into horizontal shallow connections devoid of depth. In this respect, Eastern philosophy has rich ideas on the depth of reality.[1]

The Eastern philosophy of holistic education presented in this study, however, did not intend to oppose the Western ideas of holistic education. But rather, this study has tried to initiate a dialogue between them to develop an integrated framework of holistic education that is able to encompass both perspectives. In this regard, I have presented the multidimensional theory of holistic education as a model of such an integration. In this integration "Eastern" no longer signifies a regional and cultural concept but an existential ontological category that can be united with other categories including "Western." If we see both "Eastern" and "Western" as existential and ontological categories, it becomes possible to create a new philosophy of education based on their integration, in which we can avoid such relative concepts as "Eastern" and "Western."

In the following I will summarize what has been undertaken and revealed in this study. In the process of this work, the first difficulty was to find how to approach the body of Eastern philosophy, which initially seemed to be so chaotic and diverse. The work of Eastern philosophers—D. T. Suzuki, Kitaro Nishida, Shin'ichi Hisamatsu, Keiji Nishitani, Shizuteru Ueda, Masao Abe, and Toshihiko Izutsu—helped me considerably in understanding the heart of Eastern philosophy (Chapter 1). Among them, the work of Izutsu was crucial for my study; his attempt to reconstruct Eastern philosophy as postmodern thought has provided me with a systematic understanding of Eastern philosophy as multidimensional thought.

Eastern philosophy has two remarkable aspects. First, it acknowledges the deepest dimension of reality, which has been called *Brahman, nirvana, sunyata, Tao, wu, wu-chi, li*, and also called "Eastern Perspective" by Suzuki, "Absolute Nothingness" by Nishida, "Eastern Nothingness" by Hisamatsu, and "the ultimate Zero Point" by Izutsu. As we have seen, this deepest dimension plays a decisively important role in both theory and practice of Eastern philosophy.

Second, in Eastern philosophy, the ultimate reality has been the object not of intellectual speculation but of contemplation; that is to say, we need to realize what Eastern philosophy reveals in our existence with the help of contemplative practice. What is more, Eastern philosophy is unique in its emphasis on the returning path of contemplation. Contemplation has a twofold movement of seeking and returning. The path of seeking represents the aspect of deconstruction of all beings to delve into the infinite depth of reality, and the path of returning involves the aspect of reconstruction of all beings that are radically transformed in the infinite depth. In this regard, the Eastern approach to a human life is not an escape from this world of everyday living but an attempt to radically transform the world so that we can realize there the profound depth of our life.

As its foremost characteristic holistic education is an attempt to unfold a comprehensive ontology or worldview of education. I have formulated an ontological model of holistic education as the *five dimensions of reality* (Chapter 2). The five dimensions include the objective reality, the social reality, the cosmic reality, the infinite reality, and the universal reality. This model has arisen in interaction among holistic education, Eastern philosophy, and Western theories. Indeed, the first three dimensions were formulated chiefly on Western thought, whereas Eastern components find their relevant places in the last two dimensions.

This multidimensional model does not address a hierarchical strata in which each stratum is discretely separated from each other but denotes the wholeness of reality, a particular aspect of which each dimension reveals. Any being is simultaneously an objective, social, cosmic, and infinite reality. All dimensions are ultimately identical in a non-dualistic way, which is the universal reality. However, this fullest realization of wholeness arises in Awakening or Enlightenment. In other words, the first four dimensions portray the degrees of realization towards the deeper dimensions of reality.

This multidimensional framework provides a simple definition of holistic education: *holistic education is an attempt to explore multidimensional reality in our own existence.* Holistic education helps us attain the depth of our existence and thereby recover the wholeness of reality. The wholeness of reality as such potentially exists prior to Awakening, because it cannot be produced but only be discovered. But the difficulty for the human being is that exclusive identification with the first two dimensions (the objective and social reality) through the dominating function of the mind obstructs this recognition of the wholeness. Therefore, the primary task of holistic education is to help us release ourselves from these identifications and realize the deeper dimensions of reality.

As any identification brings about fragmentation, the movement towards wholeness arises only in a ceaseless movement of disidentification. In this regard, Eastern philosophy is unique for it has celebrated Emptiness or Nothingness (the infinite reality) as the ceaseless movement of disidentification with anything. The Eastern Self peculiar to Eastern philosophy arises through this movement as the universal reality. It is a uniquely Eastern model of the awakened one who is radically emptied and negated (disidentified) in the infinite reality and then reemerges as a selfless Self. This view of the selfless Self gives us a totally new image of a selfhood. Education for Awakening intends to cultivate such a selfless Self.

The multidimensional theory also provides a perspective for the theories of holistic education that have so far been presented. Many of the contemporary holistic education theories (especially ecological thought and systems theory) have enlarged the ontological basis of education to embrace the cosmic world as well as the objective and social worlds. However, from the multidimensional theory, they are still not comprehensive enough unless they involve the infinite and universal realities. Questions on eco-spiritualism in ecological orientation and on the cosmological assumptions devoid of the anti-cosmos in the systemic orientation have been raised in this relation (Chapter 3).

Furthermore, to clarify a basic difference between contemporary holistic education and Eastern holistic education, I have explored their ideas of relationships—Interconnection and Interpenetration (Chapter 4). This consideration has to do with the essential aspect of holistic education, for the idea of Interconnection has become the ontological basis for contemporary holistic education. In my view, the idea of Interconnection describes the cosmic reality that can be explored by ecological and systemic sciences. By contrast, the idea of Interpenetration refers to the universal reality that means absolute freedom in all relationships. These two concepts of relationships are different in their qualities, so the apparent similarity between them does not justify an easy equation.

To clarify Eastern views on relationships, I have examined the concept of "dependent-arising" developed in Buddhism (especially Nagarjuna's Madhyamika philosophy and Hua-yen philosophy). In particular, Hua-yen philosophy has achieved the most comprehensive view of relationships in the idea of Interpenetration. Hua-yen philosophy and the concept of Interpenetration have immense potentialities for the philosophies of holistic education that are to be further explored.

Eastern philosophy is able to provide different views on the basic concepts of education. Some of them I have revisited to make explicit constructive contributions of Eastern philosophy to holistic education (Chapter 5), which include the aim of education conceived in Hindu philosophy and the concept of nature in the Taoist perspective. We have seen the aim of education as the non-dual realization of multiple dimensions through *Atman-Brahman* realization, and we have understood the Taoist nature as the fundamental spontaneity flowing from *Tao*.

Furthermore, I have examined issues such as language and silence, learning and unlearning, and human development from the perspectives of Taoism and Buddhism. Eastern ideas about these issues initially seemed to be paradoxical to our conventional ideas; however, the multidimensional theory has helped us acknowledge that they are oriented towards the deeper dimensions of reality. Silence and unlearning in education will become very important antidotes to our excessive obsession with language and learning. Also, an analysis of the *Ten Oxherding Pictures* has given us a significant view of human development that highlights transpersonal development after the ego-formation and also includes insights beyond the stage-specific models of human development.

Eastern philosophy is not a speculative system of thought but a very practical system of cultivation in which theory and practice form reciprocal circles to mutually transform each other. In reality, Eastern philosophy has many potential contributions to make to the practice of holistic education. This study has examined the ways of contemplation and art as representative forms of the Eastern way of practice (Chapter 6).

The way of contemplation is essentially the art of awareness that can lead through the transformation of consciousness to a great awakening. Instead of detailing various methods of contemplation developed in the East, this study has tried to describe an integral view of the way of contemplation that incorporates the Western somatic education as well as the Eastern meditation, following the multidimensional theory. What we need in the practice of holistic education is an integral vision of the practice such as this. Aldous Huxley's pioneering ideas of the "nonverbal humanities" are still important in this direction. Also, we have seen that education for awareness and awakening will reveal an essential aspect of holistic education. In this regard, we need to pay more attention to the work of Socrates and Krishnamurti.

The way of art will also occupy an important domain in the practice of holistic education. In the Eastern context, art has been a form of contemplation, a way of spiritual cultivation, and an exploration into, and an expression from, the deeper dimensions of reality. Examining the Herrigels' reports on their practices, three stages in the way of art have been articulated.

This study has finally focused on the ways of action and compassion to reveal social implications hidden in the Eastern way of practice (Chapter 7). To question the social implications of holistic education has been one of the focal issues in the discussion of contemporary holistic education, because holistic education seems to have been concerned more with the personal and the inner than with the social. This seems to be the case in the Eastern way of practice as well. However, a closer look at Eastern ways of action has revealed that they have their own social implications distinct from those found in Western social activism; that is, contemplation is a social criticism, and every action including social action can be a contemplation. And it has also clarified how the actions of Enlightenment take place in the social world. The point is that Eastern ways of action can open avenues to the deeper dimensions of reality so as to bring about a social transformation from the very bottom of reality. We need to see the way of social action in a multidimensional way.

The way of compassion represents an altruistic aspect of Enlightenment to be realized in the social domain. This study has highlighted caring—a basic concept of contemporary holistic education—in relation to compassion. Noddings' idea of caring was examined with reference to the Pure Land and Shin Buddhist notion of compassion, which has provided an ontological foundation for caring.

At last, in favor of a society for Enlightenment, I have raised awareness of our imbalanced perceptions of social reality, in which social reality has priority over the deeper reality. On the contrary, the multidimensional theory requires a sort of Copernican revolution, in which the social dimension comes to support the deeper reality to emerge in the social domain. In this sense, we need to have the politics and education of Enlightenment.

This study has attempted to reveal what Eastern philosophy can bring to the discussions of holistic education. However, it does not claim that this is the only possible form of the Eastern philosophy of holistic education. On the contrary, I am aware of the following unavoidable limitations of this study.

This study has tried to focus on the fundamental structure of Eastern philosophy, and, as a result, it has had to overlook differences between various perspectives of Eastern philosophy to some extent. In this regard, I am sure that it is both possible and significant to develop a theory of holistic education based on each perspective.

Also, as a whole, my discussion has been inclined to rely on some of the Buddhist ideas rather than others in Eastern philosophy. But there are still many resources in Eastern philosophy from which we can draw various ideas of holistic education.

A conceptual work like this has left untouched many concrete and practical approaches to holistic education that have appeared in the East, most of which are unknown to holistic education studies. It would be a significant task for us to explore them in the light of holistic education.

This study has put forth a multidimensional view of reality inspired by Eastern philosophy. Yet this notion of multidimensionality as such belongs not only to Eastern philosophy but also to other trends of thought (for instance, Kabbalah in Western mysticism). This study welcomes different ideas of holistic education appearing from these other fields of thought.

The ideas of Eastern holistic education as presented in this study may look alien to the present situation of modern schooling systems. Indeed, Eastern holistic education does not seem to match the systems of child education in many respects; however, it would be at least possible and appropriate in the systems of adult education (including youth education and teacher training), for it provides ideas and methods for the spiritual growth of adults after the formation of their ego. It would become an important contribution in this field, for modern education has failed to offer visions of spiritual growth and caused spiritual crises from which many of us have suffered. It is a further task for Eastern holistic education to identify how to implement and fulfill its ideas and practices in the existent educational systems.

However, what is more important than the practical application is to recognize that the Eastern philosophy of holistic education can deepen our understandings of reality. It is the deepest understanding of reality that will bring about a new vision of education.

NOTE

1. I raised this issue in a preliminary fashion in my article "Holistic Education and Spirituality" (1996a). The present work is a development of this work.

Bibliography

Abe, Masao. 1985. *Zen and western thought.* Edited by W. R. LaFleur. Honolulu, HI: University of Hawaii Press.

Abe, Masao. 1990. Introduction to *An inquiry into the good,* by K. Nishida, translated by M. Abe and C. Ives. New Haven, CT: Yale University Press.

Abe, Masao. 1992. *A study of Dogen: His philosophy and religion.* Edited by S. Heine. Albany, NY: State University of New York Press.

Abe, Masao. 1997. *Zen and comparative studies.* Edited by S. Heine. Honolulu, HI: University of Hawaii Press.

Alexander, F. Matthias. 1923/1985. *Constructive conscious control of the individual.* Long Beach, CA: Centerline Press.

Alexander, F. Matthias. 1932/1984. *The use of the self: Its conscious direction in relation to diagnosis, functioning and the control of reaction.* Long Beach, CA: Centerline Press.

Angel, Leonald. 1994. *Enlightenment east and west.* Albany, NY: State University of New York Press.

Armstrong, Thomas. 1985. *The radiant child.* Wheaton, IL: Quest Books, Theosophical Publishing House.

Assagioli, Robert. 1965/1971. *Psychosynthesis.* New York: Viking Press.

Aurobindo, Sri, and The Mother. 1956. *Sri Aurobindo and The Mother on education.* Pondicherry, India: Sri Aurobindo Ashram.

Aurobindo, Sri, and The Mother. 1992/1995. *A new education for a new consciousness.* Pondicherry, India: Sri Aurobindo International Centre of Education.

Bailey, Alice A. 1954. *Education in the new age.* New York: Lucis.

Bateson, Gregory. 1972. *Steps to an ecology of mind.* New York: Ballantine Books

Bateson, Gregory. 1979/1980. *Mind and nature. A necessary unity.* New York: Bantam Books.

Bateson, Gregory, and Mary Catherine Bateson. 1987/1988. *Angels fear: Towards an epistemology of the sacred.* New York: Bantam Books.

Beck, Clive. 1990. *Better schools: A values perspective.* Lewes, UK and Bristol, PA: Falmer Press.

Bennet, John. G., et al. 1984. *The spiritual hunger of the modern child.* Charles Town, WV: Claymont Communications.

Berger, Peter L., and Thomas Luckmann. 1966/1967. *The social construction of reality: A treatise in the sociology of knowledge.* Garden City, NY: Anchor Books.

Berman, Morris. 1981/1984. *The reenchantment of the world.* New York: Bantam Books.

Berry, Thomas. 1988. *The dream of the earth.* San Francisco: Sierra Club Books.

Beukes, Piet. 1989/1991. *The holistic Smuts: A study in personality.* Cape Town, South Africa: Human and Rousseau.

Bloom, Alan, trans. 1968. *The republic of Plato.* New York: Basic Books.

Bohm, David. 1980/1995. *Wholeness and the implicate order.* London and New York: Routledge.

Bollnow, Otto Friedrich. 1959/1977. *Existenzphilosophie und Pädagogik: Versuch über unstetige Formen der Erziehung.* 5th ed. Stuttgart, Germany: W. Kohlhammer.

Bollnow, Otto Friedrich. 1970/1981. *Philosophie der Erkenntnis: Erster Teil, das Vorverständnis und die Erfarung des Neuen.* 2d ed. Stuttgart, Germany: W. Kohlhammer.

Boorstein, Seymour, ed. 1996. *Transpersonal psychotherapy.* 2d ed. Albany, NY: State University of New York Press.

Boorstein, Seymour. 1997. *Clinical studies in transpersonal psychotherapy.* Albany, NY: State University of New York Press.

Bowers, Chet A. 1993a. *Critical essays on education, modernity, and the recovery of the ecological imperative.* New York: Teachers College Press.

Bowers, Chet A. 1993b. Implications of the ecological crisis for the reform of teacher education. In *The renewal of meaning in education*, edited by R. Miller. Brandon, VT: Holistic Education Press.

Bowers, Chet A., and David J. Flinders. 1990. *Responsive teaching: An ecological approach to classroom patterns of language, culture, and thought.* New York: Teachers College Press.

Brooks, Charles V. W. 1974/1982. *Sensory awareness: The rediscovery of experiencing.* Santa Barbara, CA: Ross-Erikson.

Brown, Joseph Epes, ed. 1953/1989. *The sacred pipe: Black Elk's account of the seven rites of the Oglala Sioux.* Norman, OK: Universiity of Oklahoma Press.

Brown, Norman O. 1959/1985. *Life against death: The psychoanalytical meaning of history.* 2d ed. Middletown, CT: Wesleyan University Press.

Brown, Richard C. 1991. Buddhist-inspired early childhood education at the Naropa Institute. *Holistic Education Review* 4(4): 16-20.

Brown, Richard C. 1998, December/1999, January. The teacher as contemplative observer. *Educational Leadership: The Spirit of Education* 56(4): 70-73.

Buber, Martin. 1958/1988. *Hasidism and modern man.* Edited and translated by M. Friedman. Atlantic Highlands, NJ: Humanities Press International.

Buber, Martin. 1960. *The origin and meaning of Hasidism.* Edited and translated by M. Friedman. New York: Horizon Press.

Buber, Martin. 1965. *Between man and man.* Translated by R. G. Smith. New York: Macmillan.

Buber, Martin. 1970/1996. *I and thou.* Translated by W. Kaufmann. New York: Simon and Schuster. (Originally published 1923).

Cajete, Gregory A. 1994. *Look to the mountain: An ecology of indigenous education.* Durango, CO: Kivaki Press.

Callicott, J. Baird, and Roger T. Ames, eds. 1989. *Nature in Asian traditions of thought: Essays in environmental philosophy.* Albany, NY: State University of New York Press.

Campbell, Joseph. 1972/1993. *Myths to live by.* New York: Arkana, Penguin Books.

Capra, Fritjof. 1982/1983. *The turning point: Science, society, and the rising culture.* New York: Bantam Books.

Capra, Fritjof. 1993. What is ecological literacy? In *Guide to ecoliteracy*, by F. Capra, C. Cooper, E. Clark, and R. Doughty. Berkeley, CA: Center for Ecoliteracy.

Capra, Fritjof. 1996. *The web of life: A new scientific understanding of living systems.* New York: Anchor Books.

Capra, Fritjof, Carole Cooper, Edward T. Clark Jr., and Roy Doughty. 1993. *Guide to ecoliteracy.* Berkeley, CA: Center for Ecoliteracy.

Carter, Robert E. 1992. *Becoming bamboo: Western and eastern explorations of the meaning of life.* Montreal and Kingston, ON: McGill-Queen's University Press.

Carter, Robert E. 1997. *The nothingness beyond God: An introduction to the philosophy of Nishida Kitaro.* 2d ed. St. Paul, MN: Paragon House.

Cassirer, Ernst. 1944. *An essay on man: An introduction to a philosophy of human culture.* New Haven, CT: Yale University Press.

Cenkner, William. 1976. *The Hindu personality in education: Tagore, Gandhi, Aurobindo.* New Delhi, India: Manohar Book Service.

Chan, Wing-tsit, ed. and trans. 1963. *A source book in Chinese philosophy.* Princeton, NJ: Princeton University Press.

Chang, Chung-yuan. 1963/1970. *Creativity and Taoism.* New York: Harper and Row.

Chang, Chung-yuan, trans. 1975. *Tao: A new way of thinking.* New York: Harper Colophon Books, Harper and Row.

Chang, Garma C. C., trans. 1962/1989. *The hundred thousand songs of Milarepa.* Vol. 1. Boston: Shambhala.

Chang, Garma C. C. 1971. *The Buddhist teaching of totality: The philosophy of Hwa Yen Buddhism.* University Park, PA: Pennsylvania State University Press.

Chaudhuri, Haridas. 1974. *Being, evolution, and immortality: An outline of integral philosophy.* Wheaton, IL: Quest Book, Theosophical Publishing House.

Chaudhuri, Haridas. 1977. *The evolution of integral consciousness.* Wheaton, IL: Quest Book, Theosophical Publishing House.

Cheetham, Eric. 1994. *Fundamentals of mainstream Buddhism.* Rutland, VT and Tokyo: Charles E. Tuttle.

Chih-i. 1997. *Stopping and seeing: A comprehensive course in Buddhist meditation.* Translated by T. Cleary. Boston: Shambhala.

Ching, Julia. 1993. *Chinese religions.* New York: Orbis Books, Maryknoll.

Clark, Edward T. Jr. 1993. How do you design an ecoliteracy curriculum? In *Guide to ecoliteracy,* by F. Capra, C. Cooper, E. Clark and R. Doughty. Berkeley, CA: Center for Ecoliteracy.

Clark, Edward T. Jr. 1997. *Designing and implementing an integrated curriculum: A student-centered approach.* Brandon, VT: Holistic Education Press.

Cleary, Thomas. 1983. *Entry into the inconceivable: An introduction to Hua-yen Buddhism.* Honolulu, HI: University of Hawaii Press.

Cleary, Thomas, trans. 1984/1993. *The flower ornament scripture: A translation of the Avatamsaka Sutra.* Boston: Shambhala.

Cleary, Thomas, trans. 1993. *No barrier: Unlocking the Zen koan.* New York: Aquarian Press.

Cleary, Thomas, trans. 1998. *The sutra of Hui-neng, grand master of Zen.* Boston: Shambhala.

Cleary, Thomas, and J. C. Cleary, trans. 1977/1992. *The blue cliff record.* Boston: Shambhala.

Conze, Edward, ed. and trans. 1975. *The large sutra on perfect wisdom.* Berkeley and Los Angeles: University of California Press.

Conze, Edward (with I. B. Horner, David Snellgrove, and Arthur Waley), ed. and trans. 1995. *Buddhist texts through the ages.* Oxford, UK: Oneworld Publications.

Cook, Francis. 1977. *Hua-yen Buddhism: The jewel net of Indra.* University Park, PA: Pennsylvania State University Press.

Corbin, Henry. 1995. *Swedenborg and esoteric Islam.* Translated by L. Fox. West Chester, PA: Swedenborg Foundation. (Originally published 1984).

Csikszentmihalyi, Mark, and Philip J. Ivanhoe, eds. 1999. *Religious and philosophical aspects of the Laozi.* Albany, NY: State University of New York Press.

Darroch-Lozowski, Vivian. 1987. *Notebook of stone: From the Tibetan plateau and Berlin.* Kapuskasing, Canada: Penumbra Press.

Deikman, Arthur J. 1982. *The observing self: Mysticism and psychotherapy.* Boston: Beacon Press.

Del Prete, Thomas. 1990. *Thomas Merton and the education of the whole person.* Birmingham, AL: Religious Education Press.

Deleuze, Gilles. 1983. *Nietzsche and philosophy.* Translated by H. Tomlinson. New York: Columbia University Press. (Originally published 1962).

Deutsch, Eliot. 1969/1973. *Advaita Vedanta: A philosophical reconstruction.* Honolulu, HI: The University Press of Hawaii.

Dewey, John. 1916/1966. *Democracy and education: An introduction to the philosophy of education.* New York: Free Press, Macmillan.

Dewey, John. 1923/1985. Introduction to *Constructive conscious control of the individual,* by F. M. Alexander. Long Beach, CA: Centerline Press.

Dewey, John. 1932/1984. Introduction to *The use of the self,* by F. M. Alexander. Long Beach, CA: Centerline Press.

Dogen. 1975. Shobogenzo, Buddha-nature. Part I. Translated by N. Wanddell and M. Abe. *The Eastern Buddhist* 8(2): 94-112.

Dogen. 1976a. Shobogenzo, Buddha-nature. Part II. Translated by N. Wanddell and M. Abe. *The Eastern Buddhist* 9(1): 87-105.

Dogen. 1976b. Shobogenzo, Buddha-nature, Part III. Translated by N. Wanddell and M. Abe. *The Eastern Buddhist* 9(2): 71-87.

Douglas, Mary. 1970/1973. *Natural symbols: Explorations in cosmology.* New York: Vintage Books.

Dufty, David and Helen Dufty, eds. 1994. *Holistic education: Some Australian explorations.* Belconnen, Australia: Australian Curriculum Studies Association.

Dürckheim, Karlfried Graf von. 1960/1974. *The Japanese cult of tranquility.* Translated by E. O'Shiel. London: Rider and Company.

Dürckheim, Karlfried Graf von. 1962. *Hara: The vital centre of man.* Translated by S-M. v. Kospoth. London: George Allen and Unwin. (Originally published 1956).

Dürckheim, Karlfried Graf von. 1987/1991. *Zen and us.* Translated by V. Nash. New York: Arkana, Penguin Books. (Originally published 1961).

Eckel, Malcolm David. 1997. Is there a Buddhist philosophy of nature? In *Buddhism and ecology: The interconnection of dharma and deeds,* edited by M. E. Tucker and D. R. Williams. Cambridge, MA: Harvard University Center for the Study of World Religions, Harvard University Press.

Eisler, Riane. 2000. *Tomorrow's children: A blueprint for partnership education in the 21st century.* Boulder, CO and Oxford: Westview Press.

Eliade, Mircea. 1967. *From primitives to Zen: A thematic sourcebook of the history of religions.* London: William Collins Sons and Co.

Elias, Maurice J., et al. 1997. *Promoting social and emotional learning: Guidelines for educators.* Alexandria, VA: Association for Supervision and Curriculum Development.

Emerson, Ralph Waldo. 1966. *Emerson on education: Selections.* Edited by H. M. Jones. New York: Teachers College Press.

Emerson, Ralph Waldo. 1981. *Selected writings of Emerson.* Edited by D. McQuade. New York: The Modern Library, Random House.

Eppsteiner, Fred, ed. 1985/1988. *The path of compassion: Writings on socially engaged Buddhism.* Berkeley, CA: Parallax Press.

Evans, Donald. 1993. *Spirituality and human nature.* Albany, NY: State University of New York Press.

Fa-tsang, Hozo. 1989. *Kegon gokyo-sho* [Treatise on the five teachings]. Translated by K. Kimura. *Daijo Butten Series,* Tokyo: Chuokoronsha.

Feldenkrais, Moshe. 1972/1977. *Awareness through movement: Health exercises for personal growth.* New York: Harper and Row.

Feuerstein, Georg. 1974/1992. *Wholeness or transcendence?: Ancient lessons for the emerging global civilization.* New York: Larson Publications.

Feuerstein, Georg. 1990. *Holy madness: The shock tactics and radical teachings of crazy-wise adepts, holy fools, and rascal gurus.* New York: Paragon House.

Flake, Carol L., ed. 1993. *Holistic education: Principles, perspectives and practices.* Brandon, VT: Holistic Education Press.

Foucault, Michel. 1977/1979. *Discipline and punish: The birth of prison.* Translated by A. Sheridan. Harmondsworth, UK: Penguin Books. (Originally published 1975).

Fox, Warwick. 1990. *Toward a transpersonal ecology: Developing new foundations for environmentalism.* Boston: Shambhala.

Franck, Frederick, ed. 1982. *The Buddha eye: An anthology of the Kyoto school.* New York: Crossroad.

Freire, Paulo. 1970/1996. *Pedagogy of the oppressed.* Rev. ed. Translated by M. B. Ramos. New York: Continuum.

Froebel, Friedrich. 1887/1900/1974. *The education of man.* Rev. ed. Translated by W. N. Hailmann. Clifton, NJ: Augustus M. Kelley Publishers. (Originally published 1826).

Fromm, Erich. 1976/1981. *To have or to be?* New York: Bantam Books.

Fujiyoshi, Jikai. 1989. *Zen to Jodokyo* [Zen and Pure Land Buddhism]. Tokyo: Kodansha.

Gandhi, Mahatma K. 1938/1947. *Educational reconstruction.* 4th ed. Sevagram, Wardha, India: Hindustani Talimi Sangh.

Gang, Philip S., Nina Meyerhof Lynn, and Dorothy J. Maver. 1992. *Conscious education: The bridge to freedom.* Atlanta, GA: Dagaz Press.

Garfield, Jay L., trans. 1995. *The fundamental wisdom of the middle way: Nagarjuna's Mulamadhyamakakarika.* New York: Oxford University Press.

Geldard, Richard G. 1993. *The esoteric Emerson: The spiritual teachings of Ralph Waldo Emerson.* Hudson, NY: Lindisfarne Press.

Glazer, Steven, ed. 1999. *The heart of learning: Spirituality in education.* New York: Jeremy P. Tarcher/Putnam, Penguin Putnam.

Goldenberg, Naomi R. 1990/1993. *Resurrecting the body: Feminism, religion and psychotherapy.* New York: Crossroad.

Goleman, Daniel. 1977/1988. *The meditative mind: The varieties of meditative experience.* Los Angeles: Jeremy P. Tarcher.

Griffin, David Ray. 1989. Introduction to SUNY series in constructive postmodern thought. In *God & religion in the postmodern world: Essays in postmodern theology.* Albany, NY: State University of New York Press.

Grof, Stanislav. 1985. *Beyond the brain: Birth, death, and transcendence in psychotherapy.* Albany, NY: State University of New York Press.

Grof, Stanislav. 1998. *The cosmic game: Explorations of the frontiers of human consciousness.* Albany, NY: State University of New York Press.

Guenther, Herbert V. 1971/1972. *Buddhist philosophy in theory and practice.* Baltimore, MD: Penguin Books.

Guenther, Herbert V. 1984. *Matrix of mystery: Scientific and humanistic aspects of rDzogs-chen thought.* Boston: Shambhala.

Guenther, Herbert V., and Chögyam Trungpa. 1975/1988. *The dawn of Tantra.* Edited by M. Kohn. Boston: Shambhala.

Hakeda, Yoshito. 1972. *Kukai: Major works*. New York: Columbia University Press.

Hamilton, Edith, and Huntington Cairns, eds. 1961. *The collected dialogues of Plato*. Princeton, NJ: Princeton University Press.

Harvey, Andrew. 1994. *The way of passion: A celebration of Rumi*. Berkeley, CA: Frog.

Harvey, Andrew, ed. 1996. *The essential mystics: The soul's journey into truth*. San Francisco: HarperCollins.

Harvey, Peter. 1990. *An introduction to Buddhism: Teaching, history and practices*. Cambridge, UK: Cambridge University Press.

Haskel, Peter. 1984/1989. *Bankei Zen: Translations from the record of Bankei*. Edited by Y. Hakeda. New York: Grove Weidenfeld.

Hasumi, Toshimitsu. 1962. *Zen in Japanese art*. Translated by J. Petrie. New York: Philosophical Library. (Originally published 1960).

Hayakawa, S. I. 1939/1978. *Language in thought and action*. 4th ed. New York and London: Harcourt Brace Jovanovich.

Hayakawa, S. I. 1950/1963. *Symbol, status, and personality*. New York and London: Harcourt Brace Jovanovich.

Hayashi, Nobuhiro. 1993. *Cho-jitsuzonteki-ishiki* [Trans-existential consciousness]. Kyoto, Japan: Horitsubunkasha.

Hazrat Inayat Khan. 1960. Education. In *The Sufi message of Hazrat Inayat Khan*. Vol. 3. London: Barrie and Rockliff.

Heidegger, Martin. 1996. *Being and time: A translation of* Sein und Zeit. Translated by J. Stambaugh. Albany, NY: State University of New York Press. (Originally published 1927).

Heidegger, Martin. 1998. *Pathmarks*. Edited by W. McNeill. Cambridge, UK: Cambridge University Press. (Originally published 1967).

Helminski, Kabir. 1999. *The knowing heart: A Sufi path of transformation*. Boston: Shambhala.

Hendricks, Gay. 1981. *The centering teacher: Awareness activities for teachers and their students*. Englewood Cliffs, NJ: Prentice-Hall.

Hendricks, Gay, and Thomas B. Roberts. 1977. *The second centering book: More awareness activities for children, parents, and teachers*. Englewood Cliffs, NJ: Prentice-Hall.

Herrigel, Eugen. 1953/1999. *Zen in the art of archery*. Translated by R. F. C. Hull. New York: Vintage Books. (Originally published 1948).

Herrigel, Gustie. 1958/1974. *Zen in the art of flower arrangement*. Translated by R. F. C. Hull. London: Routledge and Kegan Paul.

Hiromatsu, Wataru. 1982. *Sonzai to imi* [Being and meaning]. Tokyo: Iwanami Shoten.

His Holiness the Dalai Lama. 1999. Education and the human heart. In *The heart of learning: Spirituality in education*, edited by S. Glazer. New York: Jeremy P. Tarcher/Putnam, Penguin Putnam.

Hisamatsu, Shin'ichi. 1939/1987. *Toyoteki-mu* [Eastern nothingness]. Tokyo: Kodansha.

Hisamatsu, Shin'ichi. 1971. *Zen and the fine arts*. Translated by G. Tokiwa. Tokyo: Kodansha International.

Hisamatsu, Shin'ichi. 1982. Zen as the negation of holiness. Translated by S. Merrill. In *The Buddha eye: An anthology of the Kyoto school*, edited by F. Franck. New York: Crossroad. (Originally published 1937).

Hisamatsu, Shin'ichi and Carl G. Jung. 1992. Self and liberation: A dialogue between Carl G. Jung and Shin'ichi Hisamatsu. In *Self and liberation: The Jung-Buddhism dialogue*, edited by D. J. Meckel and R. L. Moore. New York: Paulist Press.

Holistic Kyoiku Kenkyukai, ed. 1995. *Holistic kyoiku nyumon* [Introduction to holistic education]. Tokyo: Hakujusha.

Holistic Kyoiku Kenkyukai, ed. 1995. *Jitsseen holistic kyoiku* [Practices of holistic education]. Tokyo: Hakujusha.

Hutchison, David. 1998. *Growing up green: Education for ecological renewal*. New York: Teachers College Press.

Huxley, Aldous. 1937/1966. *Ends and means: An inquiry into the nature of ideals and into the methods employed for their realization*. London: Chatto and Windus.

Huxley, Aldous. 1944/1972. Introduction to *The song of God: Bhagavad-Gita*, translated by Swami Prabhavananda and C. Isherwood. New York: New American Library.

Huxley, Aldous. 1946/1968. *The perennial philosophy*. London: Chatto and Windus.

Huxley, Aldous. 1956/1975. *Adonis and the alphabet*. London: Chatto and Windus.

Huxley, Aldous. 1962/1972. *Island*. London: Chatto and Windus.

Huxley, Aldous. 1965. Human potentialities. In *Science and human affairs,* edited by R. E. Farson. Palo Alto, CA: Science and Behavior Books.

Huxley, Aldous. 1969. Education on the nonverbal level. In *The healthy personality: Readings,* edited by H. Chiang and A. H. Maslow. New York: Van Nostrand Reinhold.

Huxley, Aldous. 1977. *The human situation: Lectures at Santa Barbara.* Edited by P. Ferrucci. London: Chatto and Windus.

Huxley, Aldous. 1992. *Huxley and God: Essays.* Edited by J. H. Bridgeman. San Francisco: HarperCollins.

Illich, Ivan. 1973/1980. *Tools for conviviality.* New York: Harper Colophon Books.

Inada, Kenneth K., and Nolan P. Jacobson, eds. 1984. *Buddhism and American thinkers.* Albany, NY: State University of New York Press.

Izutsu, Toshihiko. 1966. *Ethico-religious concepts in the Quran.* Montreal: McGill University Press. (Revised edition of *The structure of the ethical terms in the Koran,* 1959)

Izutsu, Toshihiko. 1977a. Naive realism and Confucian philosophy. In *Eranos 1975 yearbook, Vol. 44: The variety of worlds,* edited by A. Portmann and R. Ritsema. Leiden, Netherlands: E. J. Brill.

Izutsu, Toshihiko. 1977b. The temporal and a-temporal dimensions of reality in Confucian metaphysics. In *Eranos 1974 yearbook, Vol. 43: Norms in a changing world,* edited by A. Portmann and R. Ritsema. Leiden, Netherlands: E. J. Brill.

Izutsu, Toshihiko. 1977/1982. *Toward a philosophy of Zen Buddhism.* Boulder, CO: Prajna Press.

Izutsu, Toshihiko. 1980. The *I Ching* mandala and Confucian metaphysics. In *Eranos 1976 yearbook, Vol. 45: Oneness and variety,* edited by A. Portmann and R. Ritsema. Leiden, Netherlands: E. J. Brill.

Izutsu, Toshihiko. 1981a. Between image and no-image: Far eastern ways of thinking. In *Eranos 1979 yearbook, Vol. 48: Thought and mythic images,* edited by A. Portmann and R. Ritsema. Frankfurt am Main, Germany: Insel Verlag.

Izutsu, Toshihiko. 1981b. The nexus of ontological events: A Buddhist view of reality. In *Eranos 1980 yearbook, Vol. 49: Extremes and borders,* edited by A. Portmann and R. Ritsema. Frankfurt am Main, Germany: Insel Verlag.

Izutsu, Toshihiko. 1983. *Ishiki to honshitsu: Seishinteki toyo o motomete* [Cunsciousncss and essence: Explorations of the spirit of the east]. Tokyo: Iwanami Shoten.

Izutsu, Toshihiko. 1983/1984. *Sufism and Taoism: A comparative study of key philosophical concepts.* Berkeley and Los Angeles: University of California Press.

Izutsu, Toshihiko. 1985. *Imi no fukamie: Toyo-tetsugaku no suii* [Into the deeper dimensions of meaning: The levels of eastern philosophy]. Tokyo: Iwanami Shoten.

Izutsu, Toshihiko. 1989. *Kosmos to anchi-kosmos: Toyo-tetsugaku no tameni* [Cosmos and anti-cosmos: For eastern philosophy]. Tokyo: Iwanami Shoten.

Izutsu, Toshihiko. 1991. *Choetsu no kotoba: Islam, Judaya-tetsugaku ni okeru kami to hito* [The language of transcendence: The God and the human being in Islamic and Jewish philosophies]. Tokyo: Iwanami Shoten.

Izutsu, Toshihiko. 1993. *Ishiki no keijijyogaku:* Daijo-kishinron *no tetsugaku* [Metaphysics of consciousness: Philosophy of *the Awakening of Faith*]. Tokyo: Chuokoronsha.

Jackson, Philip W. 1986. *The practice of teaching.* New York: Teachers College Press.

Johansson, Rune E. A. 1969. *The psychology of nirvana.* London: George Allen and Unwin.

Johnson, Aostre N. 1999. A postmodern perspective on education and spirituality: Hearing many voices. *Encounter: Education for Meaning and Social Justice* 12(2): 41-48.

Johnson, Don. 1983. *Body.* Boston: Beacon Press.

Johnson, Don Hanlon. 1994. *Body, spirit and democracy.* Berkeley, CA: North Atlantic Books.

Johnson, Don Hanlon, ed. 1995. *Bone, breath & gesture: Practices of embodiment.* Berkeley, CA: North Atlantic Books; San Francisco: California Institute of Integral Studies.

Jones, Frank Pierce. 1976/1979. *Body awareness in action: A study of the Alexander Technique.* New York: Schocken Books.

Kaji, Nobuyuki. 1994. *Chinmoku no shukyo: Jyukyo* [Religion of silence: Confucianism]. Tokyo: Chikuma Shobo.

Kamata, Shigeo. 1983/1988. *Kegon no shiso* [The Hua-yen philosophy]. Tokyo: Kodansha.

Kane, Jeffrey, ed. 1999. *Education, information, and transformation: Essays on learning and thinking.* Upper Saddle River, NJ: Prentice-Hall.

Kane, Jeffrey, and Dale Snauwaert. 1998. Toward a socially engaged holistic education. *Encounter: Education for Meaning and Social Justice* 11(4): 2-3.

Kawai, Hayao. 1996. *Buddhism and the art of psychotherapy.* College Station, TX: Texas A & M University Press.

Keel, Hee-Sung. 1995. *Understanding Shinran: A dialogical approach.* Fremont, CA: Asian Humanities Press.

Kessler, Rachael. 1997. Social and emotional learning: An emerging field builds a foundation for peace. *Holistic Education Review* 10(4): 4-15.

Kessler, Rachael. 2000. *The soul of education: Helping students find connection, compassion, and character at school.* Alexandria, VA: Association for Supervision and Curriculum Development.

Kesson, Kathleen. 1991. The unfinished puzzle: Sustaining a dynamic holism. *Holistic Education Review* 4(4): 44-48.

Kesson, Kathleen. 1993. Critical theory and holistic education: Carrying on the conversation. In *The renewal of meaning in education,* edited by R. Miller. Brandon, VT: Holistic Education Press.

Kesson, Kathleen. 1994. An introduction to the spiritual dimensions of curriculum. *Holistic Education Review* 7(3): 2-6.

Kesson, Kathleen. 1996. The foundation of holism: Some philosophical and political dilemma. *Holistic Education Review* 9(2): 14-24.

Kesson, Kathleen. 1997. Contemplative spirituality, currere, and social transformation: Finding our "way." Manuscript submitted for publication.

Kierkegaard, Soren. 1941/1954. *Fear and trembling and the sickness unto death.* Translated by W. Lowrie. Princeton, NJ: Princeton University Press. (Originally published 1843, 1849).

Kimura, Bin. 1981. *Jiko, aida, and jikan* [Self, betweenness, and time]. Tokyo: Kobundo.

Kinsley, David. 1995. *Ecology and religion: Ecological spirituality in cross-cultural perspective.* Englewood Cliffs, NJ: Prentice Hall.

Klostermaier, Klaus K. 1994. *A survey of Hinduism*. Albany, NY: State University of New York Press.

Kohn, Livia. 1993. *The Taoist experience: An anthology*. Albany, NY: State University of New York Press.

Kohn, Sherab Chodzin. 1994. *The awakened one: A life of the Buddha*. Boston: Shambhala.

Korzybski, Alfred. 1933/1958. *Science and sanity: An introduction to non-Aristotelian systems and general semantics*. Lakeville, CT: The International Non-Aristotelian Library Publishing Company.

Kraft, Kenneth. 1985/1988. Engaged Buddhism: An introduction. In *The path of compassion: Writings on socially engaged Buddhism*, edited by F. Eppsteiner. Berkeley, CA: Parallax Press.

Krishnamurti, Jidu. 1953. *Education and the significance of life*. New York: Harper and Row.

Krishnamurti, Jidu. 1954/1975. *The first and last freedom*. San Francisco: HarperCollins.

Krishnamurti, Jidu. 1964/1970. *Think on these things*. Edited by D. Rajagopal. New York: Harper Perennial, HarperCollins.

Krishnamurti, Jidu. 1970. *The only revolution*. Edited by M. Lutyens. London: Victor Gollancz.

Krishnamurti, Jidu. 1974. *Krishnamurti on education*. New York: Harper and Row.

Krishnamurti, Jidu. 1976. *Krishnamurti's notebook*. New York: Harper and Row.

Krishnamurti, Jidu. 1979. *Meditations*. San Francisco: Harper and Row.

Krishnamurti, Jidu. 1981. *Letters to the schools, Vol. 1*. 2d ed. Den Haag, Netherlands: Mirananda.

Krishnamurti, Jidu. 1991a. *The collected works of J. Krishnamurti Vol. XI 1958-1960: Crisis in consciousness*. Dubuque, IA: Kendall/Hunt.

Krishnamurti, Jidu. 1991b. *A wholly different way of living*. London: Victor Gollancz.

Krishnamurti, Jidu. 1992a. *The collected works of J. Krishnamurti Vol. XIV 1963-1964: The new mind*. Dubuque, IA: Kendall/Hunt.

Krishnamurti, Jidu. 1992b. *The collected works of J. Krishnamurti Vol. XV 1964-1965: The dignity of living*. Dubuque, IA: Kendall/Hunt.

Krishnamurti, Jidu. 1992c. *The collected works of J. Krishnamurti Vol. XVII 1966-1967: Perennial questions.* Dubuque, IA: Kendall/Hunt.

Krishnamurti, Jidu. 1999. *This light in oneself: True meditation.* Boston: Shambhala.

Kurasawa, Yukihiro. 1983/1993. *Geido no tetsugaku: Shukyo to gei no sosoku* [A philosophy of the way of art: Identity between religion and art]. Rev. ed. Osaka, Japan: Toho Shuppan.

Laing, R. D. 1961/1971. *Self and others.* Harmondsworth, UK: Penguin Books.

Laing, R. D. 1967. *The politics of experience and the bird of paradise.* Harmondsworth, UK: Penguin Books.

Lawrence, D. H. 1921/1922/1971. *Fantasia of the unconscious* and *psychoanalysis and the unconscious.* Harmondsworth, UK: Penguin Books.

Leibniz, G. W. 1989. *Philosophical essays.* Edited and translated by R. Ariew and D. Garber. Indianapolis, IN: Hackett Publishing Company.

Leiter, Kenneth. 1980. *A primer on ethnomethodology.* New York and Oxford: Oxford University Press.

Lemkow, Anna F. 1990. *The wholeness principle: Dynamics of unity within science, religion & society.* Wheaton, IL: Quest Books, Theosophical Publishing House.

Leonard, George B. 1968. *Education and ecstasy.* New York: Dell Publishing.

Lerner, Michael. 1996/1997. *The politics of meaning: Restoring hope and possibility in an age of cynicism.* Reading, MA: Perseus Books.

LeShan, Lawrence. 1974/1975. *How to meditate: A guide to self-discovery.* New York: Bantam Books.

Levin, David Michael. 1988. *The opening of vision: Nihilism and the postmodern situation.* London and New York: Routledge.

Lowen, Alexander. 1967/1969. *The betrayal of the body.* New York: Collier Books.

Lowen, Alexander. 1972/1973. *Depression and the body: The biological basis of faith and reality.* Harmondsworth, UK: Penguin Books.

Löwith, Karl. 1928. *Das Individuum in der Rolle des Mitmenschen.* München, Germany: Drei Masken Verlag.

Macy, Joanna. 1991a. *Mutual causality in Buddhism and general systems theory: The dharma of natural systems.* Albany, NY: State University of New York Press.

Macy, Joanna. 1991b. *World as lover, world as self.* Berkeley, CA: Parallax Press.

Mahdi, Louise Carus, Nancy Geyer Christopher, and Michael Meade, eds. 1996. *Crossroads: The quest for contemporary rites of passage.* Chicago and La Salle, IL: Open Court.

Marcuse, Herbert. 1969. *An essay on liberation.* Boston: Beacon Press.

Marcuse, Herbert. 1972. *Counterrevolution and revolt.* Boston: Beacon Press.

Maritain, Jacques. 1962/1967. *The education of man: The educational philosophy of Jacques Maritain.* Edited by D. and I. Gallagher. Notre Dame, IN: University of Notre Dame Press.

Marshak, David. 1997. *The common vision: Parenting and educating for wholeness.* New York: Peter Lang.

Martin, Jane Roland. 1992. *The schoolhome: Rethinking schools for changing families.* Cambridge, MA: Harvard University Press.

Maruyama, Keizaburo. 1984. *Bunka no fetishism* [Fetishism of culture]. Tokyo: Keiso Shobo.

Maslow, Abraham H. 1971/1993. *The farther reaches of human nature.* New York: Arkana, Penguin Books.

Matsuoka, Seigo. 1984. *Kukai no yume* [Dream of Kukai]. Tokyo: Shunjusha.

Mayeda, Sengaku, ed. and trans. 1979/1992. *A thousand teachings: The Upadesasahasri of Sankara.* Albany, NY: State University of New York Press.

Mehta, Phiroz D. 1989. *Holistic consciousness: Reflections on the destiny of humanity.* Edited by J. Snelling. Longmead, UK: Element Books.

Mehta, Rohit. 1973/1979. *J. Krishnamurti and the nameless experience: A comprehensive discussion of J. Krishnamurti's approach to life.* Delhi, India: Motilal Banarsidass.

Merton, Thomas. 1995. *Thoughts on the east.* New York: New Directions. (Original works of this compilation published 1965-1975).

Metzner, Ralph. 1986. *Opening to inner light: The transformation of human nature and consciousness.* Los Angeles: Jeremy P. Tarcher.

Miller, Alice. 1983/1990. *For your own good: Hidden cruelty in child-rearing and the roots of violence*. 3d ed. Translated by H. and H. Hannum. New York: Noonday Press; Farrar, Straus and Giroux. (Originally published 1980).

Miller, John P. 1981. *The compassionate teacher: How to teach and learn with your whole self*. Englewood Cliffs, NJ: Prentice-Hall.

Miller, John P. 1983. *The educational spectrum: Orientations to curriculum*. New York: Longman.

Miller, John P. 1988/1996. *The holistic curriculum*. Rev. 2d ed. Toronto: OISE Press.

Miller, John P. 1993a. *The holistic teacher*. Toronto: OISE Press.

Miller, John P. 1993b. Worldviews, educational orientations, and holistic education. In *The renewal of meaning in education*, edited by R. Miller. Brandon, VT: Holistic Education Press.

Miller, John P. 1994. *The contemplative practitioner: Meditation in education and the professions*. Toronto: OISE Press.

Miller, John P. 2000. *Education and the soul: Toward a spiritual curriculum*. Albany, NY: State University of New York Press.

Miller, Ron. 1990/1997. *What are schools for?: Holistic education in American culture*. Rev. 3d. ed. Brandon, VT: Holistic Education Press.

Miller, Ron. 1991a. Holism and meaning: Foundations for a coherent holistic theory. *Holistic Education Review* 4(3): 23-32.

Miller, Ron. 1991b. Introduction to *New directions in education: Selections from Holistic Education Review*, edited by R. Miller. Brandon, VT: Holistic Education Press.

Miller, Ron, ed. 1991c. *New directions in education: Selections from Holistic Education Review*. Brandon, VT: Holistic Education Press.

Miller, Ron. 1992. Defining a common vision: The holistic education movement in the U.S. *Orbit, Special Issue: Holistic Education in Practice* 23(2): 20-21. Edited by J. Miller and S. Drake. Toronto: OISE Press

Miller, Ron, ed. 1993a. *The renewal of meaning in education*. Brandon, VT: Holistic Education Press.

Miller, Ron. 1993b. Vital voices of educational dissent. In *The renewal of meaning in education*. Brandon, VT: Holistic Education Press.

Miller, Ron, ed. 1995. *Educational freedom for a democratic society*. Brandon, VT: Resource Center for Redesigning Education

Miller, Ron. 1999a. Education and the evolution of the cosmos. *Encounter: Education for Meaning and Social Justice* 12(2): 21-28.

Miller, Ron. 1999b. Holistic education for an emerging culture. In *The heart of learning: Spirituality in education*, edited by S. Glazer. New York: Jeremy P. Tarcher/Putnam, Penguin Putnam.

Minakata, Kumagusu. 1991. *Minakata mandala* [Minakata Mandala]. Edited by S. Nakazawa. Tokyo: Kawadeshobo Shinsha.

Moffett, James. 1994. *The universal schoolhouse: Spiritual awakening through education*. San Francisco: Jossey-Bass.

Montessori, Maria. 1948. *To educate the human potential*. Madras, India: Kalakshetra Press.

Moore, Thomas. 1992. *Care of the soul: A guide for cultivating depth and sacredness in everyday life*. New York: HarperCollins.

Murphy, Michael. 1969. Education for transcendence. In *Transcendence*, edited by H. W. Richardson and D. R. Cutler. Boston: Beacon Press.

Murphy, Michael. 1992. *The future of the body: Explorations into the further evolution of human nature*. Los Angeles: Jeremy P. Tarcher.

Murphy, Michael, and Steven Donovan. 1988. *The physical and psychological effects of meditation: A review of contemporary meditation research with a comprehensive bibliography 1931-1988*. San Rafael, CA: Esalen Institute Study of Exceptional Functioning.

Naess, Arne. 1973/1995. The shallow and the deep, long-range ecology movements: A summary. In *Deep ecology for the 21st century*, edited by G. Sessions. Boston: Shambhala.

Naess, Arne. 1986/1995. Self-realization: An ecological approach to being in the world. In *Deep ecology for the 21st century*, edited by G. Sessions. Boston: Shambhala.

Naess, Arne. 1989. *Ecology, community and lifestyle: Outline of an ecosophy*. Translated and revised by D. Rothenberg. Cambridge, UK: Cambridge University Press.

Nagao, Gadjin. 1989. *The foundational standpoint of Madhyamika philosophy*. Translated by J. P. Keenan. Albany, NY: State University of New York Press. (Originally published 1978).

Nagao, Gadjin. 1991. *Madhyamika and Yogacara: A study of Mahayana philosophies*. Edited and translated by L. S. Kawamura. Albany, NY: State University of New York Press.

Nakagawa, Yoshiharu. 1985. Jiko to tasha no kaishakugaku 1: Doitsuka to ningenkeisei [Hermeneutics of self and others, Part 1: Identification and human growth]. *Paideia* 22: 67-83.

Nakagawa, Yoshiharu. 1986a. Jiko to tasha no kaishakugaku 2: Hi-doitsuka to choetsu [Hermeneutics of self and others, Part 2: Non-identification and transcendence]. *Paideia* 23: 60-76.

Nakagawa, Yoshiharu. 1986b. Kaishakugakuteki kyoikugaku no rinen: Heisasei to kaihousei no shomondai [The concepts of hermeneutic pedagogy: Problematic of closed-ness and openness]. *Doshisha Tetsugaku Nenpo* 8: 61-73.

Nakagawa, Yoshiharu. 1987a. Bollnow ni okeru kibou no ningengaku [Anthropology of hope in Bollnow]. *Rinrigaku-kenkyu* 17: 86-97.

Nakagawa, Yoshiharu. 1987b. Jikojitsugen to kankeishugi [Self-actualization and relationalism]. *Kansai Kyoikugakkai Kiyo* 11: 9-12.

Nakagawa, Yoshiharu. 1987c. Kaishakugaku no kozu: Kaishakugakuteki kyoikugaku no kisozuke o motomete [A structure of hermeneutics: Towards a foundation of hermeneutic pedagogy]. *Paideia* 24: 27-44.

Nakagawa, Yoshiharu. 1988. Communion to shintai [Communion and the body]. *Paideia* 25: 23-48.

Nakagawa, Yoshiharu. 1989a. Communication to communion 1: Communication kyoikugaku o chushinni [Communication and communion 1: The pedagogy of communication]. *Tetsugaku Ronkyu* 8: 51-65.

Nakagawa, Yoshiharu. 1989b. Communication to communion 2: Communion kyoikugaku o chushinni [Communication and communion 2: The pedagogy of communion]. *Paideia* 26: 24-42.

Nakagawa, Yoshiharu. 1990. Awareness no kyoiku [Education of awareness]. In *Jibunjishin eno kizuki* [Awareness to self], edited by Ningenkyoiku-Kenkyu Kyogikai. Tokyo: Kaneko Shobo.

Nakagawa, Yoshiharu. 1992a. Aldous Huxley no kyoikuron [Aldous Huxley's theory of education]. *Kyoiku Bunka* 1: 72-96.

Nakagawa, Yoshiharu. 1992b. Alice Miller no 'han'kyoikuron [Alice Miller's idea on anti-pedagogy]. *Ritsumenikan Bungaku* 524: 68-100.

Nakagawa, Yoshiharu. 1995. Holistic kyoiku no kanousei [Possibilities of holistic education]. In *Holistic kyoiku nyumon* [Introduction to holistic education], edited by Holistic Kyoiku Kenkyukai. Tokyo: Haku-jusha.

Nakagawa, Yoshiharu. 1996a. Holistic kyoiku to spirituality [Holistic education and spirituality]. *Ritsumeikan Kyoiku Kagaku Kenkyu* 7: 51-69.

Nakagawa, Yoshiharu. 1996b. Transpersonal kyoikugaku [Transpersonal education]. *Transpersonal Gaku* 1: 52-67.

Nakagawa, Yoshiharu. 1998a. Care of the soul to rinsho-kyoikugaku [Care of the soul and therapeutic pedagogy]. *Ritsumeikan Kyoiku Kagaku Kenkyu* 13: 75-87.

Nakagawa, Yoshiharu. 1998b. Holistic education in Japan: Three approaches. *Encounter: Education for Meaning and Social Justice* 11(3): 42-51.

Nakagawa, Yoshiharu. 1998c. Holistic rinsho-kyoikugaku jyoron [A holistic view of therapeutic pedagogy]. *Holistic Kyoiku Kenkyu* [Studies in Holistic Education] 1: 26-39.

Nakagawa, Yoshiharu. 1998d. John Miller no holistic kyoiku-ron [John Miller's theory of holistic education]. *Shinwa Joshi Daigaku, Kyoikusen-koka Kiyo* 3: 67-84.

Nakagawa, Yoshiharu. 2000. Eastern philosophy and holistic education. Ph.D. diss., University of Toronto.

Nakamura, Hajime. 1964/1971. *Ways of thinking of eastern peoples: India-China-Japan-Tibet.* Edited and revised by P. P. Wiener. Honolulu, HI: University Press of Hawaii.

Nakamura, Hajime. 1984. Interrelational existence. In *Buddhism and American thinkers,* edited by K. K. Inada and N. P. Jacobson. Albany, NY: State University of New York Press.

Nakazawa, Shin'ichi. 1992. *Mori no baroque* [The baroque of forest]. Tokyo: Serika Shobo.

Nanavaty, Jal Jehangir. 1973. *Educational thought.* Vol. 1. Poona, India: Joshi and Lokhande Prakashan.

Naranjo, Claudio. 1989/1990. *How to be: Meditation in spirit and practice.* Los Angeles: Jeremy P. Tarcher.

Naranjo, Claudio. 1994. *The end of patriarchy and the dawning of a tri-une society.* Oakland, CA: Amber Lotus.

Naranjo, Claudio, and Robert E. Ornstein. 1971. *On the psychology of meditation.* New York: Viking Press.

Needle, Nathaniel. 1999. The six paramitas: Outline for a Buddhist education. *Encounter: Education for Meaning and Social Justice* 12(1): 9-21.

Needleman, Jacob. 1982. *The heart of philosophy.* San Francisco: Harper and Row.

Nhat Hanh, Thich. 1987. *Being peace.* Edited by A. Kotler. Berkeley, CA: Parallax Press.

Nhat Hanh, Thich. 1987/1993. *Interbeing: Fourteen guidelines for engaged Buddhism.* Rev. ed. Edited by F. Eppsteiner. Berkeley, CA: Parallax Press.

Nhat Hanh, Thich. 1988. *The heart of understanding: Commentaries on the Prajnaparamita Heart Sutra.* Edited by P. Levitt. Berkeley, CA: Parallax Press.

Nhat Hanh, Thich. 1998/1999. *The heart of the Buddha's teaching: Transforming suffering into peace, joy, & liberation.* Edited by A. Kotler. Translated by A. Laity. New York: Broadway Books.

Nicholson, Reynold A. 1914/1989. *The mystics of Islam.* London: Arkana, Penguin Books.

Nietzsche, Friedrich. 1961/1969. *Thus spoke Zarathustra: A book for everyone and no one.* Translated by R. J. Hollingdale. Harmondsworth, UK: Penguin Books. (Originally published 1883-1885).

Nishida, Kitaro. 1958. *Intelligibility and the philosophy of nothingness: Three philosophical essays.* Translated by R. Schinzinger. Tokyo: Maruzen.

Nishida, Kitaro. 1966. Nihon-bunka no mondai [The problem of Japanese culture]. In *Nishida Kitaro zenshu* [The complete works of Nishida Kitaro]. Vol. 14. Tokyo: Iwanami Shoten.

Nishida, Kitaro. 1987. *Last writings: Nothingness and the religious worldview.* Translated by D. Dilworth. Honolulu, HI: University of Hawaii Press. (Originally published 1946).

Nishida, Kitaro. 1990. *An inquiry into the good.* Translated by M. Abe and C. Ives. New Haven, CT: Yale University Press. (Originally published 1911).

Nishijima, Gudo, and Chodo Cross, trans. 1994-1998. *Master Dogen's Shobogenzo.* Books 1-4. London and Tokyo: Windbell Publications.

Nishitani, Keiji. 1982. *Religion and nothingness.* Translated by J. V. Bragt. Berkeley and Los Angeles: University of California Press. (Originally published 1961).

Nishitani, Keiji. 1991. *Nishida Kitaro.* Translated by S. Yamamoto and J. W. Heisig. Berkeley and Los Angeles: University of California Press. (Originally published 1985).

Nishiyama, Kosen, trans. 1975-1983. *Dogen Zenji's Shobogenzo.* Vols. 1-4. Tokyo: Nakayama Shobo.

Noddings, Nel. 1984. *Caring: A feminine approach to ethics & moral education.* Berkeley and Los Angeles: University of California Press.

Noddings, Nel. 1992. *The challenge to care in schools: An alternative approach to education.* New York: Teachers College Press.

Norbu, Namkhai. 1989. *Dzogchen: The self-perfected state.* Edited by A. Clemente. Translated by J. Shane. London: Arkana, Penguin Books.

Odin, Steve. 1982. *Process metaphysics and Hua-yen Buddhism: A critical study of cumulative penetration vs. interpenetration.* Albany, NY: State University of New York Press.

Odin, Steve. 1996. *The social self in Zen and American pragmatism.* Albany, NY: State University of New York Press.

Okumura, Shohaku, and Taigen Dan Leighton, trans. 1997. *The wholehearted way: A translation of Eihei Dogen's Bendowa with commentary by Kosho Uchiyama Roshi.* North Clarendon, VT: Charles E. Tuttle.

Ornstein, Robert E. 1972/1975. *The psychology of consciousness.* New York: Penguin Books.

Orr, David W. 1992. *Ecological literacy: Education and the transition to a postmodern world.* Albany, NY: State University of New York Press.

O'Sullivan, Edmund. 1999. *Transformative learning: Educational vision for the 21st century.* Toronto: University of Toronto Press; London and New York: Zed Books.

Otto, Rudolf. 1932/1987. *Mysticism east and west.* Wheaton, IL: Quest Book, Theosophical Publishing House. (Originally published 1926).

Ouspenski, P. D. 1950/1965/1987. *In search of the miraculous: Fragments of an unknown teaching.* London: Arkana.

Palmer, Parker J. 1983/1993. *To know as we are known: Education as a spiritual journey.* San Francisco: HarperCollins.

Palmer, Parker J. 1998. *The courage to teach: Exploring the inner landscape of a teacher's life.* San Francisco: Jossey-Bass.

Palmer, Parker J. 1998, December/1999, January. Evoking the spirit in public education. *Educational Leadership: The Spirit of Education* 56(4): 6-11.

Palmer, Parker J. 1999. The grace of great things: Reclaiming the sacred in knowing, teaching, and learning. In *The heart of learning: Spirituality in education,* edited by S. Glazer. New York: Jeremy P. Tarcher/Putnam, Penguin Putnam.

Patel, M. S. 1953. *The educational philosophy of Mahatma Gandhi.* Ahmedabad, India: Navajivan Publishing House.

Pavitra, Saint-Hilaire. 1961/1991. *Education and the aim of human life.* 5th ed. Pondicherry, India: Sri Aurobindo International Centre of Education.

Pound, Ezra, trans. 1951/1969. *Confucius: The great digest; the unwobbling pivot; the analects.* New York: New Directions.

Powell, Robert, ed. 1992. *The wisdom of Sri Nisargadatta Maharaj.* New York: Globe Press Books.

Price, A. F., and Mou-Lam Wong, trans. 1990. *The Diamond Sutra and the sutra of Hui-neng.* Boston: Shambhala.

Purpel, David E. 1989. *The moral and spiritual crisis in education: A curriculum for justice and compassion in education.* New York: Bergin and Garvey.

Purpel, David E. 1996. Social transformation and holistic education: Limitations and possibilities. *Holistic Education Review* 9(2): 25-34.

Queen, Christopher S., and Sallie B. King, eds. 1996. *Engaged Buddhism: Buddhist liberation movements in Asia.* Albany, NY: State University of New York Press.

Radhakrishnan, Salvepalli. 1923/1996a. *Indian philosophy, Volume 1.* Delhi, India: Oxford University Press.

Radhakrishnan, Salvepalli. 1923/1996b. *Indian philosophy, Volume 2.* Delhi, India: Oxford University Press.

Radhakrishnan, Salvepalli. 1939/1989. *Eastern religions and western thought.* New Delhi, India: Oxford University Press.

Radhakrishnan, Salvepalli, trans. 1948/1973. *The Bhagavadgita.* New York: Harper Colophon Books.

Radhakrishnan, Salvepalli, trans. 1950/1996. *The Dhammapada*. Delhi, India: Oxford University Press.

Radhakrishnan, Salvepalli, ed. and trans. 1953/1994. *The principal Upanisads*. New Delhi, India: HarperCollins India.

Ram Dass. 1978. *Journey of awakening: A meditator's guidebook*. Edited by D. Goleman. New York: Bantam Books.

Ram Dass, and Mirabai Bush. 1992. *Compassion in action: Setting out on the path of service*. New York: Bell Tower.

Ram Dass, and Paul Gorman. 1985. *How can I help?: Stories and reflections of service*. New York: Alfred A. Knopf.

Ramana Maharshi. 1972/1988. *The spiritual teaching of Ramana Maharshi*. Boston: Shambhala.

Roberts, Bernadette. 1984/1993. *The experience of no-self: A contemplative journey*. Rev. ed. Albany, NY: State University of New York Press.

Roberts, Bernadette. 1989. *What is self?: A study of the spiritual journey in terms of consciousness*. Austin, TX: Mary Botsford Goens.

Rombach, Heinrich. 1979. Phänomenologische Erziehungswissenschaft und Strukturpädagogik. In *Erziehungswissenschaft der Gegenwart: Prinzipien und Perspektiven moderner Pädagogik*, edited by K. Schaller. Bochum, Germany: Verlag Ferdinand Kamp.

Roszak, Theodore. 1992. *The voice of the earth*. New York: Simon and Schuster.

Roszak, Theodore, Mary Gomes, and Allen Kanner, eds. 1995. *Ecopsychology: Restoring the earth, healing the mind*. San Francisco: Sierra Club Books.

Rozman, Deborah. 1976/1989. *Meditation for children*. Boulder Creek, CA: Aslan Publishing.

Rumi. Jalal al-Din. 1994. *Signs of the unseen: The discourses of Jalaluddin Rumi*. Translated by W. M. Thackston Jr. Putney, VT: Threshold Books.

Sadakata, Akira. 1997. *Buddhist cosmology: Philosophy and origins*. Translated by G. Sekimori. Tokyo: Kosei Publishing. (Originally published 1973).

Saiko, Gisho, ed. 1988. *Enjoteki-ningenkankei* [Helping relationships]. Kyoto, Japan: Nagatabunshodo.

Saiko, Gisho. 1995. Bukkyo to counseling [Buddhism and counseling]. In *Toyo no chie to shinrigaku* [Eastern wisdom and psychology], edited by A. Onda. Tokyo: Dainihontosho.

Sarmah, Jogeswar. 1978. *Philosophy of education in the Upanisads.* New Delhi, India: Oriental Publishers and Distributors.

Savin, Olga, trans. 1991. *The way of a pilgrim.* Boston: Shambhala.

Schinzinger, Robert. 1958. Introduction to *Intelligibility and the philosophy of nothingness: Three philosophical essays,* by K. Nishida. Translated by R. Schinzinger. Tokyo: Maruzen.

Schön, Donald A. 1983. *The reflective practitioner: How professionals think in action.* New York: Basic Books, HarperCollins.

Schumacher, E. F. 1977. *A guide for the perplexed.* Toronto: Fitzhenry and Whiteside.

Schuon, Frithjof. 1953. *The transcendent unity of religions.* Translated by P. Townsend. New York: Pantheon Books.

Seed, John, Joanna Macy, Pat Fleming, and Arne Naess. 1988. *Thinking like a mountain: Towards a council of all beings.* Gabriola Island, BC and East Haven, CT: New Society Publishers.

Sessions, George, ed. 1995. *Deep ecology for the 21st century.* Boston: Shambhala.

Shapiro, Deane H. Jr, and Roger N. Walsh, eds. 1984. *Meditation: Classic and contemporary perspectives.* New York: Aldine.

Sharma, Ranjit G. 1992. *The Mother's philosophy of education.* New Delhi, India: Atlantic Publishers and Distributors.

Sloan, Douglas. 1983/1993. *Insight-imagination: The emancipation of thought and the modern world.* Brandon, VT: Resource Center for Redesigning Education.

Smith, Huston. 1976/1992. *Forgotten truth: The common vision of the world's religions.* San Francisco: HarperCollins.

Smith, Huston. 1982/1989. *Beyond the post-modern mind.* Rev. ed. Wheaton, IL: Quest Books, Theosophical Publishing House.

Smuts, Jan Christiaan. 1926/1961. *Holism and evolution.* New York: Viking Press.

Spiegelman, J. Marvin, and Mokusen Miyuki. 1985. *Buddhism and Jungian psychology.* Tempe, AZ: New Falcon Publications.

Spretnak, Charlene. 1991. *States of grace: The recovery of meaning in the postmodern age.* San Francisco: HarperCollins.

Stambaugh, Joan. 1999. *The formless self.* Albany, NY: State University of New York Press.

Steiner, Rudolf. 1996. *The foundations of human experience.* Translated by R. F. Lathe and N. P. Whittaker. Hudson, NY: Anthroposophic Press. (Originally published 1919).

Suzuki, Daisetz T. 1948. *The essence of Buddhism.* Kyoto, Japan: Hozokan.

Suzuki, Daisetz T. 1949/1961. *Essays in Zen Buddhism: First series.* New York: Grove Press.

Suzuki, Daisetz T. 1953/1970. *Essays in Zen Buddhism: Third series.* Edited by C. Humphreys. London: Rider and Company.

Suzuki, Daisetz T. 1956/1996. *Zen Buddhism: Selected writings of D. T. Suzuki.* Edited by W. Barrett. New York: Doubleday.

Suzuki, Daisetz T. 1957/1962. *Mysticism: Christian and Buddhist.* New York: Collier Books.

Suzuki, Daisetz T. 1959/1993. *Zen and Japanese culture.* Princeton: Princeton University Press.

Suzuki, Daisetz T. 1960. *Manual of Zen Buddhism.* New York: Grove Press.

Suzuki, Daisetz T. 1964/1991. *An introduction to Zen Buddhism.* New York: Grove Press.

Suzuki, Daisetz T. 1970. *Shin Buddhism.* New York: Harper and Row.

Suzuki, Daisetz T. 1972. *Japanese spirituality.* Translated by N. Waddell. Tokyo: Japan Society for the Promotion of Science. (Originally published 1944).

Suzuki, Daisetz T. 1972/1994. *Living by Zen: A synthesis of the historical and practical aspects of Zen Buddhism.* York Beach, ME: Samuel Weiser.

Suzuki, Daisetz T. 1973a. *Collected writings on Shin Buddhism.* Edited by the Eastern Buddhist Society. Kyoto, Japan: Shinshu Otaniha.

Suzuki, Daisetz T., trans. 1973b. *The Kyogyoshinsho: The collection of passages expounding the true teaching, living, faith, and realizing of the pure land.* Edited by the Eastern Buddhist Society. Kyoto, Japan: Shinshu Otaniha.

Suzuki, Daisetz T. 1982. The Buddhist conception of reality. In *The Buddha eye: An anthology of the Kyoto school,* edited by F. Franck. New York: Crossroad.

Suzuki, Daisetz T. 1997. *Toyoteki na mikata* [Eastern perspective]. Edited by S. Ueda. Tokyo: Iwanami Shoten. (Originally published 1963).

Suzuki, Daisetz T. 1998. *Buddha of infinite light*. Revised by T. Unno. Boston: Shambhala. (Revised edition of *Shin Buddhism*, 1970).

Suzuki, Sadami. 1996. *"Seime" de yomu nihon kindai: Taisho-seimei-shugi no tanjo to tenkai* [Japanese modern mind in the light of "life": The birth and development of *Taisho* Life-ism]. Tokyo: NHK Books.

Suzuki, Shunryu. 1970. *Zen mind, beginner's mind*. New York and Tokyo: Weatherhill.

Swami Prabhavananda, and Christopher Isherwood, trans. 1944/1972. *The song of God: Bhagavad-gita*. New York: New American Library.

Swami Prabhavananda, and Christopher Isherwood, trans. 1947/1978. *Shankara's Crest-Jewel of Discrimination: Viveka-chudamani*. Hollywood, CA: Vedanta Press.

Swimme, Brian, and Thomas Berry. 1992. *The universe story: From the primordial flaring forth to the Ecozoic era—A celebration of the unfolding of the cosmos*. San Francisco: HarperCollins.

Tachikawa, Musashi. 1997. *An introduction to the philosophy of Nagarjuna*. Translated by R. Giebel. Delhi, India: Motilal Banarsidass. (Originally published 1986).

Tachikawa, Musashi. 1998. *Buddha no tetsugaku* [The philosophy of the Buddha]. Kyoto, Japan: Hozokan.

Tagore, Rabindranath. 1931. *The religion of man*. London: George Allen and Unwin.

Tagore, Rabindranath, and L. K. Elmhirst. 1961. *Rabindranath Tagore: Pioneer in education*. London: John Murray.

Takeuchi, Yoshinori. 1983. *The heart of Buddhism: In search of the timeless spirit of primitive Buddhism*. Edited and translated by J. W. Heisig. New York: Crossroad.

Takuan, Soho. 1986. *The unfettered mind: Writings of the Zen master to the sword master*. Translated by W. S. Wilson. Tokyo: Kodansha International.

Talbot, Michael. 1991. *The holographic universe*. New York: HarperPerennial, HarperCollins.

Tanahashi, Kazuaki, ed. 1985. *Moon in a dewdrop: Writings of Zen Master Dogen*. New York: North Point Press, Farrar Straus and Giroux.

Tanahashi, Kazuaki, ed. 1999. *Enlightenment unfolds: The essential teachings of Zen Master Dogen*. Boston: Shambhala.

Tart, Charles T. 1975/1983. *States of consciousness*. El Cerrito, CA: Psychological Processes.

Tart, Charles T. 1986/1987. *Waking up: Overcoming the obstacles to human potential*. Boston: Shambhala.

Taylor, Rodney L. 1988. *The Confucian way of contemplation: Okada Takehiko and the tradition of quiet-sitting*. Columbia, SC: University of South Carolina Press.

The Mother (Mirra Alfasa). 1984. *On education*. Pondichery, India: Sri Aurobindo Ashram.

Thomashow, Mitchell. 1995. *Ecological identity: Becoming a reflective environmentalist*. Cambridge, MA: MIT Press.

Thurman, Robert A. F. 1998. *The inner revolution: Life, liberty, and the pursuit of real happiness*. New York: Riverhead Books, Penguin Putnam.

Trungpa, Chögyam. 1969/1985. *Meditation in action*. Boston: Shambhala.

Trungpa, Chögyam. 1973. *Cutting through spiritual materialism*. Edited by J. Baker and M. Casper. Boston: Shambhala.

Tsuda, Shin'ichi. 1987. *Han-mykkyo gaku* [Anti-esoteric Buddhism]. Tokyo: Libroport.

Tucker, Mary Evelyn, and Duncan Ryuken Williams, eds. 1997. *Buddhism and ecology: The interconnection of dharma and deeds*. Cambridge, MA: Harvard University Center for the Study of World Religions, Harvard University Press.

Tucker, Mary Evelyn, and John Berthrong, eds. 1998. *Confucianism and ecology: The interrelation of heaven, earth, and humans*. Cambridge, MA: Harvard University Center for the Study of World Religions, Harvard University Press.

Turner, Victor. 1974. *Dramas, fields, and metaphors: Symbolic action in human society*. Ithaca, NY: Cornell University Press.

Ueda, Shizuteru. 1973/1993. *Zen bukkyo* [Zen Buddhism]. Tokyo: Iwanami Shoten.

Ueda, Shizuteru. 1982a. Emptiness and fullness: Sunyata in Mahayana Buddhism. Translated by J. Heisig and F. Greiner. *The Eastern Buddhist* 15(1): 9-37. (Originally published 1980).

Ueda, Shizuteru. 1982b. Nothingness in Meister Eckhart and Zen Buddhism with particular reference to the borderlands of philosophy and theology. Translated by J. W. Heisig. In *The Buddha eye: An anthology of the Kyoto school*, edited by F. Franck. New York: Crossroad. (Originally published 1977).

Ueda, Shizuteru. 1983a. Ascent and descent: Zen in comparison with Meister Eckhart (1). Translated by J. Heisig. *The Eastern Buddhist* 16(1): 52-73. (Originally published 1982).

Ueda, Shizuteru. 1983b. Ascent and descent: Zen in comparison with Meister Eckhart (2). Translated by I. Astley and J. Heisig. *The Eastern Buddhist* 16(2): 72-91. (Originally published 1982).

Ueda, Shizuteru. 1990. Freedom and language in Meister Eckhart and Zen Buddhism, Part 1. Translated by R. Szippl. *The Eastern Buddhist* 23(2): 18-59. (Originally published 1989).

Ueda, Shizuteru. 1991a. Freedom and language in Meister Eckhart and Zen Buddhism, Part 2. Translated by R. Szippl. *The Eastern Buddhist* 24(1): 52-80. (Originally published 1989).

Ueda, Shizuteru. 1991b. *Nishida Kitaro o yomu* [An interpretation of Nishida Kitaro]. Tokyo: Iwanami Shoten.

Ueda, Shizuteru. 1992. *Basho: Niju-sekai-nai-sonzai* [The place: Double-being-in-the world]. Tokyo: Kobundo.

Ueda, Shizuteru. 1994a. Nishida's thought. Translated by J. V. Bragt. *The Eastern Buddhist* 28(1): 29-47. (Originally published 1994).

Ueda, Shizuteru. 1994b. The practice of Zen. Translated by R. Hadley and T. L. Kirchner. *The Eastern Buddhist*, 27(1): 10-29. (Originally published 1993).

Ueda, Shizuteru. 1997. Suzuki Daisetz ni okeru "toyoteki na mikata." ["Eastern Perspective" in Daisetz Suzuki]. In *Toyoteki na mikata* [Eastern perspective], by D. T. Suzuki. New ed. Edited by S. Ueda. Tokyo: Iwanami Shoten.

Ueda, Shizuteru. 1998. *Nishida-tetsugaku eno michibiki: Keiken to jikaku* [An introduction to the philosophy of Nishida: Experience and awareness]. Tokyo: Iwanami Shoten. (Originally published 1994 as *Keiken to jikaku*).

Ueda, Shizuteru, and Seizan Yanagida. 1982. *Jugyuzu* [The ten oxherding pictures]. Tokyo: Chikuma Shobo.

Ueda, Yoshifumi. 1993. *Shinran no shisokozo* [The structure of Shinran's thought]. Tokyo: Shunjusha.

Ueda, Yoshifumi, and Dennis Hirota. 1989. *Shinran: Introduction to his thought*. Kyoto, Japan: Hongwanji International Center.

Uexküll, Jacob von. 1928/1973. *Theoretische biologie*. Frankfurt am Main, Germany: Suhrkamp.

Unno, Taitetsu, trans. 1984. *Tannisho: A Shin Buddhist classic*. Honolulu: Buddhist Study Center Press.

Unno, Taitetsu. 1998. *River of fire, river of water: An introduction to the Pure Land tradition of Shin Buddhism*. New York: Doubleday.

Wada, Shuji. 1995. *Kyoiku-suru yuki* [The courage to educate]. Machida, Japan: Tamagawa Daigaku Shuppanbu.

Waldenfels, Hans. 1980. *Absolute nothingness: Foundations for a Buddhist-Christian dialogue*. Translated by J. W. Heisig. New York: Paulist Press. (Originally published 1976).

Walsh, Roger. 1990. *The spirit of shamanism*. Los Angeles: Jeremy P. Tarcher.

Walsh, Roger N., and Frances Vaughan. 1980. What is a person? In *Beyond ego: Transpersonal dimensions in psychology*, edited by R. N. Walsh and F. Vaughan. Los Angeles: Jeremy P. Tarcher.

Washburn, Michael. 1995. *The ego and the dynamic ground: A transpersonal theory of human development*. 2d Rev. ed. Albany, NY: State University of New York Press.

Watson, Burton, trans. 1968. *The complete works of Chuang Tzu*. New York: Columbia University Press.

Watson, Burton, trans. 1993. *The Zen teachings of Master Lin-chi*. Boston: Shambhala.

Watson, Burton, trans. 1997. *The Vimalakirti Sutra*. New York: Columbia University Press.

Watsuji, Tetsuro. 1926/1992. *Nihon seishinshi kenkyu* [Studies in the history of Japanese mind]. Rev. ed. Tokyo: Iwanami Shoten.

Watsuji, Tetsuro. 1996. *Watsuji Tetsuro's rinrigaku: Ethics in Japan*. Translated by S. Yamamoto and R. E. Carter. Albany, NY: State University of New York Press. (Originally published 1937, 1942, 1949).

Watts, Alan. 1961/1975. *Psychotherapy east & west*. New York: Vintage Books.

Watts, Alan. 1966/1989. *The book: On the taboo against knowing who you are*. New York: Vintage Books.

Watts, Alan (with Al Chung-liang Huang). 1975. *Tao: The watercourse way*. New York: Pantheon Books.

Weerasinghe, Henry. 1992. *Education for peace: The Buddha's way*. Ratmalana, Sri Lanka: Sarvodaya Book Publishing Service.

Welwood, John. 1979. Meditation and the unconscious: A new perspective. In *The meeting of the ways: Explorations in east/west psychology*, edited by J. Welwood. New York: Schocken Books.

Welwood, John, ed. 1979. *The meeting of the ways: Explorations in east/west psychology*. New York: Schocken Books.

Wilber, Ken. 1977/1993. *The spectrum of consciousness*. 2d ed. Wheaton, IL: Quest Books, Theosophical Publishing House.

Wilber, Ken. 1979/1985. *No boundary: Eastern and western approaches to personal growth*. Boston: Shambhala.

Wilber, Ken. 1980/1996. *The Atman project: A transpersonal view of human development*. 2d ed. Wheaton, IL: Quest Books, Theosophical Publishing House.

Wilber, Ken. 1983/1996. *Eye to eye: The quest for the new paradigm*. 3d ed. Boston: Shambhala.

Wilber, Ken. 1995. *Sex, ecology, spirituality: The spirit of evolution*. Boston: Shambhala.

Wilber, Ken. 1996. *A brief history of everything*. Boston: Shambhala.

Wilber, Ken. 1997. *The eye of spirit: An integral vision for a world gone slightly mad*. Boston: Shambhala.

Wilber, Ken. 1998. *The marriage of sense and soul*. New York: Random House.

Wilber, Ken. 1999. *One taste: The journals of Ken Wilber*. Boston: Shambhala.

Wilber, Ken, Jack Engler, and Daniel P. Brown. 1986. *Transformations of consciousness: Conventional and contemplative perspectives on development*. Boston: Shambhala.

Wilhelm, Richard. 1950/1977. *The I Ching* or *Book of Changes*. Translated by C. Baynes. Princeton, NJ: Princeton University Press.

Wilhelm, Hellmut, and Richard Wilhelm. 1960/1979/1988/1995. *Understanding the I Ching: The Wilhelm lectures on the Book of Changes*. Translated by C. Baynes and I. Eber. Princeton, NJ: Princeton University Press.

Wolf, Aline D. 1996. *Nurturing the spirit in non-sectarian classrooms.* Hollidaysburg, PA: Parent Child Press.

Yanagi, Muneyoshi (Soetsu). 1955/1986. *Namu-amida-butsu* [Namu Amida Buddha]. Tokyo: Iwanami Shoten.

Yanagi, (Muneyoshi) Soetsu. 1972/1989. *The unknown craftsman: A Japanese insight into beauty.* Adapted by B. Leach. Tokyo: Kodansha International.

Yanagi, Muneyoshi. 1991. *Myokonin ronshu* [Papers on *myokonin*]. Edited by B. Jugaku. Tokyo: Iwanami Shoten.

Yanagi, Muneyoshi. 1995. *Bi no homon* [A gateway to beauty]. Edited by H. Mizuo. Tokyo: Iwanami Shoten.

Yano, Satoji. 1996. *Sokurates no double bind: Imiseisei no kyoiku-ningengaku* [Double bind of Socrates: A pedagogical anthropology of the sense-generation]. Yokohama, Japan: Seori Shobo.

Yoshida, Atsuhiko. 1995a. Holistic kyoiku no kihonteki kanten [Fundamental viewpoints of holistic education]. In *Holistic kyoiku nyumon* [Introduction to holistic education], edited by Holistic Kyoiku Kenkyukai. Tokyo: Hakujusha.

Yoshida, Atsuhiko. 1995b. Holistic kyoiku riron no shatei [The scope of the theory of holistic education]. In *Holistic kyoiku nyumon* [Introduction to holistic education], edited by Holistic Kyoiku Kenkyukai. Tokyo: Hakujusha.

Yoshida, Atsuhiko. 1996a. "Holistic kyoiku ningengaku" ni mukete no shiron [An essay towards holistic pedagogical anthropology]. In *Kyoikuteki nichijo no saikochiku* [Reconstruction of educational reality], edited by S. Wada. Machida, Japan: Tamagawa Daigaku Shuppanbu.

Yoshida, Atsuhiko. 1996b. "Holistic kyoiku-ron" saiko [A revision of "The ideas of holistic education"]. In *Ningenkeiseiron* [Theories of human formation], edited by A. Okada. Machida, Japan: Tamagawa Daigaku Shuppanbu.

Yoshida, Atsuhiko. 1998. Kison no kyoiku-shogakusetsu eno holistic kyoiku kenkyu no kiyo [A contribution of holistic education studies to educational theories]. *Holistic Kyoiku Kenkyu* [Studies in Holistic Education] 1: 40-54.

Yoshida, Atushiko. 1999. *Holistic kyoiku-ron: Nihon no doko to shiso no chihei* [A theory of holistic education: Movements in Japan and the horizon of thought]. Tokyo: Nihon Hyoronsha.

Yuasa, Yasuo. 1987. *The body: Toward an eastern mind-body theory.* Edited by T. P. Kasulis. Translated by S. Nagatomo and T. P. Kasulis. Albany, NY: State University of New York Press. (Originally published 1977).

Yuasa, Yasuo. 1993. *The body, self-cultivation, and ki-energy.* Translated by S. Nagatomo and M. S. Hull. Albany, NY: State University of New York Press. (Originally published 1986).

Yuasa, Yasuo. 1994. *Shintai no uchusei* [Cosmology of the body]. Tokyo: Iwanami Shoten.

Ze-ami. 1968. *Kadensho.* Translated by C. Sakurai, S. Hayashi, R. Satoi, and B. Miyai. Kyoto, Japan: The Foundation of Sumiya-Shinobe Scholarship, Doshisha University.

ABOUT THE AUTHOR

YOSHIHARU NAKAGAWA (1959–) studied philosophy of education in Kyoto and taught courses on teacher education at several universities in Japan. Then he studied in Toronto from 1996 to 2000 and holds a Ph.D. from the Ontario Institute for Studies in Education of the University of Toronto. Currently he offers lectures and workshops in Japan and will be Associate Professor at Ritsumeikan University in Kyoto starting in 2001. He is the vice-president of the Japanese Association for Holistic Education. He is the author of numerous articles, co-author of several books on holistic education, and translator of many books including John Miller's *Holistic Curriculum* and *Holistic Teacher*.